Random Families

RANDOM FAMILIES

GENETIC STRANGERS,
SPERM DONOR SIBLINGS,
AND THE CREATION OF NEW KIN

ROSANNA HERTZ AND
MARGARET K. NELSON

OXFORD
UNIVERSITY PRESS

OXFORD
UNIVERSITY PRESS

Oxford University Press is a department of the University of Oxford. It furthers
the University's objective of excellence in research, scholarship, and education
by publishing worldwide. Oxford is a registered trademark of Oxford University
Press in the UK and certain other countries.

Published in the United States of America by Oxford University Press
198 Madison Avenue, New York, NY 10016, United States of America.

Library of Congress Cataloging-in-Publication Data
Names: Hertz, Rosanna, author. | Nelson, Margaret K., 1944– author.
Title: Random families : genetic strangers, sperm donor siblings, and the creation of new kin /
Rosanna Hertz and Margaret K. Nelson.
Description: New York, NY : Oxford University Press, [2019] | Includes bibliographical references.
Identifiers: LCCN 2018004453 (print) | LCCN 2018003058 (ebook) |
ISBN 9780190888275 (hardcover) | ISBN 9780190888282 (updf) | ISBN 9780190888299 (epub)
Subjects: LCSH: Families—United States. | Children of sperm donors—United States. |
Parents—United States. | Kinship—United States.
Classification: LCC HQ535 .H465 2019 (ebook) | LCC HQ535 (print) | DDC 306.850973—dc23
LC record available at https://lccn.loc.gov/2018004453

3 5 7 9 8 6 4 2
Printed by Sheridan Books, Inc., United States of America

For everyone we interviewed.

CONTENTS

ACKNOWLEDGMENTS

THE NATIONAL SCIENCE FOUNDATION (NSF) allowed us to go on an amazing journey. This book is a tribute to that journey. We thank the NSF for funds (Social and Biogenetic Factors of New Forms of Family, Grants 1355726 [Nelson] and 1355740 [Hertz]); Saylor Breckenridge and Kevin T. Leicht (both at NSF); Franci Farnsworth and Alison Darrow (both at Middlebury College); and Laurel Smith-Doerr (University of Massachusetts, Amherst) for their support.

We thank the Brocher Foundation and our colleagues there for the wonderful month of July 2016. We thank Joshua Gamson, Naomi Gerstel, Karen V. Hansen, Debra Umberson, Robert Zussman, and the anonymous reviewers who read drafts of our manuscript. Special thanks to Naomi Gerstel and Robert Zussman, who read several drafts and Ilana Offen for the figure in chapter 3. Other thanks go to Jane Mattes, James Sulloway, Elizabeth Lund, Anna Weick, and the Wellesley alum network.

Todd Siler generously provided the illustrations for each donor sibling network. His visual representations captured our imagined renditions of these modern families. James Cook, our editor at Oxford University Press, expertly shepherded the manuscript through the stages of publishing. He provided sage advice to our queries with enthusiasm and colleagueship. We also thank the first-rate production team at Oxford, including Emily MacKenzie, Julia Turner, and Rachel Perkins.

Rosanna thanks the research assistants, who were hired on the Wellesley side of the NSF grant, for their important contributions: Jacqueline McGrath, Jordan Parker, Rebecca Schwarz, Gabriela Hartmann, Dharani Persaud, Alyssa Thomas, Katherine Khanna, Sophia Temkin, and Jamie Yang. Wellesley College Summer Student Research Program in the Social Sciences (2014, 2015) awarded additional student funding. A small Wellesley grant in 2012–2013 funded by the Class of 1932 Research Fund for the Social Sciences provided seed money. The Marion and Jasper Whiting Foundation awarded additional funds (2016–2017). The Petrie-Flom Center for Health Law Policy, Biotechnology, and Bioethics, Harvard Law School, and the University of Massachusetts, Amherst (Department of Sociology), provided intellectual homes.

Rosanna thanks the following colleagues and friends: Nancy Marshall, Jenny Musto, Elena Creef, Leigh Gilmore, Susan Reverby, Irene Mata, Elizabeth Tiro, Elizabeth Demski, Ravi Ravishanker, Jordan Namerow, Jane Mattes, Martha Ertman, Glenn Cohen, Naomi Cahn, Beth Fisher, Orly Benjamin, and Sonia Nix. She also thanks Robert J. Thomas big time not only for being her life partner but also for contributing in numerous ways to the sociology in this book, and, finally, Alyssa, who is always amazing company.

Margaret thanks the research assistants hired at Middlebury College through the NSF grant and matching grants. These students (and former students) made wonderful contributions to the research: Emily French, Chelsea Jerome, Sarah Koch, Haley Tetreault, and Rosalie Wright-Lapin.

Margaret also thanks Middlebury College for providing additional funds through a matching grant and the Faculty Research Assistant Fund (2017). Special thanks to Jim Ralph for his assistance in procuring these funds, and to Franci Farnsworth, Lynn Dunton, and Mari Price for careful budget support.

Finally, Margaret is grateful to numerous colleagues, friends, and family for support of various kinds. In alphabetical order, they are Emily K. Abel, Margaret L. Anderson, Kitty Calavita, Svea Closser, Judy Dickson, Rebecca Freedman, Naomi Gerstel, Karen Hansen, Elizabeth and Seymour Hersh, Barbara Hofer, Michael Katz, Bill Koulopoulos, Robert Moeller, Jeff Nelson, Sam Nelson, Ilana Offen, Sonja Olson, Ellen Oxfeld, Burke Rochford, Robert Schine, Rebecca Tiger, Nicholas Townsend, Polly Young-Eisendrath, and Maxine Baca Zinn. As always, and especially, thanks to Bill Nelson.

RANDOM FAMILIES

Introduction
Unprecedented Relationships

*Margo's son, Spencer, was eager to show us the family tree he had composed as a class project.** Like many twelve-year-olds in suburban Chicago, he had been asked to depict his genealogy, but unlike his classmates' diagrams, his wasn't exactly symmetrical. The top of the poster had a familiar branch shape that grew wider with each generation. However, the bottom had just one very long branch—labeled Margo (his single mom) and "X" (the donor). Beneath this branch were seventeen separate twigs, each corresponding to one of the donor's offspring.*[1] *Spencer proudly listed himself the first of the seventeen, but as he pointed out, "We don't know how many there'll be eventually."*

Jennifer and Leslie, partners in a same-sex couple, were in their early thirties when they decided to have a child. Initially overwhelmed by the range of options available from a sperm bank they had found on the internet, they prioritized what they wanted in a donor: someone who would agree to have his identity released when their child turned eighteen, who would not be uncomfortable meeting the child of lesbian parents, and who would look a little bit like Leslie so that she would be represented in the child. Had they started down this path in 1992 or even 2002, Jennifer and Leslie would not have had many choices. But in 2012 when Callie was conceived, sperm banks were entirely receptive to same-sex couples. By the time we interviewed them several years later, Jennifer and Leslie had met five families who shared the same donor, and Leslie was actively planning a summer gathering near their home in Minnesota.

Abigail and Don were high school sweethearts who learned after many frustrating years of failed attempts at pregnancy that Don was sterile. It was 1995, and agency fees and legal bills put adoption well beyond their means.

---

* All names in this book are pseudonyms. We have sometimes altered specific features of an individual (e.g., place of residence or occupation) to conceal the person's identity.

Fortuitously, Abigail's family doctor offered another option: for $500 (at that time), they could purchase two numbered vials of sperm and she could be inseminated in his office. Buoyed by assurances that the sperm came from a reputable source, they asked no more questions and went ahead with high hopes. Eighteen years later, to Abigail and Don's surprise, their teenage son Scott stumbled on an online registry through which he could locate other people who shared his donor number. Privately, Abigail and Don debated what to do: pursue more information themselves or leave it to him to decide. They finally opted to give him a birthday present of a year's membership in this registry. "It's your call, Scott," Don said. "You decide if and when you want to know more." Eleven months slipped by before he made his choice and then, remarkably, within thirty minutes of going online Scott made contact with one of his donor siblings.[2] Within days, a young man from Arkansas, who had been an only child for eighteen years, found himself introduced via Facebook to a national web of children and adults.

* * *

THESE THREE FAMILIES that vary in structure (single mom and same-sex and heterosexual couples) and circumstance share some very important and quite novel experiences. They represent several of the major transformations that have occurred in modern life through the use of donated reproductive gametes. First, because they were able to conceive their children by purchasing vials of sperm from a sperm bank, each now enjoys the intimate rewards of a parent-and-child relationship based, at least in part, on a genetic link.[3] Heterosexual couples were the primary users of sperm banks in the mid- to late twentieth century.[4] Today, the members of a wide range of families—including Margo, Jennifer and Leslie, and Abigail and Don—find themselves welcome to acquire donated gametes, including eggs, sperm, and whole embryos.[5] Second, disclosure to children (and others) about reliance on a donor is commonplace among all kinds of families and even among those (like Abigail and Don, and Margo) who could have concealed that fact.[6] In these three families, parents and children openly discussed the donor.

Third, and even more unexpected, all three of these families are currently embedded in networks of "donor siblings" structured around relationships that originate from genetic links alone. Most of the early users of sperm banks were unlikely to know who the donor was; none could know anyone else who had relied on the *same* sperm bank donor. As part of the move toward greater openness, identity-release donors—individuals who agree to some form of contact when a donor-conceived offspring turns eighteen—are available through most sperm banks. And, most surprising, contact with a child's genetic strangers from the sperm side ("donor siblings" and their parents) can be made even before a child's birth. That is, once parents have purchased a vial of sperm from a particular donor, *they can use the unique number assigned by the bank to begin to locate others who purchased sperm from the same donor*. The donor number itself thus becomes the mechanism for organizing activities that lead to meeting a child's donor siblings. (Soon these activities may be available also to those who use donated eggs and those who acquire whole embryos.)

As a result of these events, all three families are engaged in figuring out what it means to be part of a donor sibling network—something that is in many ways not only unprecedented but also uncertain. We began this research well aware of these events. What we did not know was how parents and their children would respond to the brand-new possibility of incorporating the parents of the donor siblings, the donor siblings, and sometimes even the donor himself into their lives. Nor did we know what kind of relationships they would forge with these strangers.

In this book we explore these unprecedented relationships as they emerge from networks of strangers linked by genes, medical technology, and the human desire for affinity and identity. We chronicle the chain of choices that parents make—from conceiving with donors through de-ciding what to do when it suddenly becomes clear that there are children out there who live in other families but share half their child's DNA. And we ask what happens next. Do parents and children believe shared genes make you family? Do children look for and find anything in common with their donor siblings? What happens within the networks that arise once parents and donor siblings find and meet one another? To answer these— and related—questions we traveled across the United States interviewing parents and their donor-conceived children. We draw on interviews with 212 parents and 154 donor-conceived children (aged ten and older).

We show that when these networks of genetic strangers emerge, they sometimes prove to be meaningful to children and parents. Some have blossomed into lively and long-standing Facebook groups of people who hold regular "reunions" and enjoy close friendships.[7] Others, however, simply contain a roster of members in an online directory. Whatever var-iations exist, each of the networks creates opportunities to make meaning out of connections that begin when parents with no preexisting relationship to each other happen to purchase vials of sperm from the same donor. Even in a world in which kinship has become more voluntary, this sequence of a random group of parents finding each other and telling their children about their genetic relatives, and then parents and children getting to know one another on the basis of shared genes is a startlingly new occurrence. We focus our inquiry on the conditions determining whether and how genetic strangers understand and use one another to create meaningful and enduring forms of social organization.

We refer to donors, donor siblings, and their families as "genetic strangers" as a way to bind together something that usually connotes familiarity with something that symbolizes the opposite.[8] On the one hand, nothing could be more familiar than the notion that kinship is created by the genes that flow in the blood (or are contained in a vial of sperm). On the other hand, nothing could be more peculiar than to learn (in some cases suddenly) that one member of a family shares half her genes with a gaggle of unknown "others" who cannot be placed on any known shape of a family tree. And this is precisely the case here: before interaction, the members of these networks are bound by genes *and* are strangers to one another. As strangers they might create particular unease for one another, even in a world in which the internet provides numerous opportunities for us to become intimate with people we do not know well and may never have met.

We also intentionally use the generic term "network" rather than the term "extended family" as a starting point to describe the groups that emerge. The only thing that originally linked the members is that they relied on (or believe they relied on) the same donor gametes.[9] By way of contrast, an extended family is a tangle of long-standing relationships into which one is born or married, like it or not. Whereas some people completely dismiss the notion that genes create kinship, the members of donor sibling networks often start out believing that they now have new relatives. In fact, when bonds do emerge it is because people have gone beyond their ideas about the significance of genes as the taken-for-granted basis for the creation of kinship and moved on to use them to create intimacy.[10] The traits that appear to be common among the donor siblings and between a donor and his or her offspring merely start a conversation. Sometimes that conversation ends quickly, without creating any new connections. But the conversation may also lead to the choice to form an entirely new kind of voluntary family.

Genes Start Kinship: Genetic Conversations

We are at a particular moment in history when public opinion leans toward the belief that genes are determinants of looks, behavior, and personality.[11] Public opinion also holds that genes create kinship. Genetic testing sites rest on, and promulgate, both of these beliefs; their recent growth is evidence of the popularity of these ideas. For a ninety-nine-dollar membership on 23andMe, that site tells us, you can "experience your ancestry in a new way!" For another hundred dollars you can "get an even more comprehensive understanding of your genetics. Receive 75 + online reports on your ancestry, traits and health—and more." AncestryDNA offers something even "better" for only seventy-nine dollars: "The DNA test that tells a more complete story of you. AncestryDNA provides richer connections to people, places, and possibilities."[12]

When people (like those in our introductory sketches) make the decision to sign up on a registry in order to contact genetic strangers, they are operating on the basis of one—or both—of these beliefs. But whatever consequences genes may actually have, they shape identity and create relationships only through socially constructed understandings. For most people, knowledge about the operation of genes stops with what they have learned in high school or college biology.

Those who choose a sperm donor and then sign up on a registry to interact with genetic strangers open conversations that rest on a cultural narrative about the significance of genes. We want to understand how parents and children use this cultural narrative. For instance, when *deciding among alternative sperm donor profiles*, do parents believe that purchasing sperm from a man who is in law school will ensure that they give birth to a smart child? Similarly, we want to understand how children develop a *self-identity* when one of their biological parents is an anonymous sperm donor. How does a donor-conceived child understand the origins of her athletic ability? Does knowing that a donor came from Scotland make a child believe that he is Scottish?

When genetic strangers interact with each other, we want to know what they say about whether genes create *resemblances* among the children.

Do people find a shared physical appearance or personality among the children who have the same donor? What do parents and children say about similarities and differences? Finally, as we explore these topics, we are especially attentive to the possible emergence of a sense of *relatedness* between the donor and his donor offspring, among donor siblings, and among the parents of these donor siblings. Do participants in these networks think that children who share a donor but are raised in separate families are some form of kin? What expectations and obligations develop from the interactions among these various parties?

In our analysis of these issues we do not consider what geneticists or sociobiologists might say; we focus on what the people we interviewed believe and how they act on those beliefs. In short, our interest is in these various uses to which ideas about genes are put as those ideas underwrite a variety of actions: the choice of a donor by parents, the ways a child imagines her own identity in relation to that of the donor, the perception (or not) of similarities, and the manner in which people relate to people who start out as genetic strangers. We are interested as well in how these ideas circulate within individual networks and influence the relationships that develop there.

Kinship in Choice: Voluntary Families

As we will see in this book, as much as people point to genes as being shared with a parent, a donor, or a donor sibling and then claim resemblance and family membership on that basis, it is their wish to affiliate with others that gives rise to these creative inventions. At one level, this is no surprise. Both the "families of choice" described by Kath Weston and the "fictive kinship" described by Carol Stack are testimonies to the importance of voluntary "kin" ties.[13] But the choice in these relationships is quite different from other sets of "chosen" kin. This difference applies both to the issue of the donor *and* to the issue of donor siblings and their parents.

Choice and the "Problem" of a Donor

The parents in these networks initially choose a donor from among the available options because they believe his genes will not prevent their establishing a connection with their own children. That donor, however, is neither an emotional nor a social partner for them. He has no under-standable role to play in any family created by parents relying on donor conception; he is nothing more than a vial of sperm.[14] Single mothers who are heterosexual often leave space for getting married in the future and thus eventually having an exclusively social father for their children.[15] The members of lesbian couples already have partners; so too do the members of heterosexual couples. All these parents are opting (whether out of unfettered choice or not) to challenge the equation of biolog-ical with social parenthood. But they are decidedly *not* making a calcu-lated decision to create new boundaries for their families; for all those we interviewed, family membership is contained within the "nuclear" unit of acting parents and their children.[16] Moreover, although we dis-cuss the donor in terms of "choice," we might note that these choices are constrained. Parents purchasing sperm have to depend on the market that determines what is available (chapter 1).[17] Parents who want contact with a donor—for themselves or their children—have to depend on what the donor himself chooses to do.

Of course, no more than any other child do donor-conceived chil-dren either choose to be born or choose their biological parents. And, like other children, they learn that it takes a man and a woman to make a baby. (In chapter 2, we discuss how the sex education curriculum is insuf-ficient for donor-conceived children.) Yet the donor, or the man whose sperm helped create them, is absent.[18] Parents selected him. Children may not initially understand what a donor is; they may also have a need to understand which genetic part of themselves came from the donor. And if children later opt for—and attain—contact with him, they cannot by themselves dictate the terms of that contact. (See especially chapters 4 and 7.) Boys and girls confront similar issues in these regards even if oc-casionally they differ in how they resolve those issues for themselves. For example, as we show in chapter 2, girls tend to be more imaginative than boys in their invention of the donor; girls also appear to use the donor more actively in a process of separation from their parents.

Choice and the "Problem" of Donor Siblings

Scholars who write about "voluntary" kin ties describe them as being close and supportive relationships. Carol Stack, for example, explains fictive kinship as emerging within a community among people who help each other out in both material and nonmaterial ways. Kath Weston describes the intimacy that developed within tight networks of gays and lesbians who formed strong friendships that become their families of choice, especially when traditional kin rejected them. As is true of these other relationships, the creation of chosen kin in networks of donor siblings begins with a decision to reach out to others (chapter 3). But these others are *not* people one knows: they are random families who just happened to have selected the same donor out of the available pool. They may live close to one another or they may be divided by geographic distances. They may be socially similar to each other, but they may also differ in family form, social class, race/ethnicity, religion, and values. Although the parents and children manage to find deep (even mystical) reasons to explain why they have come together, the affiliation begins with entirely separate purchases of the same genetic material. Biology—not sociability—opens the connection.

New Types of Voluntary Families in Contemporary Times

When parents choose to interact with the families of donor siblings, they are creating a kind of "kin" that is both "voluntary" and unusual. They and their children suddenly have a set of previously unexperienced "relatives." And although for anyone the discovery of a new relative can be an eye-opener, for most people those relationships are usually pretty easy to sort out. There is both the language with which to describe even the most distant relation *and* existing social norms that dictate behavior.

Genetic strangers encounter something quite different. They have no easy labels (like "aunt") or familiar measures of distance (like "second cousin, once removed"); they share no ancestors with a designated kin term who can serve as landmarks for the relationship. They have only a shared number assigned to the donor by a sperm bank. They might initially try to squeeze themselves into familiar, preexisting kinship terms to suggest models for interactions. That is, not surprisingly, when they are thrust into this novel situation, parents and children struggle to find a foothold of familiarity. For example, they try out the language of "half-sister" or "sibling." Children also often draw on categories that exist within

"ordinary" families—categories like birth order—to help them understand where they stand in relation to others. But they do so in the absence
of any actual family context. The terms both make good sense *and* make
no sense at all. That is, as genetic strangers push themselves into these
older concepts, they find they have to break out of them as well.

Perhaps even more significantly, the available models for interaction
are clearly insufficient. As they do with language, parents and children
initially draw on the categories that are already available to them. This
is not all that different from what we all do when we encounter new
people or a new situation. That is, as just about anyone would do, they
try to figure out what properties (and ideas and ways of interacting) of
this new situation are shared with what they have already experienced.
For example, when the family members of a donor sibling network get
together, they describe the occasion as a "reunion." (See the definition of
this term in chapter 6.) Yet, unlike people joining together at a reunion
of kinfolk, they have no shared memories or family traditions on which
to draw.

To be sure, the links within a donor sibling network might have the
same *structural* form as do the links among women who have children
with the same biological father. Low-income single mothers often live
in communities where other women have children with the same man.[19]
Similarly, women whose divorced husbands subsequently remarry and
have more children might share with the new wives the parenting of
half- or stepsiblings. In both of these situations the social norms surrounding the women's relationships to each other, the combination of
mothering and stepmothering roles, and the children's relationships
to one another are still murky; the social rules for interaction are not
institutionalized.[20]

However, in both of these more familiar situations, the connections
are created through relationships with the same known man. They are
not random. Moreover, the women might start out as adversaries, especially because several women have had sex with the same man and because separate families have to divide the resources of time with children
and the support that a single father can provide. By way of contrast, the
parents of donor siblings have no reason to regard each other as adversaries. Four other facts establish the difference. First, no legal obligations
exist among the parents in donor sibling networks. Second, a far greater

number of families are joined together within the networks of donor siblings. Third, even on those rare occasions when the families of donor siblings live near each other, unless they already know about each other, neither the mothers nor the children are likely to recognize one another when they do grocery shopping or attend church. Finally, the women in donor sibling networks have a rough parity because, at least at the moment of choice, none of them has a relationship with the donor. In spite of these differences, a central similarity remains: donor sibling networks are also almost entirely composed of women and children. Whether hegemonic ideas about gender in kinship persist even without the "father" is an empirical question we consider as we explore the networks that emerge.

The experience of children within a donor sibling network might also have an analogy in the experience of children placed for adoption. These children may wonder about biological relatives (parents *and* siblings) when they are unknown; they may have no easy language or models for interactions if they do meet. Moreover, the latter experience—of meeting—is becoming more likely. Within both the world of donor conception and the world of adoption a new interest in openness prevails.[21] In both worlds choice is crucial: some individuals seek contact with "genetic relatives" and some do not. It is also likely that children who have been donor conceived and children who have been adopted might have very similar reactions to meeting their genetic relatives; people in both groups might be astonished by what they perceive to be similarities *and* differences between themselves and people with whom they have a genetic connection. In these ways, the two worlds are much alike.[22] In other ways, the two sets of experiences differ sharply. A major difference is that a *birth* parent is raising a donor-conceived child, either alone or as a member of a couple. An additional issue has to do with numbers of "found" relatives. Usually only two families (and their extended kin) are involved in the connections formed through open adoption; by way of contrast the networks among the families of donor-conceived offspring can involve many different families (and their extended kin). As a result, in all likelihood, children who have been placed for adoption find fewer new genetic siblings than do children conceived with donor sperm; in the latter case the number of genetic strangers with whom one connects can extend to over fifty.[23]

As these other examples demonstrate, although the children within the networks are called "donor siblings," they are a novel form of sibling: these siblings come from outside and live elsewhere. Scholars tell us that "ordinary" siblings help in the process of constructing identity: as siblings compare themselves to each other, identifying similarities and differences, they discover who they are *and* who they are not.[24] Of course family life can provide many different types: full genetic siblings, half-genetic siblings, stepsiblings, siblings created through adoption, and siblings whose two moms each had a child with different donors. Each type can offer its own set of opportunities for interaction; those opportunities include role models, friends, rivals, collaborators, and enemies; siblings might also be important resources for emotional and material support.[25] As we show in what follows, donor siblings provide some quite similar and some quite different opportunities for children.

As their members figure out what to do and how to respond to each other, donor sibling networks join the ranks of new family forms that need to create for themselves normative structures and institutional support. Donor sibling networks are particularly interesting within these ranks because they are *created by choice and yet build on connections that are purely genetic in their origin.* They are also particularly interesting because unlike the situation in some other new family forms, the connection itself derives from something shared by the children alone—both to each other and to a donor who is an outsider to each natal family and thus to the network itself. Not surprisingly, then, the parents and the children sometimes have quite different interests in and concerns about these affiliations; they also sometimes secure quite different benefits and face quite different problems.

Shrinking and Thinning Families

Even so, both parents *and* children have reasons to pursue these relationships. Indeed, the kind of relationships that networks of genetic strangers offer might be particularly important because of recent social change. Families are shrinking in size no matter what form the family takes. In 1960, the total fertility rate per woman in the United States was 3.7 children; today, the average American woman is expected to have 1.9 children. The average family size has also dropped from 3.14 individuals in 1970 to

2.54 individuals in 2017.[26] For single mothers who have relied on donor conception, small families are especially an issue. Not only are they likely to have fewer children than the members of two-parent households, but they and their children only have one lineage from which to draw to create an extended family.[27] Moreover, as many sociologists have noted, mobility (especially among those who are more privileged in this society) means that people may not live close to the members of their extended family.[28]

Shrinking families result in generational "thinning." A few generations back it was not uncommon to find families of close to half a dozen children, each of whom produced their own children and grandchildren, creating a host of relatives on a family tree that widened in each subsequent generation. Smaller families in each generation now produce considerably thinned branches; instead of widening, the family tree tapers. These changes are especially significant in a society with a minimal safety net because under those conditions people who can be considered "kin" might be the only source for important social, emotional, and material benefits.[29]

Donor-conceived families are in a prime position to expand the set of kinfolk on whom they might rely. Ironically, in doing so, parents who defy convention by making an unusual set of choices about how to create family often end up having to deal with some very conventional issues about who belongs in their family. Moreover, donor siblings may pose a challenge to the two-parent model that usually assigns related children to the same household. Of course those parents and children who want to regard the donor as simply a mechanism for creating a child can, if they want, avoid these complexities. But those who venture into the land of donor siblings—a land in which the donor might appear along with the other new relatives—solve some problems (such as offering up genetic kin from the paternal side) but raise the complexities of figuring out how to make sense of a new kind of kin.

Locating Our Respondents

Families who conceive through the use of a donor or donors are what sociologists call a "hidden population." Public agencies do not keep track of sperm donor use or the number of offspring produced through sales at sperm banks, and while the US Census Bureau is interested in fertility, it does not ask questions about conception.[30] Thus, as we considered whom to interview, a random sample was out of the question. Nonetheless, we had reason to believe that the population of families with donor-conceived children had grown considerably. After all, the fertility industry has mushroomed in the last four decades; it now serves a variety of individuals (single mothers) and couples (in two-mother families) who once had trouble accessing gametes.[31] The question for us became one of how to find a way into this population.[32] Little did we know at the time that we would eventually come to focus on a circle within a circle: the membership within the networks that connected families with donor offspring.

As might be expected, we began by exploring known territory. Because we had been conducting research within the single mothers' community for over twenty-five years, we had ties to a variety of organizations across the United States and, for several of those organizations, ties to local affiliates in the Boston area. Some organizations gave us access to their mailing lists; others posted announcements about our research to their Facebook pages or websites. In order to ensure that we were reaching the LGBTQ population, we also leafleted at Gay Pride events, including family weekends and other marches we regularly attended. On the emails and leaflets we wrote: "We are seeking families to participate in a research study about 'donor-conceived families.' We are looking to understand how parents and their children (over age 10 and young adults in their 20s and 30s) think about being donor-conceived. We are also interested in understanding how parents and children think about donors and donor siblings and what place, if any, they may have in your life. The research is funded by the National Science Foundation."[33] This snowball approach helped us locate our first wave of parents and children, many of whom were based in the Boston area. Those interviews, in turn, alerted us to the families that, having discovered they shared the same donor, had gone on to create networks.

Choosing Sites

A grant from the National Science Foundation (NSF) made it possible for us to travel to seven states (and the District of Columbia) in our effort to maximize the diversity of our respondent group. Within each state we selected major metropolitan areas as our research sites, traveling to respondents who lived within a radius of three hours from the city center.

We chose several of our research sites because of their historical relationships to the rise of the fertility industry as a big business.[34] For example, we traveled to California to interview some of the first families
to use anonymous donors. San Francisco is also a major home to several
well-known women's collectives that helped lesbian parents and single
mothers have children when the large banks were primarily serving heterosexual couples.[35] Another site, Boston, also has a well-known clinic
that helped lesbian couples in the early years of sperm-freezing.[36] Further,
California and the Washington, DC, area house two of the largest national sperm banks in the United States, while the other areas offer re-
gional banks. We traveled to several research sites in Texas because we
wanted a location in which donor conception (whether by single women
or women in two-mother families) might be less socially acceptable.

As part of our strategy, we also focused on metropolitan areas that
organizational databases had indicated contained significant numbers
of single moms or lesbian couples (California, Massachusetts, and the
DC area, including Maryland and Virginia). Jane Mattes, the founder
of the Single Mothers by Choice organization, also pointed us to sites
outside of the two coasts with the largest number of single mothers that
her organization has identified over the course of its thirty-five-year history.[37] We relied on that information to select Minnesota, traveling to
Minneapolis and its suburbs. Initially, we chose our respondents to reflect
variations in family type and children's ages. We expected to interview
family members about their donor siblings, unaware that we would be
able to interview donor siblings within the same network. (Part I of the
book reflects this variety regardless of whether or not the members of
each family had contact with donor siblings.) However, from the very
first interviews we conducted in Massachusetts, both parents and teens in
these families offered to connect us with their donor siblings. That is, we
discovered networks *after* we began our research.

Once alerted to the fact that some families belonged to networks
created through reliance on the same donor, we extended our research
strategy to include those additional respondents. This new strategy
allowed us to reach the circle within the circle, a group within the *same*
network. As a result, in each age group of the children (early teens, high
school students, and post–high school kids, most of whom are in college)
we were able to interview families that were linked by a sperm donor. All

in all, we interviewed at least two families in twenty-five different linked networks; the total number of these linked individual families is seventy-six. (These networks are the focus of Part II of the book.) While not all of our respondents have had face-to-face contact with other families in person, in all of the networks featured in Part II, the majority of members have met offline at least once.

To better understand the context in which families and networks existed, we asked to join online forums to which our respondents belonged (such as several Single Mothers by Choice forums) and Facebook private pages that the networks had created. The openness of our respondents enabled us to observe networks groups "in vivo" and to learn how the group might have changed from when we interviewed members. (See appendix B for more detail.)

Choosing Networks

At the end of the first year of data collection we realized that we had networks that reflected different eras, different age groups of children, and different internal dynamics. Different eras allowed us to look at changes in the history of the fertility industry: the families we interviewed had purchased gametes under different conditions, such as having more or less information about the donor; they also had different possibilities for making contact with donor siblings. Different eras also allowed us to look at families at the forefront of the lesbian baby boom *and* at families for whom that family form had become far more routine.

Different age groups of children gave us the opportunity to learn about changes in children's understanding of what it meant to be donor conceived and in their reactions to encountering donor siblings. Yet donor siblings also turn out to be close in age *within* each network. For instance, a hypothetical network would consist of four children who are fifteen years old, three who are fourteen years old, and three who are thirteen years old. There might be another child who is twelve and two children who are eleven, each of whom has older siblings in the same nuclear family.

And finally, different internal dynamics of the networks themselves became evident once we had enough networks to actually document those differences. Four of the featured networks that include children ages ten and older have existed for approximately the same length of time (about thirteen years). They all formed in the early part of the twenty-first century when independent registries began. Yet each network has children who met at different ages. The dispersion *among* networks allowed us to compare how the children's ages influence internal group dynamics.

Once we had firmed up our network typology in the first year of the study, we asked respondents in specific networks to help us locate others in their group. We were fortunate that the members we had met in the first cities we visited were excited about the project and willing to vouch for us.[38] As soon as we had selected a number of different networks (not all of which are featured in this book), we were able to watch each one grow in size and observe network dynamics unfold. Even though we knew that membership depended on the fertility industry and that present membership was not fixed in size, we were always surprised when new members came forward. And usually new members arrived just as we thought that a particular network had reached the saturation point established by the bank-imposed limits on the number of offspring per donor. We came to learn that the arrival of new members was a routine feature of these networks. The youngest network (with children under the age of five) we chose as a focus in the second year of our data collection. We selected this group because it was in the early formation stages and we could capture "in motion" parents' discussions about their first planned gathering.

Features of the Respondents

The 212 parents we interviewed ranged in age from thirty-two to eighty-five; the vast majority (92 percent) self-reported as women. Among the separate families at the time of the interview, over half (58 percent) were headed by a single parent, 23 percent were headed by two women, and the remaining 20 percent were headed by both a man and a woman. Total incomes within these households ranged widely, from a low of $12,000 a year to a high of over a million dollars, with a median of about $138,000. The youngest parent we interviewed was thirty-two; the oldest was eighty-five. Among the 154 children we interviewed the youngest was ten; the oldest was twenty-nine. About half (51 percent) were girls.[39] Seventy-nine percent of these children knew about a donor sibling, whether or not they had contact with that sibling. In addition to parents and children, we interviewed 12 donors and 10 other individuals related to the children. Altogether we interviewed 388 people for this study. (See appendix A for more information about the sample characteristics and appendix B for more information about how we conducted our interviews.)

Brief Overview

The book is divided into two major parts. In Part I we explore the conditions that enable contact among donor siblings and the general patterns that emerge among the actors in these stories. We demonstrate how the parents—one set of actors—choose donors for their children (chapter 1) and then how they make the decision to involve themselves in networks of genetic strangers (chapter 3). We also demonstrate how the children— the other set of actors—make sense, at different stages in their own development, of what a donor is and construct their own ideas about how the influence of the donor is relevant in their daily lives (chapter 2); our focus on the children turns as well to the ways in which they come to understand the social meaning of the genetic bonds they have to their donor siblings (chapter 4). In Part II we put these two sets of actors together in networks of parents and children (chapters 5 to 10). We demonstrate how these actors perform in conjunction with each other when they are brought together within a network of donor siblings and, in some cases, with the donor himself.

* * *

The exchange of sperm that begins the process of network formation begins as a market transaction. The people we describe in this book do something constructive with that transaction. And perhaps they have good reason for doing so. Now that the family tree has begun to thin, people cannot so readily rely on traditional forms of kinship; the people who rely on donor conception, however, can take unique steps to counteract generational thinning, creating for themselves and their children whole new sets of "relatives." Unlike the unknown donor who is a paper profile, the donor siblings are full of life—real human beings—who might offer a new kind of connection. In what follows, we explore how two sets of social attitudes—attitudes toward kinship based in genes and attitudes toward kinship based in choice—precipitate, shape, and are shaped by the novel interactions that are the byproduct of contact with genetic strangers.

Part I

———◦◦◦◦◦———

Making Sense of the Donor and Donor Siblings

The emphasis in Part I is on sets of general processes as they are shaped by individual actors rather than on those processes that emerge as a result of network dynamics. The first two sets, involving both parents and the children, largely concern the donor. The second two sets also involve parents and children in tandem: these largely concern the arrangements for, and impact of, connection.

In chapter 1 we describe how parents make the private choice of a donor, a choice parents make either by themselves or with a partner but without reference to the existence of donor siblings. We show that all parents take into account similar factors as they select from among the available donor profiles. In chapter 3 we describe the decisions parents make with regard to having contact with a child's donor siblings. We show that from the first moment they become aware that they can communicate with other people who used the same donor, parents believe that they are forging a set of relationships that never before existed, and they develop strategies about how best to handle that new possibility.

In chapter 2 we introduce the children as they respond to the choices their parent(s) made for them. We show how they begin to understand what it means to be donor conceived. We show as well how they begin to fashion an identity for themselves—and simultaneously an identity for the donor. Parents usually make the decision to present children with their donor siblings; a few of the older children we interviewed initiated contact with donor siblings themselves. In both cases the children face their own challenge of interpreting the genetic link (as "half-siblings") to children with whom they do not share an active parent. We discuss these issues in chapter 4 as we describe how children begin to understand not only the concept of a donor sibling but also how donor siblings can help them understand themselves.

The complete understanding of some processes we discuss in this book cannot be placed neatly in either Part I or Part II. Among parents, one of those topics is the motivation for having contact with genetic strangers. Some motivations remain constant across time; we discuss these in chapter 2. In Part II we indicate that new motivations emerge and we analyze how these different motivations shape understandings of relationships within the networks themselves. Among children, one of those topics explored in both sections is the interactions a child has with donor siblings. In chapter 4 we discuss these interactions from the point of view of the child seeking to understand what it means to have donor siblings. In Part II we discuss these interactions in the context of each network. As we do, we demonstrate that the full meaning of donor siblinghood is created, and recreated, through interpersonal dynamics. Taken as a whole, then, the shift from Part I to Part II illuminates how individual processes transform into the potential for something with profoundly *social* consequences.

I

Choosing Donors

WHEN HIS INFERTILITY required that Greg and his wife, Sandy, acquire sperm, they decided to turn to the market and seek out the options at a national sperm bank. Greg, who lives in Tennessee and will appear again in the 7008er network (chapter 6), knew they were purchasing a commodity:

> I understand that [the donor] is a fully fleshed-out human being, but that's not the part of him that we have in our lives. What we have, as I see it, is a product that we purchased. So I purchased a product based upon my reaction to his profile as compared to the other profiles I chose to read.

Blunt and instrumental as he is, Greg did not purchase just any product. He liked one better than another, based on his reading of the profile, and so he bought the part he needed from that "human being." Having done so, Greg could laud himself—and be lauded by others—for his perceptive selectivity; the sperm was now "his."

The members of a same-sex couple living in Connecticut, who will appear again in the Social Capitalist network (chapter 9), were more explicit about wanting something more than "just a product." Originally, Marlene and her wife, Cara, tried to make an arrangement with someone they knew; when that fell through, they decided to turn to a sperm bank. They chose the bank they did for two reasons. First, it was far away and therefore would be less likely to be used by others in their tight-knit community. As Cara said, "At the time it seemed like a complicated journey to accidentally discover that the person you were sitting next to in the synagogue is in fact the donor sibling of our child." Second, the bank offered photos, and they wanted to see an adult photo of the donor so that they could assess whether or not they would "like" him. Acknowledging, perhaps, the foolishness of a "connection" at first sight, Marlene was conscious of making meaning out of the one object that she could relate to through her own visual sense. As was the case for Greg, in choosing, she acquired ownership of the sperm and, by extension, the intended child:

> When we were looking, I really wanted to choose a donor whose adult picture I could see. I really wanted to feel a sense of connection with the donor, just sort of like an ineffable connection that I couldn't really describe why—which obviously is based on nothing but me looking at his photo. . . . I always had this thing for dark, curly hair, and this guy had dark, curly hair and just had these very kind, empathic eyes.

Like Cara and Marlene, Margo, a single mother by choice living in Chicago, who appears in the Soul Mates network (chapter 8), had considered using a known donor: she quickly rejected that option because she wanted to have no competition for claims on her child; she wanted the child to be hers alone. As she narrowed her choices among the sperm donors listed at a major US sperm bank, she focused on looks—and genetic diversity—so as to get what she thought would be an attractive and healthy child:

> I think that nature gives us a lot of hints that we should mix up the gene pool, so that's part of why I didn't want someone from my own heritage background. I didn't want an Eastern European Jew. . . . Also, I think that often people with mixed heritage can be very beautiful, depending on how the genes mix, because you sometimes get unusual combinations of eye color and hair color and stuff. And I like Latin men. I think they're very handsome.

All these respondents—in different family forms—used as many pieces of information as they had available to them to make the selection of a donor. In the past, even before Greg and his wife were choosing sperm with which to conceive their now seventeen-year-old daughter, and many years before Marlene and Cara began their process of selection to conceive their one-year-old son, banks offered only limited profiles (age, race, height, weight, level of education, medical history) on paper. Over time, and in response to consumer demand and technological developments, the profiles moved online and became more extensive, including essays written by the donors. Eventually some banks started to add photographs of the donor as a child; some added audio recordings of answers to a standard series of questions asked by a "neutral" interviewer; some banks now offer adult photos of sperm donors. These add-ons come at additional expense, and not everyone can afford to purchase them, although, for those who do, these other items become valuable resources. Greg worked with a paper profile; Margo had a long essay and a description of what the donor looked like; Marlene and Cara had those materials and a photograph. In each case, the respondents individuate the choice and, in so doing, make the child an expression of *their* tastes and values. In a more "conventional" situation these tastes and values might have been embodied in a partner or father; when choosing sperm, selectivity is the process that creates both display *and* ownership.

Our respondents made a wide array of different choices about the type of donor, the bank they wanted to use, and the particular characteristics they wanted the donors to have. Yet, for all those differences, some filtering criteria were clear. Intending parents chose traits that they believed would secure advantage for their children. Respondents chose also among the types of donors available to them, including known donors, anonymous donors, and identity-release donors. And they chose characteristics that they believed would fit with who they were and how they understood their own natal families. Finally, most respondents wanted a donor who seemed likable. Respondents sought to balance these various sets of criteria; conventional ideas about an attractive child might conflict with the kind of child they thought they could raise within their family. They also wanted to be able to imagine what they would tell their future child about the donor; when they had an identity-release donor, they considered both how their child might want updated information and whether the donor would respond well when the child reached out to him. In seeking to resolve the potential conflict among these criteria, they decided which one was most important; whichever set they chose first narrowed the subsequent choices.[1] We might note that each of the particular items that made up a filter could also be an entire illusion resting on misrepresentation, incomplete information, and mistaken assumptions about the operation of genes; what looked and felt like an informed choice might have been something altogether different.[2] We might note as well that because the donor is always male, the filtering process is likely to project onto the donor (and by extension the sperm) some stereotypical masculine qualities.

Sperm with Privilege

The vast majority of respondents told us that they wanted to secure advantage as one of their criteria: they wanted someone healthy, smart (which they assessed by educational achievement), and tall.[3] People relying on donor gametes are involved in a new way to form a nuclear family; yet, in the process, for the most part they are reproducing very traditional ideas about privilege (e.g., good health, height, intelligence, and race) as well as actual human beings who will embody that privilege. But this decision is not theirs alone. Given the options the banks and clinics provide, they can do little else. But few respondents we interviewed resisted these preordained options.[4] The choice of privilege was usually reported to us by respondents as unselfconsciously as the town in which they lived or the ages of their children. That unselfconsciousness among so many of our respondents rested on its own set of advantages: sperm and eggs are expensive, and some sperm and eggs are even more expensive than others.[5] The "priceless child" has a price, and respondents had to weigh costs as well as other factors.[6] (See table 1.1.)

Our respondents with fewer resources could not assume that they would be able to give their children quite the same set of privileges, even if they also were purchasing sperm from a bank. These less-advantaged respondents still sought privilege, and they still sought to find a donor with whom they were comfortable, but their choices might be narrower. To save money, some respondents had to choose from the "clearance sale" section of a particular bank, which might not have any identity-release donors or donors over six feet tall; some respondents saved money by locating their gametes directly from donors through online registries (like the Known Donor Registry) that did not engage in the strict testing of formal banks.[7] As another way to reduce costs, some of our respondents, rather than choosing their own gametes—either egg and

TABLE 1.1 Prices for Sperm from Different Types of Donors and Using Different Methods of Insemination

Method of insemination (preparation type)	Anonymous donor	Identity-release donor
Intrauterine insemination	$830	$935
Intrauterine insemination (Cryogenic Laboratories Incorporated)	$650	$835
Intracervical insemination	$705	$825
Intracervical insemination (Cryogenic Laboratories Incorporated)	$570	$715
In vitro fertilization	$525	$685
In vitro fertilization (Cryogenic Laboratories Incorporated)	$415	$555

Source: "Fairfax Cryobank—Fees," accessed May 5, 2017.

sperm alone or each separately—obtained embryos that were already constructed.

Type of Donor

The vast majority of our respondents purchased eggs, embryos, and sperm from formal banks or clinics rather than alternative online services.[8] Among those respondents who had purchased sperm from a sperm bank, 61 percent chose a sperm donor who would remain anonymous for their first donor-conceived child, and 39 percent chose an identity-release donor.

For some respondents, the difference between anonymity and identity release was unimportant, and they went with the donor they wanted for some other reason. Some women, however, were especially eager to avoid any possibility that the donor could make a claim on their child or become too involved in their newly created nuclear family. Respondents in all three family types expressed this concern, although it was particularly prominent among the members of same-sex couples (and especially so before second-parent adoption became possible).[9] Even when not motivated by the fear that a donor might make a claim on their child, some individuals in all types of families preferred an anonymous donor because that choice ensured that the donor would never become part of their family. On the other hand, those respondents who chose identity-release donors believed it important that their children be able to contact the donor if they wanted to. (As we explain more fully in chapter 9, offering children access to the donor is another form of advantage that contemporary parents can provide for their children.)[10]

Opting for "Fit"

Beyond privilege and type of donor, respondents wanted someone who "fit" into their conception of the family they were creating. Many respondents used precisely that expression; the meaning of the word, however, was not always the same. For some respondents, filtering donors from the lists provided by banks or clinics is about searching for the physical characteristics that will create a child who resembles either the parent who is carrying (common for single mothers) or the parent who is *not* carrying (common in both same-sex and heterosexual couples).[11] Fit, in this instance, means "matching" the donor's physical appearance (or some other characteristic about the donor, such as ethnicity or heritage) to at least one parent.[12] Almost all respondents with more than one child said not only that they did not want the hassle of having to choose a donor again but that they were especially concerned about matching a child to another child already born into the family, thus indicating that they believe that genes mattered within the family.

Fit could also mean matching a child to the membership of a parent's broad set of relatives. Among the nine African American women we interviewed, all but two had chosen a white or racially mixed donor. These women explained that choice not only in terms of limited options (which some mentioned) but also in terms of wanting to match a child to the extended family they already had. They spoke about how their understanding of race was that of a continuum rather than a black/white dichotomy; they noted that because the members of their own families (and they, themselves) were already evidence of this continuum, by choosing a white or racially mixed donor they were doing what would best "fit" their child into a family of many different skin tones. Kim, a single mother in Texas, explained that when she chose to have a donor-conceived child (after having given birth to two children conceived in romantic relationships with black men), race didn't really matter to her because her extended family had already become multiracial by marriage: "My dad has married a black woman [and then] a white woman, so I have two sisters that are biracial. I have an aunt that's from Australia; my uncle married a white Australian. My cousins are biracial. I have cousins that are part Chinese, so it's no big deal."

For many other respondents, fit goes beyond a simple matching of physical traits or even race. Fit also has to do with wanting a donor who is like oneself—someone with whom one might feel comfortable if one interacted with him in some other venue; someone who might seem familiar. Parents move back and forth between the donor profile and their own identities, now emphasizing this or that aspect of themselves and now focusing on this or that aspect of the donor. In the process they creatively reimagine themselves *and* conjure up a compatible donor. Those with partners add a layer to the process as they take into consideration yet another set of desires. In addition, as noted, intending parents sometimes consider the donor's similarity to their relatives. In this way, not only the intending parents but also their mothers, fathers, sisters, and brothers may make an appearance. In effect, this search for the ideal donor is as much about how intending parents construct their own identities (and the identities of their other relatives) as it is about what shows up on a donor profile. Intending parents funnel these various notions about fit and identities into a final choice; they hope that they will be able to form a deep connection with the child embodying these characteristics.

Donna, the nongestational mother in a same-sex couple living in Maryland, described the donor that she and her partner, Cheryl, picked. She used the same unselfconscious linking of education with intelligence, acceptance of racial privilege, and assumptions of genetic determination as did many other respondents. But Donna's focus was on her belief that the donor—who would definitely *not* be a member of their family—*could* be in the family. As she talked, she emphasized the religion she and Cheryl have in common. Whether or not these aspects of their lives are important on a daily basis, they can be drawn on as selection criteria. By widening the circle to include how the donor fits with other relatives—Donna's brother, Cheryl's dad and brother—the two women became comfortable with their decision:

The donor's an engineer, so he's really smart. He had German Lutheran background, which is what I have, and Cheryl has Lutheran background. When I read his profile, it was like that's our guy because he sounded like he could be in our family. . . . Honestly, it was a combination. It was a sense because it was the look of his handwriting—like my brother's. He could have been my brother. Then, you could read the essay: he could've been Cheryl's brother. . . . Cheryl's dad was an engineer, you know, and the donor's an engineer. It's just like all the strings that make the fabric of who we are, so it's hard to tease them out and say which string [cemented the choice] because it was more of the combination. . . . He just fit. It's hard to say details because it's like when you walk into a place and you know you're home and everything's good and safe. That's how it felt when I read his profile. But there weren't words that stuck out that made me feel that way.

At this deeper level Donna was hoping to find, fit has to do with a profound sense that the donor will provide something that is both "good and safe." And at this deeper level, goodness and safety are connected to the hope that a parent will know, recognize, and be comfortable with the child.

For the vast majority of our respondents, religion was not a key element of fit. However, most of the thirty-eight parents (20 percent of the sample) who were Jewish expressed a distinctive set of concerns. Those respondents indicated that they believed something "good and safe" could only be obtained if they chose a Jewish donor. (Margo, quoted above, is a notable exception.)[13] And this was the case even though most of the Jewish respondents we interviewed identified as "cultural" Jews rather than either "religious" or "practicing" Jews, and most of these respondents recognized that Judaism is conferred through the mother, not the father. No one suggested that genes carried religion per se, but most of these respondents suggested that if not a race, Jewishness is certainly an ethnicity. As our respondents explained why they wanted a Jewish donor, they suggested that they were looking for something about themselves that connected them to the donor as a way to reduce the strangeness of using "just any" gametes. In this way, "being Jewish" is no different from familiar handwriting or being an engineer.

For some, however, "being Jewish" went beyond casual similarities, and these imputed great weight to "Jewish genes," as did Debra, a single mother from California who wanted a Jewish donor. She suggested that she would be more comfortable with her child because that child would understand innuendo and humor and would look like her; the Jewish "part" would enable a profound connection.

> DEBRA: That would be comfortable because if I spoke Yiddish to her, she would internally get it. Not that I speak Yiddish. If I say something with a Jewish innuendo, [if] you're from that side, you get the Jewish part. If I say something like that, she'll get it genetically.... We would look alike. We would have the same mannerism.
> INTERVIEWER: ... Your daughter then becomes more familiar in some ways?
> DEBRA: Not familiar, connected. Connected soully [*sic*], spiritually, inwardly, connected genetically. Connected molecule-wise not familiar.

Love *could* have been the connection for Debra—had she become a mother with a partner's sperm in a romantic relationship. Without love, she needed a different connection to her child, a connection that she believed only Jewish sperm could provide:

> I would have reconciled to a husband not being Jewish. It would just have been the way it was supposed to be, and it would have been just fine. She would have come from love so it would have been fine.... If she wasn't coming from love, she's going to come from a Jewish sperm ... that she could connect to. It's more about her.

For other respondents, finding the donor to be "likable" was the way to make the transaction (buying a body part) something more than a commercial transaction: it actually humanized the donor both for the parent and, they hoped, down the line, for their children should those children be in a position to have contact with him. As is the case for fit, being likable is in the eyes of the beholder and thus varies from person to person.

In the final moments of selection, often a particular item helped clinch the choice of one donor over another. Margo reported that her donor seemed nice, thoughtful, and motivated to achieve:

He seemed relaxed and funny, self-confident but not cocky. He seemed to be genuine, and he sounds like a nice guy. I don't know. Whatever that means. But they asked him, "What are your short-term goals?" He said, "I don't have any short-term goals, only long-term goals." I thought, "Oh, that's interesting." He just seemed focused and driven, and so it just felt right.

Greg might have suggested that he was simply buying a "product," but he also chose that particular product on the basis of the donor's essay. Here, he thought, was someone he would actually find pleasure in knowing:

I chose one guy who wrote in such a way that at the time I thought . . . was endearing. He was being very caring and yet very—I don't know, he was promoting his goods. I thought, this is a guy I could sit down and talk to and enjoy. I found him eloquent. . . . So that was really about it.

And while Marlene loved a photo, Cara, who had many other reasons for choosing the donor they did, was won over by his essay, which revealed a "voice" she found attractive:

He has this very sort of nice, gentle, inviting voice. He talked about the importance of his family. He talked about his love for nature and the beauty of urban life. He has this lovely line about the pleasure of biting into a fresh piece of fruit, and on a perfect day what he wants to do is sit under a tree open to the sunshine and bite into the fresh piece of fruit. I don't know—there was just something very pleasant about that.

Moving On

The choices made before conception enable intending parents to express their taste and values and through that expression to make the child their own. Different processes of "ownership" (and inclusion or exclusion of the donor) occur after the child is born. Scholars write that parents vary widely in how often—and in what manner—they discuss the donor.[14]

Sometimes the sperm donor is present in the family, especially when a child has a medical issue the parents believe came from the "other" side. Sometimes the donor might appear in family discussions to be a real person but at other times be perceived as being a mere "instrument." Not only are not all families the same, but within two-parent families the two parents might differ in how they think about and present the donor. In two-mother families, the nongestational parent is often reported to be less interested in keeping the image of the donor alive. And within heterosexual couples, the father is often reported to be threatened by an active awareness of the sperm donor.[15] As a group, our respondents displayed the same variations—and some of the same patterns of difference—in attitudes toward the sperm donor. But regardless of variation, all of the parents we interviewed disclosed donor conception, giving their children the information provided by the banks. That information becomes the basis for the children's own understanding of who the donor is and how the donor's genes contributed to who they are. We turn next to that issue.

2

Inventing the Donor / Inventing the Self

ALL CHILDREN ARE curious about how they came to be born. Some parents can satisfy that curiosity with a straightforward birth narrative that tells of a baby who is wanted and special; if there are two parents, the story might also tell of a baby who is central to a very intimate relationship. Over time, the birth narrative might expand to include siblings, close relatives, and ancestors connected by the same web of belonging.[1] Of course, donor-conceived children are not unique in hearing a more complex story. Some children might have an unknown biological father. Yet when this is the case for donor-conceived children, the absence of the biological father is by a parent's (or parents') intention, and the children are confronted with a special mystery of conception. How do children go beyond a simple birth narrative to understand how they came to be? How do their parents help them understand that some aspects of the self might come from a stranger, a person they do not now—and may never—know? How do the children make sense of a parent's (or parents') choices—the choice to conceive them (sometimes against great odds) and the choice of a particular set of gametes?

What Is a Donor?

Young Children

For very young children, the "donor" is a hollow concept. Absent understanding what a donor is, children skillfully use bits of information their parents tell them. All the children we interviewed, starting with the ten-year-olds, had been told a conventional birth narrative of a wanted child.[2] Just one narrative element stood out as different: a stranger known as the donor played an important role. Usually the parents told their children that the donor was a "generous" person. Take the example of Haley, who, at the time of our interview, was an eleven-year-old living in California with her single mother. Haley could not recall exactly when she learned that she was donor conceived. However, as we talked, she recollected that she had asked simple questions and been given simple information about an individual she identifies as being a "dad": "[Mom] told me when I was little that I was born in Massachusetts in her apartment. About my dad, she told me that there was a man who helped her have me but we didn't know who he was." She added her own flourishes: "I imagined a donor to be like a really nice guy. When I was really little, he was just like a magical guy who just came and helped my mom. Then I was born." Later, her curiosity returned and she probed for more information:

HALEY: Then I don't know what age it was but I started asking more questions because I was wondering. Then she told me more to [add] depth to the whole sperm donor thing.

INTERVIEWER: What did your mom tell you then?

HALEY: She told me that there was a guy who was really nice. He took some sperm and he mailed it to a place. She took it from the place and she had me. I don't really remember what she said about that. I don't know what she did with it, but somehow I got inside of her. Then she had me.

Haley understood the sequence: her mom wanted a baby, a nice guy helped by sending sperm to a place, her mom went to a place to get sperm, sperm got into her mom, and she (Haley) was born at home. At age eleven this seemed to be all she wanted to know.

Olivia, an articulate ten-year-old from rural Texas, at first told a story of being needed: her single mom "just had to have another person to love." Then, unprompted, she went on to elaborate with the details of a slightly different story:

My mom, she got married, but then she woke up to discover he [the guy she had married] had only pretended to want a baby. She still wanted to have a baby, so a really nice guy came and he helped her have us. But he didn't marry her. He just gave her the part that she needed to have a baby.

In an upbeat way that features generosity, Olivia placed the added details into a broader context that contains all the elements of a classic fairy tale: normal people living their lives come to face unusual circumstances, a struggle against the odds, and through a combination of luck and perseverance reach their goal. When school friends asked Olivia why she and her twin brother did not have a dad, she flipped between the two accounts. Her peers did not challenge these accounts because they are wrapped in familiar themes. Olivia did not really understand how this man, a donor from a sperm bank, came to give her mom "the part she needed" or exactly what that part was. This was not important to her before she was ten. In both versions she made clear she is a very wanted child.

When parents have chosen an identity-release donor, they often tell kids that they can "meet" their donor when they turn eighteen (although this is not exactly the case). When parents have chosen an anonymous donor, they say a meeting is not possible. Haley was disappointed that she had not yet met the gift-giver (who is an identity-release donor), and Olivia (who was conceived with an anonymous donor) had not yet asked whether she could meet hers. Both girls had conventional birth stories to explain themselves, but in both cases the donor remained a mystery to be solved.

Children begin to solve the mystery of how they came to be using categories available to them. Sometimes they borrow from everyday language. For instance, both Olivia and Haley used the phrases "love," "a nice guy," "needing parts," "sperm," and "dad" to try to give substance to the concept of the donor.[3] Parents give their children these words and then assume that their children understand what they mean. In fact, parents frequently told us that they had talked about the donor from the moment a child was born; many told us they had read from the available children's books about donor conception.[4] They thought their children fully understood what they needed to know. But even clever young children like Haley and Olivia confessed that it was a long time before they fully understood what a donor was and how donor conception came about.

Sex Education and the Role of Other Children

For those in single-mother or two-mother families, interactions with other children raise questions about the absent "father." Children are left on their own to find an explanation for the missing parent. When children are exposed to the "sex education" curriculum (usually in fifth grade), even more questions emerge. The biology lessons explain that all kids are created from sperm and eggs; drawing on a typical heteronormative schema, the lessons might also explain how the sperm and egg get together. Regardless of how much concrete information is provided, these conventional lessons do not include either reproductive technology (like in vitro fertilization) or the use of a donor.[5] The curriculum thus leaves a lot of room for children to invent answers for themselves.

While most of the children we interviewed knew that their donor provided gametes, the new, detailed information they learned in school created the need for further clarification about both the reproductive process through which they came to be and the "missing person." Some children were stunned to realize that they had not really understood the place of the gamete donor.

Of course, lots of information about all things related to donors and donor conception is discussed among children without a teacher or parent being present. Sometimes the donor-conceived children—whether they had accurate information or not—became the "experts." Olivia, who is featured in the opening of this chapter, had two accounts to explain only having a mom; she happily brought them out to educate her friends on the playground when they asked about her "dad." Similarly, Walker, age twelve, was very comfortable being the center of attention and answering questions from curious classmates who knew he has two moms:

> A couple days ago I had to explain what a sperm donor was. I was in study hall working on some homework and this little fifth-grader came up to me. He's a friend of mine. He goes, "Walker, how were you made?" Someone in my grade asked, "Yeah, how would that happen?" Soon enough I had five or six people standing around me. Eventually I said, "Have you ever heard of a sperm donor?" They were like, "That would explain it." That was pretty much the end of it. I had to explain to one person afterwards, but he didn't want to be that strange one that didn't know. He asked me later . . . I just explain that someone donates sperm and then they used that to create me.

Walker reported that his moms had "introduced as normal" this knowledge about donor conception. Walker and Olivia enjoyed being able to help their classmates understand something not discussed in the formal curriculum.

Children and Parents Co-Produce the Donor and the Child

Making sense of donor conception is one step in a child's understanding. Yet children who understand *how* they came to be might well want to know more. They want to know who the donor is, what he looks like, and why he made this gesture. They also want to know which—if any— parts of them came from the donor. They may have the broad outlines of the donor. They know that he is a man, and a "nice" one at that; they may assume that as a man the donor has some stereotypically masculine traits. But they want to know more about who he is. Children and parents collaborate to put together the various pieces of information (traits, characteristics, and bits pulled from the donor essays). Often the collaboration is not synchronized.[6] Sometimes children lead the way and quiz their parents for clues; sometimes parents spontaneously report on what they know about the donor from the information they were given by the sperm bank. Over time, children's curiosity and parents' efforts to be forthcoming combine to push the pieces of the donor puzzle forward. In this process children and their parents weave together information. The child comes to understand that the donor is a separate person with distinctive characteristics. The child also comes to believe that that person is the source of some of the child's own traits.[7] Parents reinforce their children's belief. Perhaps more importantly, parents try to help children see that they have qualities that come from *both* themselves and their unknown donor as parents observe the characteristics, mannerisms, or interests of their child. In this way children learn both about the donor and about how they might be like (or not like) this person.

In Los Angeles, Emily, age ten, recalled that her mother (who is single) told her the donor is "very musical," "tall," and has "blue eyes." Although Emily's mother did not necessarily use biological language, she offered a genetic explanation for why Emily has different traits and abilities than she, the mother, has. And without fully understanding genetic determinants herself, Emily collaborated with her mom's information in attributing her own characteristics to the donor because, as she said, she sang in a chorus, was tall for her age, and "no one else in [her] family has blue eyes." Thus while genes are "adult talk" and foreign to most young children, Emily had come to assume that some of her physical traits and distinctive abilities came from the donor. She enjoyed putting together these pieces with other unique bits her mother had supplied: "When I was little she told me that he liked dolphins and underwater stuff. . . . When I was little I wanted to change my last name to maybe Dolphin." Emily distinguished things about herself she could attribute to the donor; she identified things about herself that she and her mother imagined came from the donor to construct her own identity. In this process she fixed on information that made the donor less generic. Just as their parents made sense of their own identities to imagine which donor would be most "fitting" for their families, the children make sense of who they are in order to imagine a donor who matches them.

Parents and children are trying to do two things at once in this process of co-production. They are trying to make the donor less mysterious as they pick traits that the child appears to share with the donor. They are also trying to make the child less mysterious as they identify the traits that link the child to the donor. Emily and her mom found blue eyes, height, and musical abilities as traits that helped them make sense both of the donor and of Emily herself. It did not matter that these traits might not really come from the donor. What mattered is that this ten-year-old had a place from which to understand that she too, like other children, has a male progenitor whose influence is both tangible and positive.

In Florida, at the slightly more advanced age of thirteen, Parker saw his skin tones as being a combination of a white donor and a mother whose ancestral roots are in an Afro-Caribbean community. At age seventeen, Andy, who lives in suburban Boston with his single mother, had more concrete information about the donor's characteristics. Through a leap of imagination, he could see himself as a combination of his mother and the donor: "There wasn't a picture of him but there was a visual description, which was sort of tall, wavy brown hair, more of a Mediterranean skin. So I could easily see that, mixed with my mom, making me." Because none of the children we interviewed had a photo of the donor as an adult (although some had pictures of the donor as a baby), they were all guessing about what the donor actually looked like. Andy and Parker both imagined the donor blending with their mothers to produce them. As they made themselves the product of both genetic sides, Andy and Parker bound mother, child, and donor together.

Other children found a way to easily insert the donor into the story their parent(s) had already told them about how their family came to be. At age fifteen, Will, from eastern Texas, who has two moms (and has not read the donor profile but has depended on what his mothers have told him) did not blend characteristics. In fact, he guessed that he and the donor share the same build; his genetic mother did not appear to play an active part in his physical construction. As do many children, Will reversed the normal order of inheritance as he mused that the donor looks like him rather than the other way around:

> The only thing I know is that he's six foot two, blond hair, blue eyes. I guess I imagine him looking or resembling me kind of. I'm not saying identical. I'm not saying totally different. But, we probably have some of the same features. I'm kind of all legs and arms. Maybe he has longer arms, longer legs, something like that.

When Will attributed his *masculine* build to the donor, he was not disrupting the story about the tight-knit family his mothers created for him and his sister; he was finding in the donor what he saw as being the sex-linked traits he does not share with his mothers.

Other information about the donor can also be used to help sustain a family narrative. Although for the majority of children the religion of the donor is not relevant in the home, some mentioned it as being particularly important. A few children we interviewed remarked that they liked that their donor was Catholic; in a family of practicing Catholics this piece of information fit well. At age seventeen, Naomi, from a Boston suburb, was glad that her donor was Jewish because she thought this made her 100 percent Jewish and therefore just like her two mothers. Greg and Sandy's daughter, Zoe, age seventeen, from Tennessee (who appears again in the 7008er network in chapter 6), also noted that she felt more authentically Jewish knowing the donor had a "Jewish side" and therefore she did not have to feel she had simply borrowed her religion from her dad, who is Jewish but not genetically related to her.

Confirmations and Disruptions: The Role of Siblings

Sometimes siblings are collaborators in this process of figuring out who the donor is and what he has contributed. Siblings provide a point of reference that an only child like Emily, Andy, or Parker does not have. Siblings offer another source of information about traits and characteristics that could be derived from genetic material but are not explained through a parent. Shane and his twin, Finn, live in rural Massachusetts with their single mother. The three looked over the donor profile together. At age twelve, Shane discussed the parts of the donor he thought were reflected in his own and his twin's physical appearances. He also found a bit of information that resonated with his own school interests. He thus constructed an identity for himself that matched some of what he knew about the donor:

> He lives in California. He looks exactly like us; he looks more like my brother as in the way he looks facially, but the way he looks as in build, we look exactly like him. . . . He apparently got a degree in English or writing and I love English and writing.

Shane recalled some things that he felt satisfied with that both he and his twin brother seem to share with the donor as well as something distinctive for each of them. The donor is built like both of them; he looks more like his brother but he has Shane's love of writing and English. Finn, it seems, is more the science type who has their mother's interest.

Megan and her twin brother, Matt, who are from Illinois, were entering their first year of college when we talked to them and were new arrivals to the 7008er network (in chapter 6). Years ago, they had listened to the donor's audiotape their mom had purchased when she decided to conceive her children as a single parent.[8] Megan thought she was a lot like her mother but her brother might resemble the donor more. Megan told us their donor reminded her of the way her brother jokes around: "To me, he sounded like my brother because they are both funny. . . . He sort of made a joke in it. . . . The woman [sperm bank interviewer] asked him, 'What's something you most admire about yourself?' He sort of paused and he was like, 'My modesty.' I thought that was just funny and I was like, 'Yeah. My brother.'" In short, children use their siblings to help understand which of their traits might have come from the donor's genes as opposed to the genes—or nurturance—of the parent(s) with whom they live. As these examples show, sometimes children share traits they believe come from the donor with their siblings; at other times they split the donor into pieces and each claim separate ones.

Adolescents

Using the Donor to Separate

As we noted in chapter 1, in choosing the donor the parents are concerned with the issue of "fit." And, as we have just shown, children also work with that concept as they locate the donor as someone who makes sense within the family that has been created. At the same time that adolescents can use information about the donor to make him fit into a family narrative, they can also use it to create some distance from their parents:[9] Will got masculinity from his donor; Andy got wavy hair and Mediterranean skin tones from his; Parker assumed the donor was the source of his skin tone, which is lighter than his mother's, and because the donor is six foot one, he hoped he would far surpass in height his mother, who is no more than five foot two. Girls do the same distancing (perhaps with even greater vigor). As teens who push against their parent(s), donor-conceived children find support for that resistance in imagining (and identifying with) the characteristics they share with their unknown donor and *not* with their parent(s).

Paige, age fifteen, living in Virginia, used her single mother as her baseline identity. Whatever she did not share with her mom she believed must come from the donor. She simultaneously saw herself through the donor *and* created her difference from her mother:

> I think I got his nose. I have a little nose and most of my mom's side has bigger noses. Not big noses, but bigger noses. I do not play sports that well, but I am really active. My mom is not as active, so I think I got some of that [from the donor]. . . . The creative aspect—my mom is not as creative as I am. I like to draw. I am not good at it, but I like to do it. I like to dance (and Mom was never good at that) and

sing. A lot of things I would assume came from somewhere. I can only assume that is from him.

In Missouri, Jenna, age eighteen, who lived with only one of her mothers (and whom we meet again in the 7008er network), discovered some pieces of her identity that she believed came from the donor through listening to her donor's audiotape:

> My speech pattern, it's bizarre, but the way we talk is almost identical, like both of us will kind of backtrack in our sentences. I don't know if you've noticed I've done that, if I just kind of start and then restart a little differently. He seemed very thoughtful and to have put a lot of just kind of consideration into his life and the world around him, and I definitely inherited that. I think my mom is very intelligent, but I don't think she thinks very deeply or critically about things. . . . She's very good at learning and kind of figuring things out, but she doesn't sit down and actively try to learn about the world the way I do, or she doesn't sit down and try to pick things apart and figure them out mentally. I think he did.

The hesitation in the donor's speech pattern reminded her of her own uneven talk. Jenna attributed this pattern to the donor's careful thinking, which she believed she had "inherited" from him. She made a point of noting that her mom is "intelligent," but does not have the same deep and critical approach to ideas she does. Paige did something similar with the issue of a creative inclination. Both girls observed their mothers closely to find their differences from them. They also observed themselves closely and found within themselves puzzle pieces that they believed are shared with, and unique to, the donor.

In an even more dramatic move, some kids inflate and claim one part of the donor as an important way to distinguish themselves from their parents while creating a distinctive identity for themselves. Andy's donor listed his ethnicity as Scottish (which Andy's single mother does not share). In middle school, Andy decided this made him Scottish, and he crafted his own identity around this profile fact. Andy was both frank and self-aware:

One thing I have tried to do with the donor is set up—not an identity for him, but an identity for myself based around it. He's part Scottish. I identify as part Scottish, and I've learned a lot about Scottish culture. . . . I think of it as these are attributes that are part of something that is behind me. I can connect with my roots by showing those attributes in myself. So when I express those sorts of things, I feel more connected, not necessarily with the person of my father, but I feel more connected with an identity. Everyone wants to strive for that, which is comfort in the fact that you are a person who comes from somewhere. You're not just a blip on the radar.

Andy had no idea about—and did not care—whether Scottish ancestry translated into anything important for his donor. He both claimed and wanted to display attributes that he imagined were a part of his own identity. If he connected with his "roots," Andy was not cut off from his origin. As Andy said, he wanted to connect with an "identity," not a father; like everyone else, he wanted to come from somewhere, a specific geographic place with a culture and a history that he considered his own heritage.[10] Andy had also figured out a way to identify himself that separated him from his mother's ethnicity.

Using the Donor for Self-Assessment: Measuring Oneself against Choice

Over time adolescents come to understand that their parent(s) actively chose a donor profile, and they sometimes measure themselves against the traits they believe their parent(s) desired. Boys and girls alike told us how a parent's choice of specific traits factored into their self-evaluation and their understanding of who they were. While confirming a parent's choice, the child's sense of self is also affirmed.

Sometimes these confirmations involve making sense of the difficulties experienced in the world. Ben, age seventeen, who lived with his mother and a stepfather in a Boston suburb, was disappointed that he "inherited" his donor's ADHD. At age twenty-one, Devin, who lived with his single mother in Virginia, struggled with the autism spectrum disorder diagnosis that he attributed to his donor because, as he said, "Personality-wise I was different from my mother."

Far more frequently, children told us about their satisfactions with what they had thought they inherited. At age sixteen, Katie from Colorado was delighted that her donor passed on the intelligence that she knew was a big draw to her single mother. Katie's mom was thrilled that Katie's IQ is higher than her own. Katie said that her mom always liked to tell her, "That's from your donor. Not from me." Amanda and Henry are twins from a small town in Texas. At age sixteen, Amanda was well aware how very different choosing a donor is from what she calls "real life":

> When you meet a person in real life, you don't get to pick who you fall in love with. But you could pick the traits that you wanted in your progeny when you find a sperm donor. I'm glad I lived up to that [choice], because I mean, not that my mom (and grandma who helped her pick) wouldn't have loved me, but it's cool that I lived up to their whole thing. Like reading books, and being athletic, and smart, and stuff.

When teenagers like Amanda see themselves as a return on a parent's investment, they are pleased by (or disappointed with) how much they resemble what they think their parent(s) wanted. In this way, teenagers learn to see themselves based on an understanding of how others perceive them. The child might magnify the traits shared with the donor as pieces that cause parents pain or pleasure.

As part of this process of self-assessment, teenagers sometimes wonder whether the donor would be pleased to know that the child shared his traits and characteristics. With the exception of eleven children with a known donor, the children we interviewed may never know the answer to that question.[11] Although those who had an identity-release (egg or sperm) donor often believed that they would be able to correspond with the donor, the donor might not be traceable by the bank. Or, even if traceable, the donor may not honor his commitment. And, finally, the child may decide not to pursue contact. Those with an anonymous donor cannot anticipate learning more about the donor's identity unless he happens to change his mind and come forward wishing contact. (See "The Tourists," chapter 7, for more about donors who change their mind.) Instead, children with an anonymous donor have to do more long-term work of constructing by themselves who he might be—and who they are in relation to him.[12]

Completing the Donor Puzzle

As the examples above have suggested, by the time they are adolescents, kids almost entirely take over trying to make sense of the puzzle pieces. They start to fill in the space created by the broad outline with the information they have learned from their parents and the things they hypothesize they share with the donor. Guesses about the origin of distinctive physical features (e.g., height) and natural abilities (e.g., music) start the process. Teenagers add personality traits, religion, race, ethnicity and other kinds of information that overlap with their own sense of who they are in relation both to the members of their family and to the donor himself. Girls and boys similarly curate seemingly random pieces of information as they work with them to shape their donor into an imagined figure. Absent knowing the real donor as a complete person, teens skillfully use qualities from the profile to fill in the puzzle. The puzzle now has far more details that can help link them to the donor.

The kids we interviewed told us about the items that had caught their interest, such as hobbies, occupations, and other bits of esoteric information. When they believe they share those qualities with the donor, they understand themselves better because they can find a source for their passions. They locate themselves and they make the donor uniquely theirs. Kids said, for example, "He has lots of moles like I do," or "She played in a band and I do too." Emily, the ten-year-old quoted earlier, liked that her donor loved dolphins and she thought about making "Dolphin" her last name. Bailey, age fourteen, who lived with her two mothers in Virginia, was into origami, and she was surprised to find out her donor shared that passion. When she read the donor profile herself at age fifteen, Courtney, from California (whom we met when she was seventeen), was stunned to see how much she had in common with her donor:

His favorite sport is soccer and I had not known that. I play soccer too. He used to juggle, which is a really obscure talent that I had actually started. It's like this is very random. I thought this was funny—because his favorite type of music was alternative rock. We have similar music tastes. I believe if I had grown up during his time, we would have had similar taste in bands. I thought that was me. . . . Dogs are also one of my favorite animals. He says, "Especially retriever-sized."

For Courtney, it was not important that lots of people might share the same interests in soccer, juggling, alternative rock, and dogs. What mattered to her is that she uniquely shares those interests with the donor and all along they have been a part of her. Now, reading the profile, she could reaffirm that these parts of her own self came from somewhere. Around this information she could also develop an idea about the donor that made him someone like her and someone she liked. Even if she could not know him, and even if he remained a minimal representation of a person—a stick figure, one-dimensional—she knew these bits of information about him.

Ultimately, then, children who want to solve the mystery of who the donor is—and what the donor has contributed to them—have no choice but to complete the process of constructing the donor with their own imagination. Although all kids go through a process of inventing their donor as they finish middle school or begin high school, boys are more likely to limit their construction of the donor to the facts they receive. For instance, Zack, age fifteen—who will be discussed again in chapter 4 in the context of his donor siblings—put it this way: "I know some stuff about him. I know that he had olive skin and was five foot eleven. He was a doctor, I think. But I haven't created any image about him besides what I already knew based on his description." By way of contrast, girls take more liberty with the facts they know. For girls, then, even more than boys, constructing a figure involves a range of imaginative processes. Ellie, age seventeen and a high school senior from Minnesota living with her single mother, took information her mom had told her about the donor's theatrical talents and combined it with an image she borrowed when she was in middle school: "I remember I was in this play, *The Music Man*, and there was this picture in a playbill of this guy—tall, dark brown hair that's styled nicely, and pale skin. Actually, I know, he was much too young to be my father, but that's the picture. I was like, he's going to be his double, and, yeah, that's what I pictured him as looking like."

As older adolescents, kids often come to realize that the donor has aged and evolved beyond the information contained in the profile. A donor's trajectory becomes something else to imagine. At age eighteen, Jenna, who felt that her speech patterns were similar to the donor's, understood that the static donor profile was misleading. She described her donor in theoretical physics terms:

> I realized a while ago that instead of Schrödinger's cat, I have Schrödinger's father. He exists in this superposition of all of these possibilities, and if I ever meet him, like he'll collapse down into one reality, but until then, he is both charming and an ass, he is open and closed off, like he is really any possibility. He's a superposition.

In effect, Jenna knew that until she meets him, he could be anything she wants him to be. He is of indeterminate existence—everything and nothing at the same time. She wanted to know what the donor "morphed into." As she pondered her own interest in science, she wondered if he became the scientist he wrote was his ambition on the well-worn profile she had of him.

These teens knew that, at some point, they will be older than the donor was at the time of donation. As high school students or in their early college years, thinking about their own futures, they wondered what happened in their donor's future. They would have liked an update to find out what became of him. Big questions remained dangling from the dated essays their donor wrote a long time ago. A seventeen-year-old boy from Iowa wanted to know "if he achieved his dreams. If he has a family of [his] own." At age fourteen, Miya, who lived in western Massachusetts and split the week between her two mothers' households, had three questions she would ask her donor: "What do you like to do? What's your job? Why did you decide to become a donor?" She would also have liked him to tell her "stories about his life" to complete her understanding. Armed with this information, she said, "When people say to me, have you ever met your dad, I can say, 'Yes I have' and I can tell them about him." Kids, much like parents, also wish they could thank the donor, even anonymously, for giving their parents an amazing gift. And, most significantly, kids want to know if their donor thinks about them or even knows they exist.

* * *

In the next chapter we explain why and how parents make contact with a child's donor siblings. When achieved, that contact is an important event for both parents and children. As we have shown here, the donor has no expressed emotions or attitudes other than those presented in the flat paper profile itself; he is also stuck in what is now at least a decade-old context. By way of contrast, as we will see next, the donor siblings are full of emotions and attitudes. They also exist in real social contexts— in all types of families and in homes that spread from New England to California. For parents and their children alike, donor siblings thus create an opportunity for a lively connection that the donor profile does not.

3

Parents Make Contact with Genetic Strangers

TODAY, THE INTERNET is creating for the women and men who conceived with donated sperm the possibility of contact with genetic strangers. That possibility starts with the unique number the bank assigns to the donor. Indeed, from the moment parents purchase vials of sperm from a particular donor, they can use that number to begin locating others who purchased vials from the same donor. The search for a child's donor sibling is an interesting twist on the general idea of locating people. The Donor Sibling Registry was the first of these "people finding" websites in the United States. Others soon followed.[1] Marketed as a way to make connections among genetic relatives, these websites work around the fertility industry's system (and promise) of total genetic anonymity for the donor.[2]

Connecting to others involves a series of voluntary steps that follow the choice of a donor. Parents use the donor's unique number, which becomes the mechanism for contact with genetic strangers. The first step in making contact involves signing on to a registry (at a bank or elsewhere). Parents (or children under the age of eighteen with the help of parents or children by themselves if they are eighteen or older) make contact with others (e.g., by engaging in a private exchange of photos, emails, phone conversations). They then create a network (or join one that has already been created) that has its home on Facebook. Parents and children can then participate by making posts and commenting on the posts of others. Finally, the network may move offline once the members have decided to meet in person; at least some members of every network we examine in Part II have taken this step. (These various stages are illustrated in figure 3.1.)

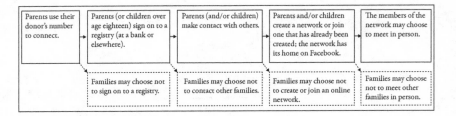

Parents use their donor's number to connect.	Parents (or children over age eighteen) sign on to a registry (at a bank or elsewhere).	Parents (and/or children) make contact with others.	Parents and/or children create a network or join one that has already been created; the network has its home on Facebook.	The members of the network may choose to meet in person.
	Families may choose not to sign on to a registry.	Families may choose not to contact other families.	Families may choose not to create or join an online network.	Families may choose not to meet other families in person.

Figure 3.1   Connecting to Genetic Strangers

Becoming a member of a *group* thus first occurs online with the Facebook page.[3] Since the families are scattered across the United States, Facebook is the group home. Unlike a personal page, the Facebook donor group is a "gated" community; a guard of sorts stands at the gates. That guard is usually a woman who was one of the first people to sign up on a registry; in no group that we studied was a man in charge of maintaining membership lists. Entry into this community is predicated on knowing the donor number and on the group controller's decision to grant membership to the holder. The majority of parents who register their children (on an independent registry or the bank's registry) become part of the Facebook group. On Facebook, parents (and children if they are old enough) make initial plans to hold a gathering of the known donor siblings and their parents. In this chapter we explore these various moments from the perspective of the parents we interviewed; we end the chapter with a brief discussion of how contact with genetic relatives acts as an affirmation of the parental choice of a particular donor.

Motivations for Contact

The parents we interviewed expressed a variety of reasons for transforming the solitary act of choosing a donor into the social act of reaching out to other people who have made the same choice.[4] Some were simply curious about who these genetic relatives are and what they are like. Some wanted to know who these people are so that their children could avoid inadvertent romantic or sexual relations with someone who might be a genetic half-sibling. Some were seeking to normalize what still felt like an odd or unusual method of family creation. Closely connected to that motivation was a desire to make connections with others who could confirm the decision to rely on a donor and, more particularly, to choose the specific donor they did. Some parents who wanted to conceive another child from a donor no longer available through a bank or clinic got online to find someone willing to sell "extra" vials of sperm; conversely, those with extra vials got online to find someone interested in purchasing them. Still others were seeking to find more information about the donor; this was especially the case when concerns about developmental or medical issues arose and people wanted to know whether those issues had a genetic origin. And finally, whether or not there were specific questions about the donor, some parents wanted more understanding of, or information about, the paternal lineage so as to have a more complete family tree for themselves and, even more so, for their children. Parents in all family forms—and of all different ages—might mention one or more of these reasons for reaching out to a child's genetic relatives.

As we show in Part II, parents within a single network did not all express the same motivations for making contact with each other. As we show there as well, some motivations shifted across the four eras we discuss. Yet, one *possible* interest never appeared: no single respondent (either parent *or* child) sought to disrupt the "insular" (legal) family created with donor gametes. None of the parents intentionally purchased sperm vials from the same donor with intending parents in another family.[5] And none of the children became siblings who lived together (as would be the case in collectives or cooperative parenting arrangements we might have found if we had selected our respondents differently). In each network, parents still determined for their own children resources, religion, culture, values, and beliefs. Meetings with people who are originally genetic strangers might raise questions about alternative ways of being in the world, but those meetings were not designed to—and actually did not—transform daily family life.[6] Still, as we will see in what follows, the members within donor sibling networks were deeply affected by their participation in them even as the dynamics of the various groups shaped the nature of that experience.

Whatever initial motivations led to signing up for a registry and whatever impact that action ultimately had, the individual decision to make a connection became, like the decision about which donor to use, another significant moment for parents. Some hesitated for long periods of time between learning about the possibility of signing up and actually reaching out to someone. Many of those with whom we spoke had worried that making contact with genetic strangers would disrupt in some way the insular family they had already created. Angie, a single mother in Minnesota, expressed this concern. She had looked at her bank's registry and discovered another mother with a child from the same donor as her two children. Initially she did not want to move forward: "I think it was the idea that my kids have 'family'—note my air quotes—that is not me or our family. . . . I'm very protective of the three of us as a unit. The idea that they might have really close connections that have nothing to do with me, I have no control over, and have no connection to—that put me off a little bit." For the present, Angie decided not to meet donor siblings in person; it was enough to exchange an occasional email with the parents.

Some parents—and this was often the nongenetic parent—feared that contact with genetic strangers would highlight the issue of genes in a household that was predicated on the assumption that nurture is as important as—if not more important than—nature. Other parents worried that their child might be more interested in connections than would the child's donor siblings and that their child would be hurt by that relative indifference. For some, donor sibling families were not a priority in their busy lives. Every sibling network we describe in Part II had essentially silent members, people who simply listed minimal information about their child or made only brief contact with the other network members.

A Whole New World

Those who overcame their hesitation and made contact described it as venturing into new, unscripted territory.[7] As they did, they struggled for language; the usual words available to them did not adequately describe these new kinds of relationships. Julie, an otherwise articulate college professor in urban California, made up a word to describe the strange experience of having a child with links to many different families: "It still feels a little pioneerish and a little freaky . . . I don't know other people who've done this."

Parents also struggled—as people do in other new family forms—to figure out what norms should apply. Cara and Marlene (introduced in chapter 1 as having been attracted to the photograph of the donor, and a couple we encounter again in chapter 9) described meeting the parents of their son's donor siblings almost as they would a first date: they wanted to be liked and they wanted to like the parents. But they didn't know what rules to draw on to guide their interactions:

> CARA: Well, we had set this plan, and we chose to make a spinach feta frittata, and we thought about what dishes to use. It suddenly felt like a date. We were both nervous an hour before they were showing up. I didn't know what to wear. My wife didn't know what to wear. We had to check each other's outfits to make sure everyone wasn't overdressed or underdressed. How do we want to present ourselves to these people we don't know, or people with whom we share a connection, but have never met in person? It was that moment that was, "What are we doing?"
>
> MARLENE: When they walked in, it was, well, we hugged, but it was sort of awkward.
>
> CARA: There was a moment, "Do we hug? Do we shake hands?" We did hug. We actually did hug. I think we all felt this shared curiosity, excitement, and discomfort because this is not a relationship we'd ever been part of. There are no expectations for how you're supposed to behave or not behave. You don't really know what the norms are when you're meeting your donor sibling family. At least I didn't know what the ones were.

Like Cara and Marlene, Donna (who chose a donor who was an engineer to match her partner's family) said she and her partner engaged in the same anxious preparation because, as she said, "here's this person that you're, like, biologically related to, so there's meaning and they're coming over." Interestingly, Donna explained that when her daughter met yet another new family, that family had also been uncertain about appropriate attire:

> [The girls in the donor sibling family] had wanted to wear dresses, and their moms were like, "No, don't wear dresses. You'll be overdressed." Then our daughter shows up in a dress. And that just tells me they all thought it was a special occasion, that it's something you get dressed up for.

The partners in both of these couples were in agreement about moving forward and connecting with the parents of their children's donor siblings. But this is not always the case: sometimes one parent is more ambivalent than the other. Take, for example, Kate and Claudia (who are also members of the Social Capitalist network described in chapter 9):

CLAUDIA: Kate is really into [meeting the donor sibling families]. Last weekend we went to a three-year-old's birthday party in a nearby state; she is a donor sibling of [our daughters]. I'm not as *evolved* around the thinking about it. I think that Kate is like, "Oh, can I do this?" "This is good, this is what we're supposed to do." I'm not quite there yet.

INTERVIEWER: Why do you call it evolved?

CLAUDIA: I haven't wrapped my head around it completely. I find some inconsistencies in it, and I think that's a little weird. Most of these people are far away, and I feel like we're cultivating relationships with these people when they might not have an immediate or as local of an impact in our lives when we're not doing that with other people that we know that are similar to us. Then, Kate's brother has two kids. We've never seen one of them. We don't have any relationships there. There's something that's just out of balance for me. I can't get the bricks to line up in my mind yet. If your family is really what you define it to be, then why are these people so important? Why are we making all the effort to meet them and go to a summer vacation with them?

While her questions were rhetorical, Claudia did wonder about the contradictions between valuing "families we choose" and this new emphasis on genes as the basis for creating relationships. Surprisingly, she saw the latter—a return to genes as the starting point for family ties—as being more modern or up to date; more "evolved" was how she put it. Ambivalent as she was about this move, however, she recognized the benefits to pursuing these ties: "I'm happy that [our daughters will have] those people because I was an only child and I would have loved that. It's like part of the greatness. I think it's a huge bonus of the situation that we're in."

Claudia suggested another paradoxical effect of contact with donor siblings, when she commented that as much as the donor sibling group offered them people with whom they might have something in common, it highlighted the more unusual aspect of their lives. By this she meant that she and her wife are lesbians with two children conceived with *both* a sperm donor and an egg donor:

> It's like this constant, "We're normal. We're not normal. We're normal. We're not normal." I think, day-to-day, operationally, we're incredibly just normal. We change diapers; we go to the children when they cry. . . . It just feels like everyone else with young children. Is meeting donor siblings giving donor conception too much weight? Does that put us in the realm [of being different] instead of just the "day-to-day like every other family" realm?

Angie, the single mother we interviewed in Minnesota who had been ambivalent about making contact with her children's donor sibling families, was less concerned with paradoxical effects and more concerned with boundaries. Like college professor Julie, she invented a word, in this case to describe her feelings: "I wanted to be in touch and I wanted to be friendly, but I wanted it to be boundaried [*sic*] as well because I don't know this person and I didn't want assumptions about the relationship, although I actually did want there to be some sort of relationship." In their initial confusion, excitement, and ambivalence, then, our respondents implied that they believe that meeting a genetic stranger is like opening Pandora's box, a box that once opened will unleash whatever forces lie within and then cannot be closed again.

Open Discomfort and Strategies of Control

Parents attempt to make sense of the experience of being "pioneers" in this new land populated by genetic strangers. They experience some anxiety as well. They do not necessarily want to be embroiled in relationships of intimacy with people they do not know, and they do not necessarily want to acquire obligations of either friendship *or* family. Having created a way both to understand their own family form among themselves and to present it to others, they may want to continue to control that understanding and that presentation. Genetic strangers might upset the apple cart. Not surprisingly, then, parents engage in a number of strategies for controlling what happens in these interactions. For instance, Donna, who had been anxious about meeting "this person that you're like biologically related to," said that when two sets of parents of their children's donor siblings got together for the first time, they immediately agreed on ground rules: "And you know, they said basically what we felt, that this is a connection for our kids, but we're still the parents and we're not combining or merging our families in any way."[8]

However they move forward, each stage of contact opens up new possibilities for intimacy and obligations; each stage of contact might challenge the nuclear family's definition of its boundaries.[9] Parents thus move into new liminal spaces that have no precedent.[10] Sandy, the wife of Greg (discussed in chapter 1 in terms of his careful choice of a donor) and the mother of two children, Zoe and Joseph (members of the 7008er network), described her worries as each transition point marked an occasion where the members of her family tried to grasp the import of donor siblings in their lives:

> SANDY: It was one thing to be connected through an online registry where it's in the ether and you've got a machine being the intermediary contact. It took me a bit to get comfortable with meeting [the mother and child in a donor sibling family] in 2005 when the kids were young. You're putting yourself out there. You're losing a little bit of anonymity. But also, what is that going to mean . . . for the kids and the relationships, and how are they going to react? What is this going to signal? Is it going to upset the order of the universe?
>
> INTERVIEWER: Did it upset the order of the universe?
>
> SANDY: It didn't. It didn't. That was [only] one family. Fast-forward to 2012 and you're talking about half a dozen families. What does all of that mean? I didn't want to necessarily open myself up to all of these people, as I am painfully shy. But I went along with it to support the kids because they wanted to go to the group gathering at this point (at ages fourteen and twelve), and all the other families were going. The kids were all at an age where they were all very curious, and they were very curious about each other. I think

it was very important for them. It has evolved since then where, just like with anything, as you get to know people, you get to determine whether or not you like someone as a person as opposed to the fact that there is a biological connection. Is there something that we have in common because of that?

Her children's curiosity drove her willingness to take each step toward meeting a full complement of donor siblings.

Each time these pathbreakers cross the threshold into a new liminal space, they worry about what might emerge next. And, at each shift, they struggle for understanding. That is, they are not just nervous; they are at sea. Occasionally parents search for reasons that they are meant to have contact with each other, to be forming some new kind of bond. One mother found special totemic significance in the fact that many of the children in the network had been given the same names—a fact easily explained by trends in naming in their generation. Moreover, and perhaps not surprisingly, parents initially try to map familiar understandings of friendship and kinship (e.g., "like a cousin") onto these new relationships.[11] (As we show in Part II, that mapping sometimes helps and sometimes hinders the creation of a strong network.)

Sandy represents the many respondents who actually moved from identification of a child's donor sibling family through online contact to participation in a large network gathering. But, of course, not everyone takes the next step.[12] And sometimes, people stop—either for years or even permanently—at one step or another. Members in each network reported that there were people who changed their minds and left the Facebook page within weeks of joining. Even a face-to-face meeting might not result in further contact. Two mothers in an upscale Boston suburb described one such meeting, pursued because they did not want their children (who were toddlers at the time) to "blame" them for not having gotten together earlier. Having done what they thought was their duty, in the absence of any particular interest in the other couple, they chose not to repeat the experience:

Two moms, their son, came over, we had ice cream, we played. I was waiting for that magical moment for it to feel like there was some connection between our two toddler boys, and we did a little bit of the physical similarities. . . . [We found] some similarities between the moms and us. . . . It was a nice gathering, but nothing that made it feel like . . . Kismet. . . . There was nothing magical about it.

(We might note that even though there is no "magic" here, the host couple did sell extra vials of sperm from their "shared" donor to the second couple. The fact that they preferred to sell the vials to people within their donor sibling network suggests that they assigned some meaning to this connection, even if they did not want to pursue it as a social one.)

Serendipity Happens

In contrast with the careful decision-making that characterized most actions around contact with genetic strangers, some individuals we interviewed found that contact with donors *and* donor siblings occurred entirely by chance, with no forewarning whatsoever. In fact, we found seventeen discrete examples of unanticipated contact. The stories of what seemed to their participants to be sheer serendipity took two basic forms. In one form a third party inadvertently let drop a piece of information that was sufficiently identifying to reveal the common "donor number" to people the parents knew casually. Equally often the participants themselves discovered the connection while in conversation with each other. In some cases the parents found this connection first; in other cases it was the children. In one case both scenarios happened in tandem: the parents serendipitously learned they had used the same sperm donor; several months later, when they were about to tell the children about this affiliation, the children discovered the same fact.

We actually heard this story from three different sources (although it counts as one example). One source, Janet, explained that she was "chatting with a bunch" of the lesbian mothers who were watching their sixth-grade daughters play soccer in Northampton, Massachusetts, when either she or another mother, Holly, said something about her donor. The two women paused, looked at each other, and recognized their commonality, confirmed by sharing the donor number. Holly's mother (the grandmother), who was there, immediately said, "Welcome to the family." For her part, Janet was not so ready with a response, and she stepped off the viewing stands to call her wife, Nadine, to tell her what had happened. Nadine said that they "were very freaked out," especially by the "welcome comment" because, although they knew the other couple, they had no interest in "spending Christmas with them." She noted also that they had never wanted their daughters "to be confused about who [was] family," and that she feared the "unknown kind of a thing." After talking on the phone with Nadine, Janet came back to the stands to discuss next moves with Holly; the two women agreed to wait before telling the kids. During the months that followed, Nadine and Janet went to a therapist to get guidance on handling the situation. As Nadine said, "We didn't want to cause any damage psychologically." Using the language of an unknown landscape that we have heard before, she then added, "It was new territory." On the advice of the therapist, Nadine and Janet opened a conversation with their daughters about the concept of donor siblings; they also signed up on a registry and told their daughters about some of the donor siblings in other states they had discovered. But they did not identify Holly's daughter, Joy, as a donor sibling. Sophie, the soccer player, who had never even imagined this concept of donor siblings, wanted to meet anyone and everyone right away; Cameron, their younger child by two years, was more hesitant.

Meanwhile, Holly and her partner, Hannah, apparently were having some of the same conversations with Joy, who, they suggested, would have been happy to meet her local donor sibling because she already knew of, and had met, several others. Indeed, Holly and Hannah were much less taken aback by the situation because they had already joined the Facebook group and had thus incorporated the notion of donor siblings into their understanding of their family.

Six months later, the two sets of parents had agreed on how to move forward and had settled on the very next weekend as the time to tell their children about the donor sibling connection. Three days before that scheduled event, Joy and Sophie were chatting in band practice, comparing notes on being donor conceived: they each mentioned a donor sibling sister, Danielle, who lived in Florida and a donor who had written in his personal essay that he liked rainbows and dolphins. The cat out of the bag, the parents had lost control. One of the girls described that moment:

> I was really excited. I was like, "This is the coolest thing to happen to anyone." We were laughing, and were screaming, I guess. We went to the lunchroom, because we were in the band room practicing during lunch. We went to the lunchroom, and were like, "Oh, yeah, guys, we're related, we're sisters, donor siblings." . . . It was this whole jumping-up happiness thing.

After several months of close affiliation, the girls went back to what they were before—friendly acquaintances with overlapping, but separate, friendship circles. Janet summed up the evolution of that relationship, saying that, although the two girls were friendly, "there's a reason why they weren't friends in the beginning. . . . They are just really different people. They don't have as much in common; they're different."

As this story suggests, parents might want to maintain the borders of a relatively conventional family. Because genetic strangers might threaten those borders, when parents find the information, first they have to decide what to do with it. Even among our respondents, selected largely from among those who sought to connect with genetic strangers, not everyone we spoke with who experienced a moment of "serendipity" chose to "connect." In fact, some parents, like Janet and Nadine and Holly and Hannah, concealed the information from their children unless the children asked if they had donor siblings. Other parents we interviewed probably never would tell their children about the donor siblings they had discovered by chance.[13]

As we heard these stories of unanticipated contact, we came to realize that what felt like sheer chance to the participants might well have been predicted. Families with two mothers (like Janet and Nadine and Holly and Hannah) chose to live in communities that welcomed them and their children. They then sent their children to the same day-care center, school, and summer camp; they joined the same synagogue, mosque, or church; they were thus bound to have friends in common. Their similarities also made it likely that they would learn about the same sperm banks and even, perhaps, that they would emphasize the same criteria or be drawn to some of the same features when choosing a donor from those banks. And, given a finite number of donors at any moment in time, especially when one has narrowed down the donor pool (e.g., by desiring a Jewish donor), the likelihood of making the same choice as someone else in one's social network is increased.

Affirming Choice

Regardless of when—or how—parents made connections with the parents of a child's donor siblings, those connections ultimately could offer the parents the chance to reassess their earlier construction of the donor as they came to know (whether through photographs, a parent's description, or face-to-face contact) the other children in any given donor sibling network. And parents do perceive similarities among the children of the same donor when they see them: they might observe that all the children have the same lanky build, prominent forehead, or deep-set eyes; they find shared personalities, abilities, behaviors and, sometimes, health concerns. At the first moment of contact, all they can see is what they believe to be the imprint of a shared genetic lineage; at the first moment of contact, ideas about nature assume prominence over ideas about nurture.

Parents draw on these perceived similarities to confirm their assessments of their own children. They see other smart children and they are more confident in their own child's intelligence; they see other musical children and they are more certain of their own child's talents in that arena. Parents also sometimes draw on these similarities to confirm their belief that some particular traits (both positive and negative) have their origin in the genes that came from outside the family. One mother in Kansas indicated that she believed that intelligence united the donor siblings:

> That's a trait that all the kids share, because they were all smart. . . . One of the children graduated from high school early. . . . I think she's going into elementary education, to be a teacher, but every one of them seem like they were academically driven and very smart. I'd say that probably came from the donor.

Another mother, in Connecticut, with an elementary school child, felt that the donor siblings had many of the same behaviors and preferences; she now had an explanation for her son's choices. She also could now believe she understood his differences from her; she relieved herself of a sense of responsibility for behaviors that were occasionally troubling. The donor siblings thus became a way to make a distance of sorts between herself and her children:

> We find that a lot of the kids, because they're so good at their reading and math, they get bored very easily, and that could be misconceived as behavioral issues. However, when the kids are challenged, they more than meet their goals. For example, Hayden . . . is in second grade, and he's already reading chapter books, fourth-grade level. Another thing that's really funny is most of these kids are excelling in individual sports, not team sports. They like the team sports, like my son plays ice hockey. But when it comes to tennis and taekwondo, he's exceptional. He's very focused and he really tries harder than anywhere else. I think in team sports he becomes overwhelmed and intimidated by the other kids, and after talking to some of the other moms, that's the same thing going on with their children as well. The kids are all exceptional swimmers. They love the water.

* * *

Interestingly, as the parents talked about observed similarities among their children, they did not always make a vertical leap upward to the donor. That is, as the parents spoke with us, they did not necessarily draw on resemblances to make a more vivid image, or a more complex understanding, of the donor: for the most part the donor remained the person they had imagined him to be when they made that choice many months or years before. The parents made the donor "real" when they bought the advantage the donor offered and created the elements of "fit" and "likability." Meeting a child's donor siblings does not require that the parents redraw or reinvigorate that earlier creation. Yet when the children meet donor siblings, not only do they begin to construct a more complex donor, but they begin to reevaluate what they understood to be the influences that made them who they are.

4

The Surprise of Donor Siblings

CHILDREN TRY TO fashion an identity in conjunction with an image of a donor that is partly surmised and partly taken directly from the donor profile. Parents participate actively in this process. Until donor sibling registries became commonplace, both parents and children spoke about the donor himself as if he belonged only to their family. Even if the parents might have considered the possibility that they were not the only people purchasing this donor's vials of sperm, they had no place to put that thought and no reason to share it with a child. And that is not so surprising: consider the many times we feel we have made a distinctive purchase that reflects our personal taste (e.g., a new evening dress) and ignore the basic reality that others are making the same purchase; even if these others rise to consciousness, we hope they will not show up at a wedding wearing precisely the same outfit. Children have additional reasons for believing the donor is only theirs: they have been told about the "nice man" who gave something special to their parents that led to making them; he thus belongs to them alone.

The explosion of the internet is shattering these illusions. For parents, as we have seen, the possibility of contact with the families of a child's donor siblings is challenging—startling, exciting, and scary, all at the same time. For children, this possibility offers similar challenges as well as some different ones. For both parents and children, new challenges emerge when they actually meet these genetic relatives. They have to take a creative leap and make sense of connections that begin with genes alone. In this chapter, we consider what insights donor siblings offer children about the donor, how they contribute to understandings of the separate and conjoint influences of nature and nurture, and how the experience of being a donor sibling differs from that of being a sister or brother.[1]

As we discuss these issues, we focus initially on those children who remember distinctly the moment they met donor siblings for the first time.[2] Most of those children are teenagers; several of them will appear in the 7008er network in chapter 6. We then turn to a thirteen-year-old (a member of a network described in "Connected Soul Mates," chapter 8) who has known her donor siblings essentially her whole life. At the end of the chapter we return to the question of what donor siblinghood means.

The Impact of Donor Siblings

Even if some of the older children we interviewed had come to realize that the donor might well have a family of his own before they were told about donor siblings, they usually did not imagine a donor who gave liberally to anyone who asked.[3] For the children who did not know of donor siblings until they were in their teens, learning about them was often a shock. At nineteen, Isabel (a member of the 7008er network), who was raised as a single child by a single mother in Southern California, recalled that she was stunned to learn three years earlier that she had donor siblings. She used familial terms—"father" and "siblings"—as she described her amazement:

> I didn't even know it was an option. I had not a clue. I really had no handle on the life of being a sperm donor child at all. I knew nothing. This was a really huge emotional blow. Not in a bad way. It was just a very strange experience. . . . I had siblings who had the same father as me, which I didn't even know was possible and I didn't even know they existed.

Yet there they were. And Isabel, along with others, suddenly had new resources she could call on as she attempted to make sense of several related issues: who belongs in her family, what it means to be donor conceived, and how to imagine both who the donor might be and what he has contributed to her. She thought she had figured these things out. She now knew she had more work to do on all fronts.[4]

Children like Isabel draw selectively on these new resources. For the most part, they do so without regard to gender. In fact, many boys and many girls openly embrace donor siblings as potential relatives; in similar ways, both boys and girls work through how to distinguish between these new bonds and those they recognize with siblings. However, we find some evidence that boys are especially likely to worry that forming relationships with donor siblings will involve them in an obligation to take responsibility for others, an obligation in which they have little interest (see chapter 6).

At the same time, among *both* boys and girls, knowledge of, and contact with, donor siblings makes the donor side more real, more complex, and more vivid. Children also use information they obtain from donor siblings about the donor to identify the source of their own traits; again, this is the case for both boys and girls, although the donor is always a man and although once they are in groups, boys are granted a special "likeness" to the donor.[5] As they observe similarities and differences among the donor siblings, children almost invariably come to reflect on how nature and nurture operate.

New Perceptions of Genetic Origins

Some children might have thought specific traits came from a parent or relative they know; others might have thought those traits were uniquely theirs. Either way, children may learn that those traits are shared with others and that therefore they might well have their origins in the genetic material inherited from the unknown donor. Isabel was not only astonished to learn that she had donor siblings but also astonished to learn that some of what she had attributed to her mother's influence might well have come from the other side. As she mused about this, she continued to call the donor a "father":

> He wrote [in his essay] a lot about how he's a very calm, centered person, a very complex thinker. Those are things that I see a lot in myself and in the group [of donor siblings]. It's like, "Oh. We have all these unifying qualities, so maybe they come from my mother *and* my father. It's not just her."

Andy, whose fascination with his Scottish roots we described in chapter 2, also referred to the donor with a kinship term. He used the similarities he found among the donor siblings to revise his understanding of which genetic parent he most resembled: "I know some of my donor siblings, and I see some of the similarities there. I think I resemble my donor father more." His comment implies that once he had photographs of the donor siblings, he realized that he looked less like his mother than like the donor, a man whose photograph he had never seen.

Not uncommonly, and no matter what kind of family they are born into, children may believe that they differ radically from their parents and siblings; such children fantasize they are adopted as a way to explain that difference. Children in donor-conceived families who feel they have different attributes in the realm of appearance or personality than the other members of their nuclear family might be able to find in the donor siblings a link to, or insight into, these distinctive attributes. This is especially the case when the donor siblings include another child who is startlingly like oneself.

Seth, who is eleven years old, told us that it was one of the best days of his life when he met his donor siblings. Until that time, he had felt unease in his own family—an unease that might have been created in part by the changing structure of that family. Seth had been conceived through sperm donation in a single-mother family. When he was four years old, his mother married and had a child with his stepfather. Even at the age of four, Seth knew intuitively (although no one told him explicitly) that the stepfather he called "dad" was not his biological father. The two did not share many interests, and Seth felt that his "dad" preferred his sister. One year before we spoke with Seth, his mother had divorced his stepfather. When she did, she told Seth that he was donor conceived. Soon after telling him, she realized that Seth had begun searching the internet on his own, hoping to find the donor: she then decided to locate Seth's donor siblings for him. Among the sixteen donor siblings she found registered on the bank's website was a family that had four children (two sets of twins, all full-genetic siblings) and two, now separated, mothers. That family lived an hour south of Seth's home in Northern California.

The day Seth met this family of donor siblings, he thought he had found answers to his question about his appearance and clues about what he might look like when he grew older: "We went to this park. I saw one of them coming in. It was Zack. I didn't realize it was him. Zack looks a lot like me. It's a spitting image. I know that that's what I'm going to look like when I'm a teenager." Seth, who had always felt that he was an "outsider" within his family, had finally met someone with whom he could identify in a way he could not with his stepfather or even his mother and sister. Soon Seth viewed Zack as being like an older "brother" to look up to.

For his part, Zack, who was then fifteen, had been meeting donor siblings during his family's travels around the country from the time he was around seven years old. But he had not considered those donor siblings to be anything more than people he would meet on a casual basis. Zack had never really given much thought to his donor. He always assumed that he was just different from his siblings because, unlike them, he had especially favored his genetic mother and her relatives. Once he met Seth, Zack's view changed:

> Meeting with Seth, I was certainly struck by how similar we were. A lot of the similarities that we share were stuff that I thought came from my mom's side, like the verbalness [*sic*] and sort of the way we thought. But it did make me realize, yeah, half of me didn't come from her. It was interesting to see just how similar we were.

Even though the two boys are several years apart, Zack believed he had discovered through this meeting (and then through other gatherings between the two families) that he had inherited genetic material from his anonymous donor that made him who he was.

In other cases as well, observations of similarity range from physical appearance to personality. We can start with Justin, who at twenty-eight was one of our oldest respondents; he makes an appearance again in chapter 5. The son of two mothers living in Berkeley, California, Justin had an enduring relationship with his donor sibling Nathan. Justin found comfort in the similarity of behavior and experience he shares with Nathan and with another donor sibling whom he has met more recently: "[The donor siblings] give me perspective. Yes, they give me perspective. It's nice to have someone else that has some similarity to you in the way you think and certain attributes that you have that are present in your life."

Milo, age seventeen and from the Boston area, also noticed commonality with his newfound donor sibling who lives in Arkansas: "Me and my donor sibling Annie, we have like the same smile. And maybe our sense of humor. We make each other laugh a lot." When they first came into contact with each other, Milo instantly felt that he could talk intimately with

Annie because she was his donor sibling. Even before their first meeting, Milo had drawn up a list of questions he felt he could have asked of any donor sibling he happened to meet: "What situation are they in? What's their school life like? Is it different? How do they react when [other kids] ask about two moms? What do they picture our dad to be like? Things like that." As they got to know each other better, Milo liked listening to Annie talk about her life in the South and about what it was like growing up in two different households after her mothers separated. But most important to him was that Annie was the only person he met who shared his donor, a connection of special significance because his brother has a different donor. Annie was not a stand-in for the donor Milo continued to wonder about. But she served as a bridge to knowledge that existed apart from his immediate family: "It was so cool to have this different side of life that was not my parents and not my brother. It was this whole other thing that only I had. I think that's cool ownership." In effect, meeting Annie allowed him to claim information about a side of his heritage that belonged to him alone, which is what he meant by "ownership."

Once Sammy, the son of a single mother living in Washington, DC, had met his donor siblings, he had more information to bring to bear as he mused about the source of his personal traits. He suggested that, as was the case for his similarity to his donor siblings, his similarity to his mother could be chalked up to either nature or nurture: "My donor sibling Kelsey and I both share a very healthy, intellectual curiosity that we can nerd out together, I guess you would say, over cool stuff. . . . I don't know if it is nurture or nature. My mom is the same—and also very smart."

We do not know (and our data do not allow us to know) what makes some donor-conceived children believe that the balance of influence tilts in one direction or the other. We do know that having two parents— one genetic and one nongenetic—often tipped the scale toward nurture. That is, children with two parents believed that they had found ways in which their personalities and interests had been shaped separately by each of their parents. Clearly, meeting donor siblings intersects with this process of trying to dissect the source of the various components of who one is—and whom one resembles. After meeting donor siblings, some children (and this is also the case for some parents, as we discuss in chapter 5) become more convinced of the power of genes as determinants of an individual's attributes and abilities because they see such great similarity between themselves and the donor and among the donor siblings; others become less convinced of that power because, by way of contrast, they recognize such great difference and diversity.

A More Complex Donor

Not only do some children come to see that their traits have an origin in the donor after they meet their donor siblings, but they may also come to see new features of the donor because they emerge within the network of donor siblings. David, the nineteen-year-old son of a single mother who lives in Northern California (and a member of the 7008ers discussed in chapter 6), explained this process: "I can guess at some physical traits of the donor by looking at other siblings." Sometimes the new portrait of the donor is a group decision. In several groups, the oldest boy—and never a girl—was designated as the one who looked most like the sperm donor they had never seen. As the kids also take the traits they find in the group and imaginatively project them back onto the donor, they invigorate the paper profile; the donor is now more like a flesh-and-blood person. The new contacts can also constrain the inventiveness we saw in chapter 2 as the donor siblings provide concrete clues to fill the remaining gaps in the portrait of the donor being constructed.

Both processes are unusual—albeit not unique—ways of making sense of an ancestor. In most kin groups, family resemblances are located as having the same source through vertical connections that go in two directions: the family picture of a grandparent can be identified as the origin of the shape of a child's eyebrows; the smile of a cousin evokes the remembered smile of a deceased uncle. Sometimes within a group of kin relations, the lateral ties *do* help re-create characteristics of an absent forbearer or bring to light something no one had previously noticed or identified. When several cousins suffer from depression or breast cancer, a family might search for genetic roots; when several cousins are born with startlingly red hair, a family might suspect the source in a grandmother of whom one had never seen a childhood color photo.[6]

Among donor siblings, the lateral connections are the only ones available. Donor siblings draw on the evidence these lateral connections provide to create one layer (and only one layer) of the vertical branch in the "family" tree. Now they suspect that the donor was an introvert; now they imagine that he has a particular facial expression. (As we will see in the chapters that follow, this evidence of lateral similarity sometimes helps the donor siblings come to see themselves as some form of "siblings" or "relatives.")

No matter how much—or how little—lateral similarity the donor siblings find, contact helps children construct a portrait of the donor in another way. Solitary constructions of the donor are sometimes scary. At fourteen, Bailey, who lives with her two mothers, Cheryl and Donna, in Maryland, told us the secret, dark image of the donor she had carried around from childhood: "I knew he was tall and I knew he was German. This is going to sound really weird but I imagined him as a Nazi soldier because I knew he was blonde and had blue eyes. Kind of a scary image." This "scary image" dissolved as soon as she saw her donor siblings, a group of girls and boys with whom she shared her slight build: "But then I met my donor siblings and even though I still imagine a lanky kind of guy— we all share the same body type—the soldier image went away."

Donor Siblings without the Surprise

Children who have known donor siblings essentially their entire lives have the resource of donor siblings to help them imagine the donor from an early age; they do not experience the "shock" of discovery in quite the same way. Yet they, too, have to make sense of who these people are and what they might mean in their lives. That understanding shifts with development. Children who have known each other for years and played together since they were toddlers might begin to think more fully about their relationships once they move into adolescence.

For example, Elena, age twelve, who has known her donor siblings since she was three years old, explained to us how her sense of who those children are has changed over time:

> I remember our mom had close friends, and she'd be like, those kids. She didn't say it as "half-siblings." She said, "Her mom was also lesbian, and they had the same donor as you." From there, when we first met them, some of them kind of looked like us. It just grew on [my brothers and me] that they were our half-siblings.

For Elena and other children in her network (chapter 8), the processes of construction and reconstruction of the donor that we find among the teens meeting for the first time *might* still occur as they reach an age where they both understand fully their connections and can draw comparisons and insights from each other (with or without interventions from their parents). At the time, Elena was still trying to absorb the meaning of this relationship that she had just begun to define in genetic terms.

What Is Donor Siblinghood?

As one of the youngest children in this study, Elena's experience stands in sharp contrast to that of older children, like Isabel, who could re-call the shock of first learning about their donor siblings. Both, how-ever, understood the inherent duality of their relationships with donor siblings. On the one hand, they noted that donor siblings both helped them feel that their experience of being donor conceived was shared with someone else in the cosmos, someone from whom they could learn about their paternal side. On the other hand, they knew that these were not "ordinary" siblings. They used a variety of different terms to capture this duality: sometimes they drew on the familiar language of kinship; sometimes they emphasized the familiar language of friendship; some-times they relied on a different language that highlighted only the genetic connection.

Those who grow up with siblings in their household (whether or not they are genetically related to them) can—and do—explain clearly that it is not necessarily love or liking, but shared experience (including conflict and competition) that makes being a sibling both meaningful and pro-foundly different from being a *donor* sibling. That is, they easily distin-guish between the different meanings of "siblinghood." Take, for instance, Brooke (age twenty-one), who lives an hour north of San Francisco with her twin brother and two mothers. She did not call her donor siblings her "siblings," although other people in the same network used that term. Brooke enjoyed getting to know her donor siblings, and she participated in posting to the shared Facebook page. At the same time, she wanted to make a distinction between the brother with whom she was raised and these genetic relatives she met a mere three years earlier:

It is sort of weird just because I wouldn't ever say that they're my siblings. I would say half-siblings always, or donor siblings. [My twin] Brody's my sibling, and that's it. When [my donor sibling] Cassandra and I met up, we posted a picture on the Facebook page and she was like, "Sisters," or something like that. I was just like, "Whoa."

The issues of significance and definition were somewhat different for Sienna, age seventeen (a member of the Tourists network discussed in chapter 7), who lives in suburban Boston and has an anonymous donor. Sienna's older sister has the same two mothers but a different—and "known"—donor. The difference from her sister left Sienna feeling that no one in her immediate world could understand her exact situation— that she knew nothing about *her* donor other than what is written on the paper profile. Her discovery of donor siblings—which she referred to as "the group of half-sibs" or "the others"—provided her with comfort in knowing that there are others like her. But that discovery did not foster intimacy or a desire to develop a relationship. Like Brooke, Sienna was explicit about the distinction between these other people and the sister who is part of her daily life:

They've added a feeling that I'm not alone. They've had a similar experience. But aside from that, I don't feel any connection with them and I don't feel a need to pursue a connection. . . . It was weird to me to think that I'm the same amount related to these kids [donor siblings], who I have no interest in, as I am to the sister who I've grown up with. I think the whole experience really taught me that, at least in my life, genetics is so much less of a part of it than who you've actually grown up with and who has had an impact on your life.

Much as Zack came to believe that more of his personality came from his donor side after meeting Seth, he did not think about Seth in the same way he did the three siblings with whom he was being raised. As Zack put it:

The siblings I have here [in the house] are full siblings. But more so than that, I've grown up with them and I know them very, very well.

We've shared a mother and countless experiences. We live together, and I love them, and I know them very, very well, whereas my half-sibs are my friends and I know them to an extent. They are like me in some ways, but there's much less of that sense of family. . . . Certainly they can give me some more information about my donor. . . . When I grow up I might move away. It may be that they stay with us more through my mother because Seth and Adam (another donor sibling close by) are going to live here. But if I move away and Adam and Seth are on different sides of the country, I don't know if we would meet up just to meet up. I would with my siblings who I live with constantly.

* * *

The children we interviewed who have siblings who live with them (as members of their nuclear family) considered those siblings to be more important than the donor siblings. They also described their relationships with siblings as people who share history, parents, and everyday life. For them, donor siblings are not the same. The children we interviewed who are only children do not have this comparison, and they did not apply the same functional definition to their concept of siblings. They are often more open to the use of sibling language to refer to (and claim) donor siblings. But, as we will see more clearly in what follows, they too acknowledged that they need to develop a rich relationship with their donor siblings in order to transform the genetic tie into a meaningful relationship.

All the children in this study—whether they have siblings or not—were trying to figure out how to negotiate the terrain of these new and unnamed relationships. As we discuss in Part II, the dynamics created by joining together in a larger group raise entirely new sets of complexities. Tensions sometimes arose within a single network when some donor siblings wanted to use sibling language and others did not (as was the case for Brooke). However, like the parents, the adolescents generally proceeded with caution as they figured out how to make social ties out of genes. Sometimes teens had high expectations that there would be some kind of intuitive understanding of, and immediate sense of ease with, genetic siblings. They soon found out that genetic links did not automatically determine the social behavior of being either "siblings" or friends. Strikingly, many of the older teens we interviewed did not know any other kids (outside their own family if they had siblings) who were donor conceived.[7] Even those who had no interest in forming connections with people they considered genetic strangers could find comfort in simply knowing that there were others out there with the same experience of being not only donor conceived but also being conceived from the *same* donor.

In Part II of this book, as we explore five different donor sibling networks, we demonstrate the variety of types of responses to donor siblings and the variety of types of relationships that emerge even within a single network, among the people bound by a shared donor. We show as well that these very different responses and relationships emerge from two separate sources: the group dynamics (especially insofar as they revolve around what it means to be donor siblings) *and* the distinctive needs and desires of the individuals involved.

Part II

Five Featured Networks
of Donor Siblings

We now shift our focus from the acts of individuals to networks that include parents, donor siblings, and, occasionally, donors. These networks represent an entirely new form of social organization. There is no obvious organizing framework that participants can easily graft onto the web of genetic connections they discover. Groups differ markedly in such facets of their organization as their comfort and willingness to adopt labels like "father," "brother/sister," or even "sibling." Labels, like relationships, have to be invented or redefined.

In the upcoming five chapters we explore the different organizing strategies random families of parents and donor siblings adopt once they find each other and begin building a network. Each network represents a distinct set of solutions.

At the beginning of each chapter there is an illustration of the featured network. These illustrations show each separate family and its links to the other network members. They also provide the reader with a guide to the names we use in the narratives. As the reader will see, the children constitute the linkages between the individual family trees. When the children do not constitute these linkages, their names appear only on the bushy part of the tree. This modern rendition of the family tree approximates how donor siblings and donors are located within a broader network.

The networks we selected for closer examination all represent occasions when people moved offline and met in person. The five networks vary in important ways:

1. Era in which donor conception occurred
2. Age of kids in the network
3. The value participants attribute to their connection to each other
4. The interpersonal dynamics of networks

The first two criteria are related, but they offer different insights. Together they give us a window into the process of network formation and they need some explanation.

Parents who have children born before 2003 did not anticipate that they could connect with donor siblings because donor sibling registries either did not exist or were in their infancy. Participants in these networks did not have other examples to learn from or compare themselves to. In fact, few people in the broader society had ever heard of such arrangements. This was the situation for the members of the first three networks we examine. Most of the children in these networks did not meet until they were at least adolescents, and donor siblings came as a surprise. The ages of the children had much to do with their interpersonal dynamics.

Parents in the last two networks, whose children were born after 2003, had access to contact through donor sibling registries from the very beginning; they might have even known other people who had made that kind of contact. The older children in these families (all of whom were preteens) had sometimes known about donor siblings from the time they were toddlers; over time they formed deeper connections. The youngest children (under five years old) were happy enough to play with their donor siblings without even being able to understand how they were related. In short, by observing networks that began in different eras we can better understand how the process of network formation may have changed as more information about this phenomenon of donor siblings became available, especially through media reports, and as the contact among donor siblings occurred at younger ages.

In order to find out more about the five networks featured in chapters 5 through 9, we corresponded with the staff at several national sperm banks; no bank was willing to tell us how many children had been born from our respondents' donors. Therefore, the data on network membership is missing those families who have chosen to have no contact with donor siblings. These families would only be listed in the bank's records. If we had this information about individual donors from the bank's records, it would be possible to estimate the proportion of children conceived from a specific donor whose families have chosen to join a donor sibling network. In the absence of that information, no one knows either what percentage of the donor-conceived population is searching for donor siblings or what percentage has found them. We do know that interest in finding others has increased in the last five years and is likely to continue to increase in the future.

The first network we examine, Michael's Clan (chapter 5), is distinctive in two important ways: first, the network members all reside in the same geographic area and, second, they all know the donor. In fact, he is a central figure in this network. He plays the role of a "father" who convenes the various participants. In this network, donor siblings are a by-product of the donor's appearance. Born between 1986 and 1990, the kids in this network were between twenty-four and twenty-eight years old at the time of the interviews.

We next introduce (chapter 6) the 7008er network at the occasion of a significant gathering, when seven families came together at a hotel in the Midwest. From the beginning, the children in this network sought to construct themselves as a family. However, as the group expanded to incorporate new members, the original narrative of family membership failed to describe the reality of competing allegiances among teenage kids. Born between 1995 and 2001, the kids we interviewed were between fifteen and nineteen years old.

The members of the third network we discuss, the Tourists (chapter 7), are not really sure what they are looking for when they connect with one another. The fact of donor siblings is a novelty, but like tourists who are only curious about the sites in a different land, a brief visit suffices. Interestingly, the donor makes himself known to this network, but he too is a tourist who sets clear limits on what he has to offer these kids. The Facebook group and holiday cards sent within the network are reminders of membership, but there is little other interaction. Born between 1994 and 2001, the kids we interviewed were between sixteen and nineteen years old.

The Soul Mates network (chapter 8) differs from the previous two networks in that among its members we find neither group cohesion nor bland disinterest. Rather the network provides opportunities for pairs of parents and pairs of children to find particular meaning in their relationships with each other. The fact that there is a medical issue (which might come from the donor) running through some offspring, complicates—and sometimes intensifies —these relationships. Born between 2003 and 2006, the kids we interviewed were eleven- and twelve-year-olds.

While their children are too young to participate in the network formation, the parents in the last network we examine—the Social Capitalists (chapter 9)—recognized from the beginning that their donor purchase might be transformed into a resource for gaining social capital. They are not looking for family-like intimacy. The donor number connects the group, but the donor is little more than a form of "privilege" they can provide their children. Born between 2011 and 2014, these children were under age five.

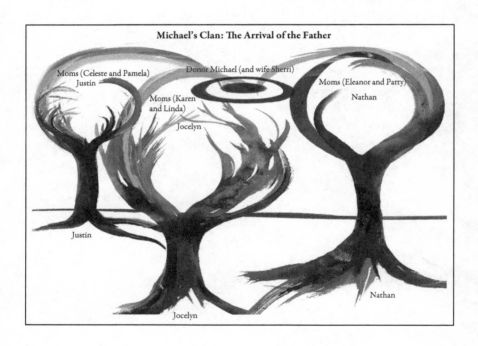

Michael's Clan: The Arrival of the Father

Moms (Celeste and Pamela)
Justin

Donor Michael (and wife Sherri)

Moms (Eleanor and Patty)
Nathan

Moms (Karen and Linda)

Jocelyn

Justin

Jocelyn

Nathan

5

Michael's Clan
The Arrival of the Father

THE SAME-SEX COUPLES highlighted in this narrative are members of the "families of choice" cohorts that arose during the 1980s. Even though they were establishing a new family form, Justin's two mothers told him while he was growing up that he had a sperm donor "father," a man he could meet when he turned eighteen. During that momentous meeting, Michael, the sperm donor, became "Pops" to Justin as the two men formed a limited father-child bond. After Justin's donor siblings called the same sperm bank hoping to contact their sperm donor, Michael introduced the donor siblings to each other. The members of this network reconsidered ideas about the relative influence of nature and nurture once Michael and the donor siblings met each other. Yet ideas about chosen families remain central to the manner in which the members relate to one another.

* * *

We were lucky to arrive in the Bay Area to conduct interviews in a linked network during a weekend when Michael, the sperm donor, was in town. And we were lucky that almost everyone in this network (including Michael and his wife, Sherri, who had accompanied him from their home in Washington to California that weekend) was willing—even eager—to be interviewed. The three young adults we spoke with ranged in age from twenty-three to twenty-eight; since they first met ten years before the interview, the two donor sibling brothers (Justin and Nathan) have become very close. They are less close to their donor sibling sister (Jocelyn), whom they met only recently. We also interviewed some of the parents of these three "offspring": Justin's parents, Celeste and Pamela; Jocelyn's parents, Linda and Karen; and one of Nathan's two mothers, Eleanor. Finally, we spent some time talking with Rosie, an old friend of Justin's parents, who stopped by while we were at their home.

We were especially lucky to meet this network of genetic relatives because theirs is a story of being pioneers. Not only was Michael among the first donors at a boutique sperm bank serving lesbian couples and single women, but he was among the first donors at this new bank to be registered as identity release. Moreover, he was only the second donor at that bank who actually made contact with an "offspring." Not surprisingly, given Michael's low donor number, Pamela and Celeste and Eleanor and her partner at that time, Patty, were among the bank's initial clients. Eleanor and Patty were also one of the earliest couples in their county to have a second-parent adoption. Their experience of being pioneers was echoed in different ways across the bay. Justin was among the first children of (out) lesbian parents to attend his Berkeley, California, elementary school. And although Nathan was actually six months older, Justin was the first among the three offspring now known to Michael who made contact with Michael and probably, therefore, one of the first children of a lesbian couple in the United States to meet a previously unknown donor.

The pioneering components of their separate but connected experiences come through as these various individuals describe what they did— and how they made their decisions along the way. Even as we emphasize the pioneering aspect of this account, we want to note that it is far from being unique. Other respondents with children of approximately the same age shared many aspects of this story, including especially the belief that the donor constituted some sort of "father." We start with Pamela and Celeste because that is where Justin's story begins.

Among the First to Have a Donor-Conceived Child

Justin's parents are well aware of the many ways in which they were among the first to do what they did. In fact Pamela explicitly noted that she is proud to have been among a small group of pathbreakers, creating a lesbian household with two mothers and easing the path for the considerably younger women in same-sex couples who used sperm donors.[1] And she suggested that an eagerness to share her experience as a "lesson" is why she agreed to be interviewed: "So it just seemed to me that it was a story worth telling in terms of 'This is how things used to be, and look how different they are now.' And 'This is how our life was, to help get to where we are now.'"

At the start of their journey to parenthood, Pamela and Celeste first considered using a known donor. They quickly realized that route had too many complications: the girlfriends of straight men "would get all weird about it," and the gay men they knew were "party boys and [we] didn't want to be parents with them." Another woman in the same network had similar experiences, noting that negotiating with both straight and gay men resulted in "one horrible scenario after another." Moreover, as these parents were considering using their friends as sperm donors, there was something—no one yet knew quite what—emerging among gay men that these parents wanted to avoid; that something, of course, turned out to be AIDS, and Pamela and Celeste now count among their blessings that they escaped that problem.[2]

All in all, then, as so many others did three decades ago—and continue to do today—the parents of Jocelyn, Nathan, and Justin all decided that an unknown donor made the most sense for them. Justin's mother Celeste said that she and Pamela were not necessarily seeking to be nuclear and insular about their family form. After all, this was California in the 1980s, the heyday of what Kath Weston called "families we choose" within the gay and lesbian community.[3] When Celeste's parents had not been accepting of her lesbianism, she and Pamela had moved on to creating what they thought of as their own family. In fact, Celeste used Weston's language to describe the relationships among a tight-knit group of parents and their children: "In our community we call it the 'family of choice.'" When the interviewer suggested to Celeste that she and Pamela had been trying to build a family wherein they could have their child all to themselves, Celeste corrected her:

It's not that I'm wanting my boy all to myself and I'm not willing for him to experience other people and other ideas and other things in life. I think that my overall spirit, I would have loved to have that extra set of hands around. There were times I can promise you that would have been helpful.

But Celeste and Pamela were also unwilling to take the risk of having a known donor show up and claim their child, especially since there was no second-parent adoption in their state until Justin was three. After consulting a friend who was an attorney with a specialization in family law, Celeste said, she had learned enough to be very cautious:

> I had no parental rights . . . until Justin was three years old. There was no way we were going to run any risk of [using a known sperm donor such as] my best friend or Pamela's best friend or her brother or somebody else's brother. There was no way I was going to run the risk of somebody coming in and saying, "I want him every other weekend. I want that kid every other week."

When the search for a known donor ended, Pamela and Celeste were lucky to have found a progressive nurse-midwife who was just starting to offer insemination with donor sperm to lesbian women.[4] They were enormously relieved to find her, especially after their experience at the more conventional sperm banks, where, as a same-sex couple, they had felt uncomfortable:

> So first we went to the regular sperm banks, and it was just excruciating. We'd go in there, and there'd be the straight couples, and everyone looked at us like we were weird, and it was really uncomfortable. Then we heard that there was a woman in the city who was beginning to work with the lesbian community. So we went to her.

Celeste seconded Pamela's feelings and perceptions: "We didn't like the sperm banks. They looked at us like we were a little odd back then."

Pamela and Celeste had two interests in addition to wanting a more comfortable environment for selecting sperm. First, they wanted fresh sperm, which, in the pre-AIDS era, was still an option. Pamela attributed this choice to the time period and its values: "Because I was a hippie then, frozen sperm seemed to me to be like inorganic, you know. So I just couldn't fathom using it. I wanted, like, the real deal." Second, they wanted a donor who was willing to be identified when their child turned eighteen. They felt it was important for their child to be able to have contact with his donor, and they were delighted that this new bank offered that opportunity. Five men met their criteria, and Michael seemed the best among them in part because of the personal attributes they thought he revealed in his essay.

Pamela recalled that Michael's essay was "sweet" and that he stated that he was committed to helping others. This self-presentation helped Pamela make the transition from someone she knew to someone she might like to know. Eleanor, Nathan's mother, who is now a retired schoolteacher, remembered that she could make the same transition more easily when she recognized a connection to Michael in a shared love of folk dancing. For Eleanor, a Jewish donor who represented her "half" of the child's heritage was another deciding factor. Jocelyn's moms, Linda, a fundraiser, and Karen, a physician's assistant, also wanted a Jewish donor because they were both Jewish themselves. And although being Jewish was not important to either Pamela or Celeste, Pamela now jokes that they might have thought through more carefully what that could mean: "So I figured, okay, good. Jewish, smart, nice, Woody Allen, Bob Dylan, they're okay. A little neurotic. I should have paid a little more attention to that part." Finally, for these parents, the recommendation of a staff member at the sperm bank itself clinched the deal: Pamela and Celeste said that the secretary there told them she thought Michael was perfect for them; Eleanor recalled that the nurse-midwife "really liked him."[5]

Fortunately, Michael was willing to donate to this new program that helped lesbians have children and equally willing not to be a part of a child's life until that child turned eighteen and sought him out. Michael had been raised in what he called a "liberal family," and he was living in San Francisco when he saw an advertisement for sperm donors. He said that the idea appealed to him because it satisfied his distinctive interest in being of service to the lesbian community:

> I saw a little notice on a board in the college and I read it, and it said, "Looking for a man of Jewish heritage who would be a donor, for a completely new program." I thought about it for a little while, and I made contact with [the owner of the sperm bank]. . . . I felt that it was just, you know, the exact right thing, because I felt that at that time if a woman . . . chose to have a child and they really wanted a child, then they should have an opportunity to have a child, and if you're lesbian, you shouldn't have to have sex with a man to do it.

Among the First to Meet

From the time he was first told his birth story, Justin had known that he could contact the bank and find his donor once he turned eighteen. He acted as soon as he could with the call to the bank.[6] He then hesitated before contacting Michael. Justin worried that his donor "basically . . . would be this jerk guy that didn't want anything to do with me when I'd have questions and maybe want to develop some sort of relationship."

For his part, Michael had his own nervous anxiety about what contact with his offspring would mean. The year of waiting between giving his information to the bank and Justin's contact with him felt long and frustrating: "Months go by. Months go by and nothing happens, and I'm getting a little restless and just thinking . . . 'Oh, I'm getting really excited about this.'"

Justin focused on their first face-to-face meeting as being the moment of connection. He had chosen a café as the location for his first glimpse of Michael because his own private fantasy had always included a public, but warm, setting:

> Man, I was so nervous—so, so nervous to meet him. Then I met him at a café. We had breakfast. We were there literally talking. As soon as we met, we kicked it off. Everything was great. I mean we literally were sitting there through all of breakfast, through all of lunch, and everyone had left. We had been there through two meal periods. We left. I don't remember what we went to go do. We didn't get back until nine at night or something like that.

Michael had not needed to wait for a face-to-face meeting to feel something powerful. It had taken just one brief conversation on the telephone to cement his sense of strong, intimate connection: "He calls, and it was remarkable. I mean, the very first words, and I thought, 'I'm listening to myself. This young man sounds like me, and his sentence structures are my sentence structures. Now he's describing things in ways that I might describe things.'"[7] The relationship bloomed from the café, and over the past decade Michael and Justin have spoken regularly on the telephone and met on numerous occasions.

Raising Justin to Expect a Father

From the very beginning of imagining their family, Justin's two mothers cared a lot about the possibility that their child would be able to have contact with the sperm donor, a man to whom they always referred as a "father" or "dad." Celeste, who is a psychologist, explained the nomenclature decision as being based both in their desire to give Justin an answer to the questions he might be asked and in their not having a ready-made script that could provide alternative answers:

> When your little kid goes to school and they say, "Who's your mom and who's your dad," you don't want him to say, "I don't have a dad." Of course, he's got a dad. [So we told him,] "Yes, you have a dad." [We taught him to say,] "We don't know my dad. He doesn't live with us. We don't know him yet. We don't get to know him until I'm eighteen." It was important from the point of view that I wanted Justin to be able to have an answer to that at an early age. It was also important for us. I know Pamela will speak for herself, but we were in uncharted waters. . . . We didn't have any role models. . . . We didn't know two lesbians that had had children together at that time.

Pamela and Celeste thus armed Justin with the notion that he had a "dad" even if that dad did not live with them. They used the language of paternity to describe the donor with other people in their social milieu as well. Intent on educating first Justin's day-care providers and then the principal of the elementary school he attended, they explained that Justin "has a father, who[m] he'll get to meet when he's eighteen." They then laid out in concrete detail their ideas about how they should be treated as a family. Fortunately, Celeste said, "everyone behaved" because, she added with a wry smile, "this is Berkeley."

Pamela and Celeste might not have known any other lesbian couples who had children together when they started to create their own family, but within a few years their lives were enriched by contact with many other such families. And if Justin was one of the first children of "out" lesbian parents in his school, he found many others at the "family camp" he and his parents attended each summer. For Celeste and Pamela—as for many other parents we interviewed in that cohort—places like this were important to help "normalize" the experience of being donor conceived.[8] Celeste explained:

> Every year we went to family camp, the gay and lesbian family camp. We went from the time Justin was tiny little. We keep going and we keep going. We even went back there when he was an adult. . . . We all went. . . . We thought it was important that he see other families with same-sex parents, with different family configurations so that he didn't grow up thinking moms and dads have families and everybody else is just different and weird. We didn't want him to feel different and weird.

They also rented a summer cabin with another lesbian couple and their young child both because that couple were among their closest friends and because doing so offered another opportunity to "normalize" the situation of donor conception in a two-mom family for Justin.

Meeting Michael: Affirming (and Disconfirming) Genes

Bringing up Justin challenged Pamela's ideas about the relative importance of nature and nurture. He was a difficult child who raised lots of questions. In fact, Pamela, a philosophy professor, said she soon gave up her "progressive" notion that she could nurture against what she was coming to see as Justin's essential nature:

> I had this notion that everything was about nurture; that's sort of sixties and early seventies. And as soon as he was born, it was really clear he was his own person. . . . I thought, this nurture stuff doesn't have anything. This kid is wired to be the way he is.

Meeting Michael created a brand-new belief in *genetic* influences. Pamela had already determined that "this nurture stuff doesn't have anything." But she had not yet come to believe that Justin's nature came from the genes passed down by his biological father. All that changed at the intense moment when she first saw Michael and Justin together:

When we met Michael, the first thing that was so striking is they looked so much alike. So when Michael and Justin walked in the front door of this place in Seattle where we were staying when we went up to meet him, my jaw dropped. It was just like, "Oh my God, you look just like him."

Moreover, for Pamela, finding a source for Justin's difficulties was a great comfort because she suddenly felt free of responsibility for his behavior:

How did I feel? There's a way in which I felt somewhat, kind of re-lieved, because there was a period of time when Justin was doing his teenage rebellion, where he blamed us for absolutely every problem in his life. Of course, that's what kids do. And there was a way in which I felt . . . some of his issues were just the way the genes fell. And some of them were from Michael and not me. And so there was an element of relief.

Her newfound conviction that nature was preeminent was confirmed when she noted another odd similarity between Justin and his donor sibling Nathan:

When Justin met Nathan, he was thrilled. Just thrilled. They look alike too. I think the first time we met Nathan, he came here to the house with Eleanor [his mother]. Justin and Nathan had already met. And here's this weird story—I don't know if anybody's told you this, about the things they do that are the same. Justin has this thing that he does—he loves to pull on ears. To the point that . . . I finally said, you got to cut this out, it's weird. . . . So Nathan walks into the kitchen, with Eleanor, and they sit at the table, and I look up and Nathan is reaching up and pulling on Eleanor's ear. . . . No kidding. Celeste and Justin and I are sitting at the table and we all looked at each other, and . . . I said, "You do that all the time?" He said, "Yeah, I love to pull on my mom's ear." How weird is that?

Justin also identified strongly with his donor, Michael, finding vast realms of similarity between the two of them, confirming his own belief in the power of nature over that of nurture. His donor sibling brother, Nathan, had the same experience concerning similarities between himself and Justin:

> I noticed patterns in Justin's voice that reminded me of my voice. Just little things about the way that the brain develops, that I think we have things in common, because of our genetics, about thought patterns, and the way we lay things down to the neural hard drive. There's definitely something in common there. It's hard to really put a finger on it.

Michael's wife, Sherri, also became more convinced about the influence of genes once she saw Michael with Justin. Sherri had believed that the determinants of personality were threefold: environment, genes, and spirit. Observing Michael and Justin when they were together strengthened her belief in the middle one of these, especially with respect to issues of addiction and other patterns of behavior. When we asked her what she thought Michael's offspring had gotten from him, she responded:

> Addiction and mental health issues, and even just thinking. Some of the thought patterns and stuff. . . . I can't tell you specifically anything [that is an] example of this, but the way that Justin perseverates about things the same way Michael does. His moms don't. It didn't come from them. It's like there's just certain patterns of behavior that are—oh my God, I can't believe how much he's like Michael, you know? He in particular because he's so open. You can just read him straight out. . . . Physical for sure. There's that. That, I would never have denied, the physical similarities. But it's more the internal stuff that I was just amazed by.

Meeting Justin did for Michael what it did for the others: "I had never realized how much this whole 'nurture and nature' thing could be in the way of developing your personality, and how that could connect to genetics. Yet I was looking at somebody who thought in ways like I did." Michael sees different sides of himself in different offspring. When it comes to Jocelyn, he appears to stretch to find those commonalities. We cannot tell whether that stretching is because he met her only recently, because he less readily identifies with a "daughter," or because she actually is less similar to him than the boys are: "I think with Jocelyn, . . . her interests are similar, very similar interests—like her interest in music and animals and art. Those are things we share. And she likes the outdoors. I like the outdoors."

Not everyone is quite so willing—or eager—to place such weight in this genetic tie as are Justin, Nathan, Pamela, and Michael. According to Pamela, Celeste, as the nongenetic mother, has had moments of distress about all the focus on inherited traits that accompanied seeing Justin and Michael together for the first time: "She said, 'God, all this gene stuff, I don't know how I fit into this.'" However, Pamela also suggested that "the next day, it was sort of like gone." As this example suggests, meeting donor siblings can have the unsettling effect of highlighting genes in a family, an effect that is particularly problematic in a family that has downplayed the importance of biological parenthood to create two, relatively equal, social parents. Several genetic parents (in this network as well as in others) reported on how distressed their same-sex partners had been at the moment of meeting the donor or donor siblings. Each of them also commented that the distress was short-lived and that, on the surface at least, everything went quickly back to normal.

Michael the Father

Justin has not only identified his similarities to Michael in looks and personality (and vice versa), but after ten years of the relationship, Justin has come to regard Michael as a paternal figure:

> It's turned into he's my guide. He's my mentor. He's very much of a
> father figure. . . . I've developed something with him where I'll go to
> him with questions seeking wisdom and advice. He really just spills
> it out in a way I can understand that just is very helpful and has been
> a very great addition in my life.

Jocelyn is the youngest offspring in this group and the one who met Michael most recently; her parents are more ambivalent about her interactions with him than are the other parents we interviewed. These factors probably contribute to her being much less comfortable than Justin

and Nathan in accepting the language of family to describe her relationships. While she said she "wouldn't talk about certain things in front
of Michael," as would be the case for her own parents (or any adults for
that matter), she is not entirely easy with the notion that the genetic link
means anything much. She has gone along with the name "Pops" that was
Michael's invention for how to represent himself in correspondence with
his offspring: "He signed, 'Love, Pops' on a text." As she told us this, Jocelyn
hesitated because she is neither looking for, nor ready to claim him as, a father. She is also not ready to call Nathan and Justin her brothers. She ended
up calling them "the boys" instead: "The boys call him 'Pops,' I think. I don't
know if they call him 'Dad' too." She also went along with the "love" part.
Although it startled her at first and may even have felt intrusive, she was not
ready to reject entirely another source of love in her life:

> INTERVIEWER: Who said love first?
> JOCELYN: Michael did.
> INTERVIEWER: How did you feel about it?
> JOCELYN: I was like, "I love you too." I guess I was like a little
>   surprised, but then I was just like, okay, cool. I have a dad that loves
>   me. . . . It was weird, but it's nice, I guess.

Jocelyn might have been a little ambivalent, but Michael wore his new position as the father proudly; he also accepted limits to, or boundaries around,
his position. He was respectful of the fact that he didn't raise Justin, that
Justin was raised by two parents (whom he refers to as an "adoptive parent"
and a "biological parent"). But he then verbally put himself on a par with
Pamela, describing himself also as a "biological parent." And he hasn't shied
away from developing a relationship with Justin in which he gives advice:

> Justin and I have a very deep, more intense relationship. We can
> really get into personal dialogue about self-development, and he
> really wants to have somebody to throw things against to get reflec-
> tion and things like that.

Still, he was clear that he believes he gives advice to Justin only because
Justin wants it; he is trying to be a good father, and a different one at that,
to each of these three young adults:

I only give advice if somebody asks me or says that they want it. So I'll ask, "Are you saying that you want some advice right now, and you want me to give you some of my thoughts about this?" Then I'll give them, but I don't generally give advice when it's not requested.

And like the "good father" he is trying to be, he claimed not to have a favorite: "I really have cherished each connection that I've been able to make with each one of the three." But, of course, Michael's fatherly role is limited: he might give advice, but he does not offer financial support to any of the three children.

Sherri is delighted to see him in this new role. Watching him confirms her "understanding" of her husband, that "he's just this amazing, big-hearted, generous person." She likes as well that she now has the "big messy family" that she had always wanted. Delighted as she is, she was also clear about limiting the kind of support that she and Michael offer: "There's nothing financial about any of this."

Some Parents Welcome the Father

Along with Michael and Sherri, Pamela and Celeste were ready to acknowledge Michael as Justin's father, even in a limited capacity. They claimed that meeting this "father" has been entirely positive for Justin himself and for their family dynamics. After Pamela described how jaw-dropping it was to see the physical similarity between Michael and Justin and the relief she felt now that she was not "responsible" for his behaviors, we probed a bit deeper. She admitted only to joy because that is what she saw on the face of Michael and Justin:

INTERVIEWER: How was that for you?
PAMELA: Just stunning. It was like overwhelming. Stunning. . . . It was just, like, so sweet to see him standing there with his father, and they were both so happy. I was so happy. I could hardly stand it. It was one of the best days of my life. Yeah. Oh yeah, I was so happy.

When asked, "Who is Michael to Justin," she readily answered, "He's Justin's father." But Pamela also modified this initially straightforward response. She and Celeste, she said, remain the first port of call when Justin is in trouble; Michael is a "sometimes" relationship for Justin:

> I think that Justin still relates to us as the day-to-day. . . . He doesn't call Michael when he has a crisis with the roommate, but he does call Michael sometimes when he has to figure something out and he wants some advice. But not a lot. When they're together, they are together. But Justin's an "out of sight, out of mind" kind of person. . . . He's not big on communication when somebody's not present in his life. I think sometimes he contacts Michael, but not a lot, but when Michael's around, he wants to be with him as much as he can.

Celeste agreed with Pamela that Michael has been a "plus" in Justin's life, not only because they are happy together but because Michael supplies Justin with another person who cares about him and to whom Justin can turn when he has a problem: "He brings his own person to the table and he's available and he's caring and he's conscientious. I like for Justin to think if Justin has a problem, he has a choice of people to call. His choices just got broadened." Celeste even accepted the nomenclature of "parent" for Michael, claiming that the more one has, the better off one is.[9]

Pamela and Celeste's happy father story was not reflected quite so fully among the other members of the clan that Michael is trying to pull together. Linda, the nonbiological mother of Jocelyn, was troubled by the newfound relationship between Michael and her daughter. Perhaps because she feels more threatened by the sudden emphasis on a genetic tie than does her partner, Linda made an analogy between Michael and a "divorced father" who can sweep in, after all the work is done, and be the "fun" parent:

> Maybe I'm jealous. Maybe. I'm not sure, really, that's it, but it might be a little bit of that. It's more like—I don't want to make the analogy to the father who comes on the weekend and takes the kids to Disneyland, and then brings them back, and then the primary parent, there, or the mother, or whomever it may be, taking care and having to be responsible, and, "Okay, now you owe me; you have to pay this and you have to do that." You know for us it's more the daily routine of "Do your laundry." And then he comes rolling in and it's like everything's

good-time, and everything's great. Everything's not great. . . . I'm not having as much fun with Jocelyn these days as he is.

A difficult (and strange) situation was given a familiar analogy (the divorced dad) even as Linda denied its utility and insisted that she was not making that comparison. Linda might feel especially protective because Jocelyn is still young, having just graduated from college. By way of contrast, neither Celeste nor Pamela seeks to control the relationship between Justin and Michael. After all, Justin is in his late twenties, and, as Celeste said, because he lives on his own, her direct influence is limited at best.

In any case, everyone agreed that meeting Michael had always been Justin's ambition and goal and that he has embraced the relationship with Michael as his father more fully than have the other donor siblings. Eleanor said, "I think that Justin relates more to Michael as a father than Nathan does." Rosie, Pamela and Celeste's friend from the summer cabin, knows Justin well. Her own son, she said, was never interested in his donor and wasn't interested when he met "a couple of his half-sibs." For him, the existing relatives and their chosen family members were sufficient. Justin, she said, was always different: "Justin was interested. . . . He's a dog with a bone. He was really wanting to find his donor." Rosie said as well that she was "so jealous that Michael's children have come back to him." Poignantly, she added, because she had never had biological children of her own, there were none "coming back" to her.

Chosen Family

Pamela and Celeste have not only embraced the relationship between Michael and Justin and introduced Michael to their "chosen family" but they have become fast friends with Michael and Sherri. Pamela described their web of relationships this way:

We have people like Rosie who are part of this sort of extended family, and so I don't really need more extended family. . . . So I guess I'm saying yes, there's our family, and our extended family with our people, and Michael's part of that, and Sherri's part of that . . . because we loved each other instantly. Seriously, it was instant.

Celeste gave much the same answer about both Michael and Sherri ("They're family"); she would also like to see a relationship develop between Justin and the members of the family Michael shares with Sherri:

> I would definitely encourage his relationship with Michael, with Sherri, with Connor [Sherri's son]. They're wonderful people. We hit a royal flush. We got lucky. I'm not saying we didn't deserve it. I'm not saying we didn't set it up to happen that way. I don't know what caused it, but we couldn't have done better.

Michael brought Celeste and Pamela into his family as well, but he did not include Nathan's mothers in that close circle of kinship:

> We were going to go get T-shirts ... that said, "My Big Messy Family." I mean, who is in my family? My family is [my wife] Sherri and myself, [Sherri's son] Connor and his wife—they just got married—and then my family is Justin and Nathan and Jocelyn. And Pamela and Celeste are absolutely family, and I get the impression that maybe Jocelyn's moms will be more in the fold of family. I will say this, that it has not been the same with every child. Nathan's two moms ... I have almost no contact with, and neither party has wanted or tried to really develop that. That's been more separate, so we've kept it that way, and it's just been natural to keep it that way. That doesn't mean that Nathan doesn't want it. Nathan wants it. He sees it as we are all family, and he would love it if we were all together.

For her part, Eleanor (the only one of Nathan's mothers we interviewed) is happy enough to remain excluded from this tight circle. Although, like Pamela and Celeste, she believes in families of choice, Michael is not part of her choice and neither is Justin: "I don't think Michael is part of my family. I would say Michael is my son's donor dad. Justin is my son's half-brother."

We Never Knew about Donor Siblings, but There They Are

When Justin contacted the sperm bank as soon as he turned eighteen, he was hoping to locate his biological father. Donor siblings were not part of his plan; in fact, neither he nor his parents had ever heard this term or imagined this set of relationships. But these relationships have delighted Justin since he first met Nathan when the two were both nineteen. Now Justin and Nathan maintain a strong relationship that survives through occasional episodes of difficult behavior on each side. And they do not hesitate to call each other "brother" and to introduce each other to their friends in that way.

Nathan described his relationship with Justin as one that is more than friendship, as a relationship that rests on a deep sense of connection: "I try to share as much as possible with Justin. Like I said, I've taken him more in like family in my sense and feelings, so I share more of my life with Justin, and I try to let him understand who I am and what I'm going through and how I'm feeling. I think he does with me, too." Eleanor confirmed the significance of this tie for her son; she also commented—as we will see other parents do—on the physicality of the relationship, on how the donor siblings engage in rough-and-tumble play:

> What was interesting was that Nathan and Justin became really good friends. That was very fascinating. When I would say to Nathan, "Do you want to go shopping?" he'd say, "No, I'm going to see my brother." Not "Justin." "My brother." Justin did the same thing. They would use names for all their friends and they would say "My brother." They were very tight. For a while they were just constantly together. When we went over, at some point . . . to meet Celeste and Pamela . . . the kids were like puppies. Nathan and Justin were like puppies romping all over. It was really a trip watching them.

Although the relationship between Justin and Nathan is symmetrical, with each caring a lot about the other, their independent relationships with Michael are not the same. Nathan explained that he and Justin have different attitudes: "Justin has been more fascinated than I have been in meeting Michael, and more obsessed with the idea of having both a father and a mother." There is also asymmetry in the relationships of Justin and Nathan to Jocelyn and she to them. Justin and Nathan happily call her their sister. But, as already noted, although she reported that it's been "exciting, fun and interesting," to meet them, she insisted she has no personal or intimate relationship with them and she said she is not sure she would keep in touch with them were it not for Michael.

Once again, as he did for the original meeting of Justin and Nathan, Michael has facilitated the relationship between Jocelyn and the two young men. As Michael suggested, he is the focus of this set of relationships:

> Jocelyn's the one that has said, "I really need to establish the relation-ship with you, and I'm not ready to establish a relationship with my other siblings yet." Yet. That went on for three or four months, okay, and then all of a sudden she changed. I say I'm coming down on the tenth. [She said,] "Oh, I'm going to be doing my concert with my band. Do you want to come?" I say, "Absolutely. Of course I'll come." [She said,] "Well, then I'll introduce you to my moms." And all of a sudden . . . she's like, "I'm ready." Then I said, "Well, you know, I was thinking about getting together with Justin and Nathan. What do you think about them coming to the concert?" She writes back and she says, "Oh, I think it's a great idea, and then I can spend time with them." . . . So tonight I'm having dinner with Jocelyn and her girlfriend, and I'm then going with Justin and Nathan to hear Jocelyn's band play.

Clearly, Justin and Nathan have a stronger sense of being bound together, of being "family," than Jocelyn has with either of them. However, even Justin suggested that it is the link upward to Michael and back down to Nathan that creates that bond:

> I feel like we have this bond, this connection due to our father. That will always bring us back together. . . . Where other people might slip away, we have . . . a net, of our parents and where they live and their location and their lives and my father, and that all keeps us a little bit more combined, I think, than had it been just random: "Who is this dude? Oh, we're going to become friends."

This Is Justin's Family

Pamela and Celeste have been far less interested in the donor siblings than they have been in the donor. They were first surprised and then ex-cited to find that there were donor siblings.

Didn't even occur to us that there were siblings. We were mostly waiting to meet Michael, and when we went over to get the name of his father from [the bank's director], she said there's a sibling who wants to meet you. And we were so excited. . . . We just hadn't thought of it. It's silly, but we hadn't.

Excited as they were, they left the decisions about moving forward up to Justin, who made contact first with Michael and then, in conjunction with Michael, with Nathan. Pamela described that contact with a donor sibling as being thrilling for Justin (as he did for himself). Pamela also suggested that she has her concerns about some of Nathan's behaviors and she is comfortable with there being distance between them. She has met Jocelyn once ("She's very shy and very sweet"). But these, she reminded us, are *Justin's* relatives, not hers. Celeste shares Pamela's definition of the situation. She said that Jocelyn is Justin's "biological half-sibling," nothing more and nothing less. Celeste has only once met one of Nathan's mothers; she was "not personally drawn to [her]" and has not wanted "to make family with her." Celeste said as well that she would be "happy to [meet Jocelyn's] parents if they want to, or happy not to." Although she included this new network of people in a very broad definition of family, she denied it at the same time. As did Eleanor and Pamela, Celeste is ready to differentiate between her son's family and her own choices; she just draws her boundaries in a slightly different place:

CELESTE: If Justin considers them family, they're family to me.
INTERVIEWER: It doesn't sound like this is how you feel.
CELESTE: Let's put it this way. Justin is my family. If they're family
    to Justin, they're family to me. If he wants them here, they're here.
    If he doesn't and we want them here, they're here. Am I going
    to start inviting his [donor sibling] brothers and sisters over for
    every event? No. If he wants to invite them, that would be his
    business. That's the way I would consider it. . . . Michael is my
    family of choice. [The donor siblings] weren't my family of choice.
    They're biologically connected to Justin and they can be his family
    of choice if he wants or they're his biological family if he wants
    or they're both if he wants. It's up to him. I'll embrace whatever

he wants of that. I didn't choose to have those children. I've met Jocelyn only once I think. That's all.

Justin Draws Lines Too

In the next generation, Justin's lines are different from those of his mothers. Michael and Nathan get into his family: "At least Michael and Nathan are as close as any, if not closer, than a lot of my immediate family such as my cousins and my uncles things like that." But they are not quite as close as his mothers: "No. No. . . . You can't beat eighteen years of— well, really twenty-eight years of them being in my life."

He is also willing to embrace Jocelyn as his sister, if she will agree to it, and he adores Sherri. On the other hand, he is not particularly interested in the members of Michael's extended family. Although Michael's mother is excited to get to know someone she considers a grandchild, Justin is not so ready to be embraced.[10] Interestingly, for all the love Justin expressed toward Michael, his emotions are not straightforward. Justin also is angry that Michael was not present for most of his life. Some of that anger was brought to the surface when he talked about the rest of Michael's family—perhaps out of jealousy and perhaps out of a simple sense of having been somehow neglected:

INTERVIEWER: Were you interested in his family?

JUSTIN: Not terribly much and still not too much. I met his mother. . . . It was cool. I mean it was interesting meeting, yes, meeting his mom. I mean, to her I'm really significant because Michael didn't have any other kids. . . . I'm her first grandson.

INTERVIEWER: Do you consider her a grandparent?

JUSTIN: I mean not really. I feel guilty and bad saying that. She wasn't there for whatever. Neither was my dad. It's like, why do I need to care about my dad? I don't know. I somehow created the significance there. There has not been much desire or need to create something with his mother.

Justin thus acknowledged the "constructed" element of his relationship with Michael. Michael did not raise him and played no paternal role in his life until he was nineteen. He was "real" and not real at the same time.

Yet Justin has found a way to make Michael and Sherri a meaningful part of his current life. He is unwilling to do the same with Michael's mother, although she would like to develop a relationship with him.

* * *

Along with their peers, Pamela and Celeste have been pioneers in creating a new kind of family in which to have and raise a child: two mothers and reliance on an anonymous, identity-release donor. While engaging in something quite revolutionary, they drew on preexisting models that enabled their child to feel comfortable in a world that was occasionally, if not frequently, hostile to the idea of lesbian families and donor conception. Ironically, these models included the conventional idea of a father who would arrive to take his place amid "his" children. The "donor as father" represented a solution of sorts for parents (both in same-sex and single-parent families) who had no other language with which to explain to a child how she or he came to be and why she or he did not actually have a father. Having been raised to expect a father, Justin is lucky that Michael eagerly fills this role. With varying levels of enthusiasm, other members of this network not only embraced the language of family but also developed natal family relationships (pops, brother, sister) and enacted extended family forms (the occasional gatherings).

When Michael showed up for Justin, and then for Nathan and Jocelyn in turn, he was acting according to the schedule of the identity-release program at the sperm bank. He had agreed to have contact with each child after that child turned eighteen *and* had informed the bank that he or she was ready for contact. Michael is not an irresponsible parent or a deadbeat dad. Men dubbed "irresponsible" or "deadbeat" do not see their children, raise them, or pay child support. Michael had none of *those* obligations, but he did keep the one promise he had made.

Michael himself may not have known what to expect from that contact; he is both surprised by, and overjoyed with, his relationship to Justin. Yet the ties he developed are strictly emotional ones. He may be there for fun and advice, but he does not offer material support. And he is careful in his assessment of his position to acknowledge that the parents who raised "his" children are the real parents.

Michael's role is unique to a particular moment in time. It is not, however, unusual *within* that moment of time. We found similar actions on the part of donors, parents, and children within other networks in which donor conception occurred approximately thirty years ago. But we did not find the same thing in any of the networks that formed around younger children. Whether it is because of a larger number of offspring from a single donor (Michael has only four who have contacted him) or because they are raising their own biological children (Michael has none), no subsequent donor we interviewed was so willing to embrace his offspring as his children.

We did, however, find equally strong donor sibling ties. In this group, these ties center on the bond between two brothers. Justin and Nathan like to spend time together: they go to concerts and bars; they hang out. When we interviewed the members of this network, Jocelyn had only recently met the brothers; neither she nor they knew whether a strong bond would form there as well. The three donor siblings differed in their reaction to Michael as well as in their reactions to each other. Justin cared the most; Jocelyn was ambivalent; Nathan stood somewhere in the middle. Gender may be relevant, but it may equally well not be: in subsequent networks, we did not find that attitudes toward the donor were shaped by gender.

Since the boys met each other and the donor *after* they had moved out of their parents' homes, they manage both sets of relationships on their own. The three sets of parents had separate, and quite dissimilar, reactions to these new contacts. Pamela and Celeste were ready to add to their "chosen" family. They appreciated especially their relationship with Michael and Sherri. They were reassured that Michael has not supplanted them but that Justin still turns to them when he needs support. Nathan's mother has been less involved altogether; although she too believes in chosen family, she did not choose *these people* to be part of her family. And like their daughter, Jocelyn's mothers mostly had a "wait and see" attitude, although at least one of them was irritated by Michael's "divorced dad" style of sweeping in for the fun times while the real work of child-rearing remained hers. (The fact that she used this analogy suggests that she too had a father in mind.)

The absence of bonds among the mothers is unusual for donor sibling networks. The mothers in this network are not antagonists, but they have no reason for cooperation either. In this way, the network that swirls around Michael is quite different from the networks formed by parents who initiate interactions with each other in order to provide contacts with their children's donor siblings; in some of those networks the bonds that form among the parents can be as significant as the bonds that form among the donor siblings.

The primacy given to discussions of nature and nurture is a key feature of this network. The mothers in this network chose a donor at a time when nurture was deemed dominant over nature; they also had far more limited choices for donors than did subsequent groups of parents. For these reasons, they probably had not given much thought to the influence of genes. Thus Celeste and Pamela were surprised to find striking similarities between Justin and Michael and between Justin and Nathan. Michael and Sherri also noticed them. For Justin, these similarities offer great comfort: he now thinks he knows something more about how he came to be who he is. As we will see, in networks with younger children, the age of those children determines the manner in which the idea of genes reverberates among the children in the network.

Michael's Clan has distinctive dynamics. These reflect a particular moment in time in the fertility industry, the formation of two-mother families, the membership in the network, and the age of the children involved. The next network we examine is similar in its reliance on conventional ideas about families. Yet that model plays out in very different ways in a network in which parents and children meet when the children are much younger and when the donor himself is not an active participant.

Network update: Michael knew of a fourth child whom he was getting to know before introducing her to the other kids. He had told Justin, Nathan, and Jocelyn about this girl. The sperm bank at which he had donated told him there are two additional children who share his genes. Neither has contacted Michael.

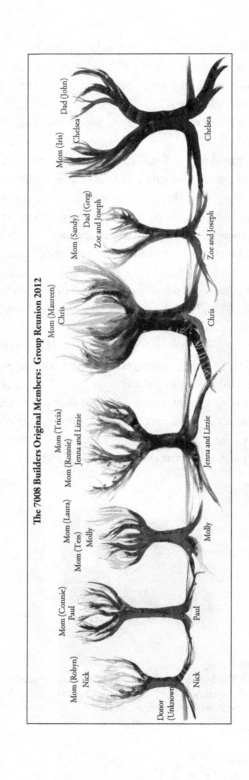

The 7008 Builders Original Members: Group Reunion 2012

6

The 7008 Builders

We Are Family

A DONOR SIBLING registry was the beginning of a whole new world. How would it feel to suddenly be part of a national network rooted in genes? Would both the parents and their children feel that genetic strangers were part of their families? Initially, many of the parents seemed to be more excited than their children about meeting new relatives. Yet it was the children who chose their donor's number as their group's name—"7008ers." And, as we will see, there are other collective symbols that remind them that they share this common ancestor.

Over time, as this network became larger, the lives of the children were enhanced by the intensity of bonds formed from a shared biology. As the children grew older, they rearranged their alliances within the network. Even with these rearrangements, the critical social ties in this network are among the children. These lateral ties are illustrated on the family tree rendition. We present this network chronologically to explore both how the social organization of this network developed and how the internal dynamics among the children changed as the children grew up.

* * *

I Really Think You Should Go

In February 2012, Nick and his mother boarded a plane for Kansas City, Missouri, where he would meet his donor siblings for the first time. As they took their seats, Nick, age fifteen, said again that he did not want to go. "Why not?" his mother asked, trying to get at the cause of his hesitation. As he remembered it almost four years later when we interviewed him, he felt ambivalent about the significance of a genetic tie. He said to his mother, "These people might be blood related to me, but I don't feel connected to them at all."

Despite Nick's concerns, his mom was not about to cancel plans. That's when his ambivalence turned into something closer to dread:

> She insisted I go. She said, "It might be a good experience," all of that kind of thing. At that point I was locked in to going. I was nervous to go and meet all of these people. The whole plane ride in, I just tried to block it out of my mind. I thought, "I'm just on the plane. It doesn't matter." There are no direct flights from Boston to Kansas City. Waiting in the lounge, I kept thinking, "These shadowy figures are about to become a reality." Chilling thought. I felt numb.

His mother, who had ignored his complaints, also remembered trying to reassure him:

> [I said,] "Nicky, what do you have to lose? This is three days. We go on this trip. You meet these kids. If you're not comfortable, if you're not interested, or if it doesn't work out, fine. But if it does, then you'll always have these people. What do you have to lose?"

Nick's "birth story" about his donor conception had always been part of his life. Whenever he asked questions about his origins, his mom added details that were, in his words, "age appropriate." Nick had been told—and repeated to us—the now commonplace "choice" narrative for single mothers: "She chose not to get married and she chose to have an anonymous donor. I just accepted that, the part about not having the dad, but as for my birth story and things like that, she always loved to talk about me, tell me about myself. She was never shy about that." Nor was she shy about involving others in Nick's life and making sure he had male role models. Through a local Big Brother program, he met a terrific college student, with whom he has a close friendship to this day. Moreover, Nick's classmates all had dads who included him in their father-son outings.

The choice narrative Nick's mother created is acceptable among those who live in the safe, middle-class, social world of suburban Boston, even though that world consists primarily of two-parent households. Perhaps because their family raised so few eyebrows, after a period of time, Nick stopped asking for more details about his origins: "I'd say probably from the age of seven to maybe thirteen or fourteen I lost interest or just didn't think about it much."

The whole story of Nick's donor siblings began one day in 2005, when Nick was about ten years old. His mother, Robyn (who never expected there would be a way to meet the anonymous donor she had selected), nearly jumped out of her chair as she watched a TV show that discussed how "donor siblings" could connect with one another. Robyn, a psychiatric social worker, had never heard that term before. However, it made intuitive sense to her that there would be other offspring from the same donor; she immediately logged on to the advertised website, where she registered her name and donor number. She had fretted for a long time about the fact that Nick was not just an only child but had an older mother. (She was forty years old when he was born.) Without much close family on her side, the idea of "others" from the same donor, or Nick's "genetic relatives," appeared to open up a new option for creating kin.

Several people had already registered with the same donor number on the site by the time Robyn signed up. Robyn exchanged some individual emails and swapped pictures of the children with these parents. From the start, Robyn said she saw the "others" as belonging to Nick, as being *his* relatives and important to her through him. Once she had determined to her satisfaction that the parents were good, well-meaning people, she decided to tell Nick about them. He reacted in a way she had not predicted:

> [I said,] "Do you want to see the pictures?" They wrote letters, and so I showed him the pictures and whatever, and I said, "Why don't you take these. These are yours. These are *your* people. You hold these." He said, "I don't want them." He's looking at me kind of crestfallen, and I said, "What's the matter?" He said, "Now I don't feel special. I thought I was his only child."

Nick's mom had never shared her suspicions that other families had also purchased sperm vials from Nick's donor. It seemed an unnecessary and confusing detail that had nothing to do with her individual donor choice. Several kids who would join this network later also imagined the donor as theirs alone; when they learned that other children had also been conceived using "their" donor's sperm, they were taken aback. Confronting the reality that these "others" were also actual people, which is what happened when Nick saw their photos, took some time.

Several years after learning about the donor siblings, when Nick had just turned fifteen, a group of seven families and their nine children agreed to meet for a long weekend at a hotel in Kansas City. This setting was chosen not only because it was a central point geographically for all the families, but because one of the girls—Lizzie—was playing in a sports tournament in that city. That event serendipitously would become the occasion for a critical bonding experience for the entire group.

On the last leg of the flight to that first gathering in Kansas City, Nick, who was still nervous, tried to focus on the contact he'd had recently with his donor siblings. The donor siblings had created a Facebook page so they would not feel like total strangers when they met. They asked him to join. He hadn't been quite sure whether they meant anything to him, whether sharing DNA made them relatives. Even after joining the Facebook page, Nick held back, hesitant to make meaning out of this novel connection:

> I wasn't sure at that point how much of an impact these people would have on my life. I thought maybe they might be blood related, but they weren't really related to me. I didn't talk to anybody one-on-one over a Facebook message or anything. . . . A lot of them would add polls to the group, just very ice breaker activities like, "What is your favorite food?" And then you could answer. I never really did any of that.

Now, full of ambivalence, he was going to meet them for the first time.

Why Others Signed Up for the Registry

The parents of the donor siblings Nick was about to meet all had different reasons for signing on to an internet registry. No one said that he or she was looking for a father for a child, and no one had waited until the child turned eighteen before making contact with genetic relatives. Connie, a real estate agent from Maryland, said she had become curious when she read an article in *More* magazine (no longer in existence) that described the possibility of contact with her child's donor siblings. She clipped the article but waited a year before signing up; she went back and forth in her mind, trying to figure out whether to act or leave well enough alone. She had divorced her husband because he did not want kids. As a single mother who conceived with both a sperm and egg donor, she wondered how the other kids would react to her son. She also worried that she was creating a situation she could not control: "What if he wanted connection and they didn't? And vice versa? Once you make the connection with someone else, the door is open. That's a whole new world. I had to process it myself." While she watched the registry fill up with new potential contacts, she debated what to do. Connie did not tell her son, Paul, anything. She saw the email contacts on the registry and reached out to another mom, Tess from California, who shared her concerns about placing their children in a difficult situation. Tess, a sales manager, and her partner, Laura, a bus driver, debated for weeks whether to tell their daughter, Molly, about these genetic strangers. After many emails and a few phone conversations, the parents decided to tell their respective children.

Another mother, Tricia, who was then partnered with Ronnie, was stunned when her daughter Jenna, who was thirteen years old at the time, woke her up from a deep sleep asking, "Can we sign up on the registry? I found five siblings online with my donor number." Jenna, who lived in Missouri, had been poking around online, trying to find information about her donor; she instead found the sibling registry. Once her mother, who worked as a physical therapist, agreed to let Jenna sign on, Jenna shared her excitement with her younger sister, Lizzie.

Maureen, also a single mother, had initially left just a thank-you note for the donor on a different registry—the Single Mothers by Choice registry that existed briefly around 1999. She told us she would never have tried to locate donor siblings if not for Greg, the father of two donor-conceived teenage children, who found Maureen through that note. When he contacted her, Maureen was still trying to figure out what to tell Chris, her son, who felt uncomfortable about the constant questions his classmates had been asking about his "dad." Greg, a home-schooling, stay-at-home dad, convinced Maureen, a lawyer, that their kids could be important to each other; otherwise, she would have given her son a "divorced and left" story—a scenario that was plausible enough for her situation:

A lot of people think donor conception is weird. Let's be honest. Synthetic children, right? A lot of people think it's weird, and, frankly, I did in the beginning. I was, "Am I really going to tell people that I used a sperm donor? Really?" I totally understood it. I was just going to follow my son's lead.

Greg had a different motive. He and his wife, Sandy, had used a donor because his sperm was the medical problem. Greg had initially thought that his children, Zoe and Joseph, would hear that they were donor conceived, digest that information, and move on emotionally. However, they could not understand their father's attempt to tell them that their genes came from a donor, *and* that this fact did not make him less of a dad. "I was just very naive. [When they were] three, four, five, six years old, I would tell them repeatedly. They really didn't want to know about it, anything that in any way smacked that I wasn't their dad." He thought that having connections with donor siblings would help his children understand that the use of donors was "normal," and that even though they shared genes with other people, he was still their "real" dad.

Maureen and Greg exchanged emails about the importance of donor siblings for about six months before they decided she would fly out to Tennessee from Washington, DC, with her son Chris to meet Greg's family. Greg's email notes had struck a deep chord with Maureen, but not for the reason he might have imagined: "When I was growing up, my mother's friends were also my family—my emotional family—and I was heartbroken when my 'aunties' died." Since Greg's kids were her son's genetic family, she wondered if they could become an "emotional family" for him. While their reasons for making a connection were somewhat different, both Maureen and Greg illustrate the importance people place on genetic inheritance. They, and Greg's wife, Sandy, hoped that the genes their kids share could become the foundation for an expanding family.

Maureen brought Chris to Tennessee in January 2005 so the three children could meet. Greg's daughter, Zoe, who had just turned seven years old, believes that she really wasn't sure that it sank in that this kid she was meeting is her half-brother. She just remembers running around the hotel lobby and having a great time. But her awareness of who Chris is blossomed over the next few years, and now she thinks about that early connection with donor siblings as having created more "family" for her: "Even if my family is huge on all sides, I got an even bigger family. I wanted a strong family connection and I got that." Her younger brother,

Joseph, who was only five at the time, doesn't remember that meeting at all. But Chris, who was six years old, recalled that it was fun. He added, "I was so young at that point. It was not something that provoked these deep questions that I was asking at that point in my development. I kind of accepted that these people are your siblings and I was like okay, great!"

Chris started to tell his friends about Zoe and Joseph, whom he referred to as his sister and brother who lived elsewhere. Zoe and Joseph made Chris feel special as opposed to weird about having been conceived with a donor. Maureen had also come around to Greg's vision that the donor siblings could counter her son's rejection of all things about the donor. She referred to the importance of the donor sibling network this way: "We've got this community to talk about this very strange situation that you're in."

A First Group Reunion

In 2012, as the seven families headed to Kansas City for their first group "reunion," parents were still the driving force. Iris, the happily married wife of an older man, directs a nonprofit organization; she made most of the arrangements. She had first learned about the internet registry around 2010, through a job-related webinar on the topic. A few weeks later, while driving her daughter, Chelsea, home from school, Iris shared the news that Chelsea might have half-siblings. Chelsea, who was in middle school at the time, retorted, "That is so gross. I mean, don't even talk to me about that again. That's repulsive." Chelsea kept another reason for being bothered to herself: "I wasn't super social and the idea of more preteens accepting me and having to care about them was not appealing." Two years later, when she was fourteen and about to start her freshman year in high school, she began to think about the donor siblings again. What if the donor siblings could help her learn about the donor, a man she imagined to be more like her than the father with whom she lived?

> In that period, I know I started to think about my donor more. There was definitely a period where I very much needed to know who he was. I still would like to, but then it was very much on my mind. . . . There was this guy out there, he would be this perfect dad, he would get me, and we'd have a deeper connection. That fantasy

has gone away, but it was there for a while. . . . Just someone more similar to me than my own dad. . . . I asked my mom about the registry and my siblings again. . . . I became much more curious about where I came from, if they were these people who would be similar to me, if they could give hints about the donor, things that we would share. Just more curiosity and less fear, I guess.

Unlike Chelsea—and much more like Nick—Paul in Maryland was reluctant to go to this first group meeting. He admitted that as an only child he was unprepared for instantaneous siblings. What if they made sibling-like demands on him, such as expecting him to help them or watch out for them? "I understood that I had half-siblings, but I didn't understand the purpose of having half-siblings. I wanted to meet them and all that, but I didn't understand what it would mean to meet them or what it would mean to be their brother." Molly, also an only child—the daughter of Tess and Laura—and "not very outgoing," as she described herself, did hope for sibling ties. As she put it, "I wished for a sibling to drag me along to do things."

Anxious Nick from Massachusetts (fifteen, a sophomore); reluctant Paul from Maryland (fifteen, a sophomore); excited Molly from California (fifteen, a sophomore); thrilled sisters Jenna (fifteen, a sophomore) and Lizzie (thirteen, an eighth-grader) from Missouri; indifferent Chris from DC (thirteen, an eighth-grader); curious Chelsea from Texas (fourteen, a ninth-grader); and the brother-sister pair Zoe (fourteen, a ninth-grader) and Joseph (twelve, a seventh-grader) from Tennessee, who were already primed to enjoy donor siblings from their earlier contact, were about to meet. The girls were the most enthusiastic about this "reunion," and they had already had more contact with each other on Facebook than the boys did. Getting together in person would raise their level of involvement with one another, opening up all sorts of possibilities.

The term "reunion" appears in the lexicon of this network and some others that have planned meetings of groups of donor siblings and their parents. The term evokes the fabricated notion that the children were together—in sperm state (in a vial)—even before they actually existed. The term further implies that now, after years of separation while being raised in different homes, they will be brought back together, reunited.

The parents who created this particular reunion, as noted, all had their own quite different motives for connecting on a website. Different as their motivations had been, the parents agreed that this reunion was about the children. Indeed, much as the parents were beginning to have personal opinions about the other parents—liking some, disliking others—they set those opinions aside (and for the most part still do) for the sake of their children. As Maureen, who describes herself as left-leaning, said, "I really try to like all of the parents because there's really no upside of getting annoyed. I ignore their political beliefs, their religious beliefs, etc. It might drive me crazy but these kids are my son's family. What I'm trying to do is facilitate anything my kid wants." Maureen and the other members of this group of parents were discovering that they had little in common with each other, aside from their kids having the same sperm donor. It is a group, like most donor sibling networks, in which the members might never choose one another as friends or even try to meet one another.

In fact, unlike Michael's Clan, the original 7008 members are geographically diverse, including families who live in rural areas and those that are city dwellers. It also contains a great deal of social diversity and a wide range of incomes (from $80,000 to $500,000).[1] While most of the kids go to public school, one family home-schools their children (and travels for educational purposes), and three families have their kids in parochial or other private schools. There is also a range of religious beliefs. Some families described themselves as agnostic, while others are practicing Baptists, Christians of other denominations, Quakers, and culturally Jewish. Some families even practice religions that are against IVF or donor use.[2] Since we first made contact with the group in January 2014, the newest members have brought even more diversity, including several hourly wage workers (whose household incomes are $50,000 or less) and more kids attending college on scholarships. For some of the less-advantaged families, a child's request for a plane ticket to meet donor siblings intensifies the economic struggles their families experience; for others, the occasional reunions barely make a dent in the family's budget.[3]

As much as these parents want to foster emotional bonds for their children, they have no need for their own relationships or any expectations about the development of closer emotional ties with one another. As one of the mothers said, "We have this connection when we see them, but everyone has their own life and their own circle, too. I have a warm feeling toward them and, as I said, if I texted one of them now, they would text me back or whatever. But I don't feel a sense of 'Oh, I'm going to call or I can't wait to tell this one or that one about this.' I just don't have that feeling. I don't think of them as part of my life, my immediate life from one day to the next. [The donor sibling group is] a very compartmentalized thing for me."

The Thrill of Meeting

Nick and his mother were the first to arrive in Missouri. They were met by Jenna, Lizzie, and their two moms, who showed them around town and drove them to their hotel. The others soon followed and, as each plane landed, that same quartet was waiting at the airport. All the parents said they felt welcome. For the kids, the moment was more complex. One of the girls summed up the feeling for others by saying it was like they were having an "out-of-body" experience:

> The first thing I saw was Jenna, and she just looks really similar to me. Not that we look like exact siblings, but we do have a lot of physical similarities and I just froze. I was like, "This is so weird." I really couldn't wrap my head around any of it.

Nick—who had not really interacted with any of the others on Facebook—said those first moments felt both strange and awkward. But those feelings soon dissipated, he said, as the group got bigger and Paul arrived to start conversations about similarities:

> At that point everybody started to relax and we came together as a group, I feel. . . . I started to feel so comfortable with these people so quickly I realized this isn't normal. This doesn't happen all the time when you meet brand-new people. I felt we had this common connection. We looked at each other and said, "Oh, you too have similar eyes, or these people both seem to have this temperament or whatever." . . . Once we started doing that, it was tough to stop. I think on the first night we stayed up until two or three in the morning just

discussing things like that and discussing our mentalities and who had similar thoughts and things like that.

Indeed, all the kids who gathered together were stunned to find that they shared commonalities that extended well beyond looks to interests and personality traits. As they watched each other and started to talk about themselves, they also referenced details they remembered from their donor's profile. Some kids like sciences (like the donor); other kids look alike (and share the donor's blue eyes, his sharp chin line, and his hair texture). They overlap with one another in interesting ways they thought they could spot as having a basis in genes. The power of the idea of genes as a source of connection reverberated through the group. And as it did, kids who had initially not known what to make of each other began to talk as if they had known each other forever.

Since the group had gathered in Missouri because Lizzie was in a volleyball tournament that weekend, one of the moms suggested that the kids make signs for her. They did, and also attended her game, where they spent time rooting for her, with each kid holding up a letter of "Go Lizzie" in unison. As they did, they felt a surge of belonging: they felt they really cared about her and about each other; they felt they had formed a group. There was a photographer at the game taking pictures. They told the photographer, "We are all siblings and we have just met. We want the photo to say on it '7008'—that's the donor's number." "The 7008ers" would become the name they called themselves.[4] (Every family we interviewed told us about that first group picture and how meaningful it was to have a copy of it.)

Each of the donor siblings may have arrived in Missouri separately with his or her parent(s), but a magical moment of connection had transpired. As they cheered Lizzie on and spent more time together, they had a growing awareness that they were part of something that was larger than themselves. Along with others, Nick described leaving with a sense that they were family:

I felt like we were a group, we were a team. . . . I would definitely call them all my family and I refer to all of them as "sister," "brother," etc. I don't say "half-sister" unless [I'm talking to] someone I don't really know. But to people who know that I have a donor for a father and are aware of my half-siblings, I just say "my sister Jenna" or "my brother Paul."

Chris also used the language of family to express his excited sense of connection within the group:

> It was kind of nuts because it was three days and all we did was spend time with each other. It was really fun bonding with people you haven't known all your life and suddenly you have more siblings. It's that feeling of like meeting family that you knew about sort of, but had never met them before, and then you suddenly meet them and you're like, "Hey! You're my people! I like you!"—that sort of idea and feeling.

As Chelsea noted about their ages, "We were at the perfect age that we weren't gross middle-schoolers anymore—the majority of us, but we weren't too old to be too cool or whatever."

Some siblings took on particular roles. For instance, Nick is the oldest, and although he is an only child, he found that he gloried in the role of older brother, protective and watchful of the younger ones when they snuck out late that night to go swimming without parental permission. As much as Paul had worried about what it would be like to be a big brother, he seemed to fall into an age and gendered pattern quickly. Distinctive connections also emerged as special sets of "siblings." Initially, Paul was drawn to Zoe and Joseph because, like them, he was also a brony, a fan of the animated TV series *My Little Pony* (as embarrassed as he was to tell the interviewer this); for their part, Zoe and Joseph loved the fact that Paul also enjoyed this iconic cartoon. Other siblings made their own connections. Chelsea clicked with Jenna almost immediately because they are similar physically and have some of the same interests, although by Chelsea's account, she is quieter and more introverted than Jenna. Jenna said she and Chelsea bonded over talking about Chelsea's boyfriend (with Jenna offering advice) and the discovery that they conduct relationships in similar ways with the same kind of expectations. Jenna, like the others, also talked about older and younger siblings with classic examples of how older siblings treat younger ones. Chelsea recalled the sweet relationship she has with Paul and how he made sure she was not afraid in the dark when the group was sneaking around late that first night.

As they observed the children, the parents noted these dynamics and were especially struck by just how comfortable the kids were with each other's bodies. The parents suggested that defining each other as siblings neutralized whatever sexual tension might have emerged:

> They're very physical and I think it's in part because not all the girls have brothers and it's very safe for them, right? To have this rough and tumble. They really enjoy it, I think, having brothers, right? The boys also like one another—they horse around a lot.

After three days of being together at that first reunion, the kids not only used the language of "brother" and "sister" to describe themselves, they also used the word "love" as an indication of their close bonds. Nick later described these postreunion attachments, which persist even during periods of separation, this way:

> I think there's some sort of unconditional love aspect there because I know they won't judge me if I say the wrong thing. We are connected at this point in our relationships. If we grow apart in the short term, we are not going to stay apart. We still can catch up, and with a lot of my friends I feel that's not the case. Once I'm disconnected from them on a regular basis they're gone—whereas with my siblings, if I don't talk to them for a while, the connection doesn't fade at all. It's still there.

Paul echoed Nick's thoughts:

> These people, if I'm busy for three weeks or even four months or something like that and I don't talk to them, it's not a big deal. They understand; I understand. Then when we come together, it's instantly like we never separated and we start just talking about very intimate issues—it's not just, "What's been new with you?"

Discovered Siblings and Chosen Family

For all the use of sibling language, the donor siblings are *not* "traditional" siblings who grew up in the same household and share continuous memories. The donor siblings grew up in separate families and share only discrete, and relatively new, memories. The assertions of love and connection made by the members of the 7008 group reflect something that does exist but, perhaps, not in the same form as among siblings who live together. In fact, as we discussed in chapter 4, those who actually grew up in the same household talked about very different levels of disagreement, forgiveness, and knowledge of one another. Zoe, who is one of two children, is no exception. She described the difference between constant communication with her brother and the intermittent contact with her donor siblings:

> Joseph and I see our annoying quirks and have to deal with annoying
> sibling things. . . . We argue and we yell at each other and all of that,
> but knowing that we love each other so much and knowing that
> when I'm upset and when he's upset we can just talk to each other,
> it's really important to me to know that I do have that and I always
> have him with me. It's not like I can just call up David [whom she
> met at a later reunion] and say, "Hey, can you swing by Memphis?
> I want to talk to you."

As Zoe suggested, while she loves David and refers to him—as she does to Joseph—as her brother, he is a plane trip away; that geographic separation leaves him in her emotional circle of caring but not in the tight sibling circle of butting heads and making up.

The "reunion" of donor siblings created the same kind of intense bond some people describe having with friends at summer camp or other brief, but intimate, encounters. Repeated interactions (another reunion, like another summer at camp) can make the feelings of being connected more powerful; the repetition can create a sense of continuous rather than discrete memories. But, for the most part, maintaining these newfound—but real— relationships at a geographical distance requires hard work; the separation is spanned only through contact with one another through some form of social media. Networks of donor siblings are no different in this regard.

Immediately after the Kansas City long weekend, the members of 7008 stayed in touch through Facebook; as social media technologies changed, so did their form of communication, with group and individual texting becoming more prominent than Facebook postings. As members of Generation Z, these kids are comfortable with technology and interact easily on social media (including Instagram and other photo-sharing technologies).[5] Once in a while someone might text a group message such as, "Hi, I miss you guys," setting off a chain reaction with both group involvement and separate interactions. As Chelsea said, "It is a fun way to stay in contact because it involves a lot of people." Jenna, whom everyone pointed to as the (social director) "glue" who had originally held the kids together, does try to stay in touch with everyone at least once a month. The rest of the kids said they also tried to maintain contact but acknowledged that they were more invested in their immediate local lives.

Several years after the initial Missouri reunion, the 7008ers were able to reflect on how the relationships in their donor sibling group differ from those with their high school and college friends. They said those connections give them latitude to be who they are. They insisted that they can drop their guard with each other and say what they want to say without worrying about what might otherwise be harsh judgment from another teenager. For the most part, they said they also accept the quite acute differences among them. Put differently, the world of donor siblings appears to offer a safe space to be who you are. Nick could not articulate how this connection happened, but he felt secure that his donor siblings are there for him:

> I don't know if it's because we all came together as a group in the beginning, but I just feel I can go up to any of them and start talking and it won't be strange, it won't be awkward if I talked about things that I'm interested in, if they talked about things that they're interested in. It wouldn't be boring to the other person. It's just nice talking to them. That's part of what makes them different than a friend.

Paul isn't as active on social media as some of the donor siblings. However, when he gets together with the others after a separation, the connections are immediately reactivated for him too: "I know that they're all siblings, but when we're all getting together, I think of it more as a reunion of lost friends."

For some, the core trust that emerged when they got together for the first time enables them to speak without worrying about jeopardizing the relationship, whereas even strong bonds among local friends feel more fragile. As Nick, who is now a freshman in college, said:

> Even friends that I met at the beginning of this year that I've been friends with now, very close friends for seven-ish months, if I started really speaking my mind about anything, they might back off and think, "Oh, I didn't know that about you," whereas [the donor siblings] wouldn't do that. They would accept me. They might not agree with me, but they would accept me.

Like Nick, they feel safe *together* in a world in which differences in politics, race, geography, gender, and sexual identity could create tension and a lack of acceptance.[6] They are available by social media to give advice, to offer a bed in another city, to help celebrate milestones, and to listen to struggles with parents about growing up. They have learned the personality quirks and strengths of each member of the group. They know how to comfort one another and make each other feel okay; they also know when to back off and what makes them feel frustrated with each other. They even bring their romantic partners to meet their donor siblings and hope for their approval.

The Importance of the Donor Tape

Some of this feeling of safety and comfort is created and re-created through the ritual experience of listening to the tape of the donor answering questions, a tape some parents had purchased either while they were selecting the donor or at a later point. When smaller groups occasionally get together, one teen often suggests that they listen to the tape again; the tape thus becomes the equivalent of a favorite story read over and over.[7] By now, not only can each kid finish the donor's sentences, but also, the *shared* experience helps bind the group together. As the kids explain the meaning of the tape, they go back and forth between the

distancing language of the "donor" and the familial language of "father."
Nick used both terms:

> Most of us have listened to the interview together. Afterwards, or
> even throughout, we would talk about different answers he had and
> which parts related to which siblings and things like that. . . . Then
> we talk about our thoughts about meeting our father and anything
> related to that. . . . We talk a lot about the actual donor and our
> similarities to the donor. . . . We don't start with "So, how's school
> going?"

As they listen again and again to this voice, the donor becomes a reminder
that they are together because of their DNA. For those kids who recall
finding the receipts from the vials of sperm their parents purchased, the
tape helps transform a financial transaction into an intimate connection
with a group of others.[8]
One of the newer members, Scott, recently talked about hearing the
tape for the first time when he met Jenna, Lizzie, and Chelsea:

> I remember we sat on their roof. I looked up at the stars while
> I was listening to it. I don't remember what it was, but he said some
> dickish thing in his interview and we all laughed at him. We just all
> sort of talked about that.

As they laughed at the same exact moment in the audiotape, Scott realized that he shares the same humor as his newly found donor sisters.
Despite the importance of the tape, the donor siblings are split in their
attitudes about how much weight they give the tape as a mechanism for
learning about the donor; these attitudes reflect feelings about whether
or not they want to meet the donor. The siblings who most like to play
the audiotape are the ones most interested in someday meeting the donor.
The ones who have limited or no interest in meeting the donor seem not
to care about the tape. Those with a moderate interest in the tape also
have a moderate interest in knowing the donor. Although they recognize
that the donor is the reason they are alive—and the reason they have attachments to the other donor siblings—they do not feel that they would
be "unfulfilled" if they did not meet him.

Interestingly, there doesn't seem to be any common factor (family form/structure, number of siblings, or gender) that determines whether the kids in this group wish to meet their anonymous donor (who is not an identity-release donor). And even those who most strongly want to have contact of some kind indicated that they believe their "rights" come second, behind the rights their parents exercised when they chose a particular donor. (At the time this group's parents were selecting the donor, there were few identity-release donors at their national bank.) They also extend the argument about rights to the donor, granting him the "right" to remain anonymous. If they blame anything for their inability to know the donor, it is the market-based, transactional system the sperm banks imposed. Jenna, for example, is resigned to her circumstances as the only person without rights in this system. But she would like to see changes:

> Everyone else signs a contract in this relationship. The parents do, the sperm bank does, the donor does, but like the people who are born, the people whose lives are created, they get no say in it. We just have to deal with whatever happens to us, and while most of us are fine and okay, it's not fair and it is not easy to not know where you come from, so I would advocate for open donors. Just donors who will agree, like if the kid wants it, they can have some identifying information when the kid turns eighteen, so there is nothing about any kind of parental issue.

Nick, who disagrees with Jenna and believes that donors should be allowed to remain anonymous in the future, would be disappointed not to meet his donor: "If he doesn't want to have a connection with us, he has that right, I feel, which is disappointing to me, but just from his rights standpoint, I think he should be able to remain anonymous if he feels this is best for him."

What these two kids agree on is that when they weigh their rights against those of other parties involved in the transaction, they come up short. Those with moderate interest in knowing the donor do not care much about *his* anonymity one way or another, and they do not think they need to protect him. These kids say they would meet the donor if he revealed himself, but they have no great enthusiasm for that idea. As Chris explained:

I wouldn't say I'm totally uninterested. I think to a certain extent it would be interesting to meet the person who fathered me. Isabel and I have talked about this. We're both like it's not something that really defines our lives, so it's not something as interesting to us.

Those with the least interest in meeting the donor said that, even if he came forward, they would not meet him because they do not feel he would add to their lives. They recognize the difference between a donor and a father (and he is not a father to them); they also believe that meeting him might make them uncomfortable.[9] None of these attitudes—toward the tape, toward donor anonymity, and toward meeting the donor—fractures the group. Other fault lines, however, have appeared.

In the Land of the Utopian Family: Choosing among My Brothers and Sisters

By the time we spoke with many of the donor siblings in this network, protestations of love and siblingship aside, all was not well in the land of this utopian family. Some of the kids were beginning to sense that they had created a fairy tale about their family and that, in truth, shared genes could only carry their relationships so far. Chelsea was both prescient and insightful when she remembered the donor siblings as being at the "perfect age" for meeting one another. Jenna also recalled that the magical moment of bonding and inclusion had been based in the shared experience of being young teens:

> We were just a group of kids and we got together, and I think the fact that we all just were comfortable to let our guard down was important. We were funny and stupid and just very transparent and we bonded quickly. I think the fact that it was a group was nice because we got to see each other and get to know each other while people were interacting with others and it wasn't just completely concentrated.

As time passed and the younger kids became older high school students and the older ones entered college, what had once seemed easy and natural became more difficult. Part of the problem was the natural

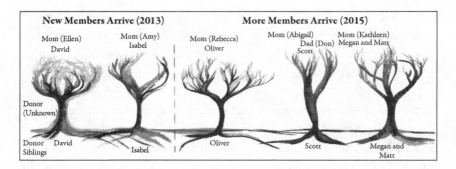

Figure 6.1 New Members Arrive (2013) . . . More Members Arrive (2015)

separations that form in any family, donor sibling or not, as children become older and find that they have more in common with friends than
with family members. Siblings might have enough shared history, and
the nudging of parents, to help keep their bonds intact. The 7008 group
did not have either because their parents, who initially fueled reunion
efforts, later took a hands-off approach. The donor siblings were very
much on their own as they explored territory that was both very new and
entirely unscripted.

A mere eighteen months after the original reunion, unexpressed feelings about who was really included and who was marginal surfaced, despite the group mantra of cemented bonds: "We are about embracing
one another, loving one another, and we all call each other brother and
sister." Another message emerged as well: "Don't be fooled by our love;
you can choose among the group participants and like some more than
others."

In 2013 another large reunion was held in California. Two additional
families attended this event, which revealed the stresses that already
existed and would eventually come to fragment the group. Ellen had
signed on to the registry in October 2012, *after* the initial gathering earlier that year. Her son, David, had just had a rare tumor removed, and
since there was no research on this tumor, the doctors did not know if
there was a genetic component. Ellen called the sperm bank she had used;
they told her there were other births from this donor and referred her
to an independent registry. Her interest in signing on to the registry was
simply to let others know about the tumor, but when she did, she found
Greg's welcoming note from years before. She, too, was stunned by how

many "Davids" there actually were because the bank had told her they capped the number of offspring at ten. Like some of the other parents, she finally told her son about the donor siblings, and the group greeted him on their Facebook page. Initially, the 2013 California gathering was to be a welcome for David, and the majority of the original families were able to attend. Ellen was upset when she realized that this group had been meeting for some time, and she was disappointed that her son, now age sixteen, had been missing out.

Meanwhile, since the group was going to hold its reunion in California, Jenna wrote an email to another mother, Amy, who years before had left minimal contact information on the registry but had not identified herself with her real name. Jenna knew that Amy and her daughter lived in California and that Amy had posted when her child was under ten. Amy had at one point talked to Tess, who lived in the same state, but she had found Tess to be "pushy." Not liking what she found, Amy decided that the whole donor siblings thing gave her a "bad vibe—not a good idea." Because she did not want to pursue that relationship, Amy had not told her daughter, Isabel, about Tess and her child; in fact, she had pretty much forgotten that she had ever registered on a website.[10] Jenna knew it was a long shot, but she decided to write to Amy anyway once the group had decided to meet in California. Amy, who liked the sweet note Jenna had written to her, felt she needed to rethink her earlier decision not to tell Isabel she had donor siblings. Isabel, who also appears in chapter 4, told us about the emotional shock of her mother's revelation.

The stories of the welcome to these two new kids—David and Isabel—reveal that choice—and being chosen—had become far more important than the mantra of love, embrace, and belonging. Zoe, who had initially created the teens' Facebook page and had considered herself like a "gate master," spent a long time revising her welcome email to David. By her own report, she wanted it to sound inviting but also realistic. As much as Zoe wanted David to feel that he was entering into a group that embraced everyone—so much so that he would be loved because he was one of them—she also cautioned him:

I remember saying to him, "You came in pretty late to all this and it's overwhelming, but I want you to know that we are all really eager to get to know you." I thought to myself like I have to say, "Yeah, it's going to be overwhelming" and then I said in my email, "Everyone is going to start reaching out to you like this and trying to get to know you and trying to be your best friend and telling you that we're all going to love you and you'll love us."

I remember telling him that because I was already over my honeymoon period with most of my half-siblings. I said, "You don't have to like all of us, you don't even have to like me. I just want you to know you have that choice to like everyone or not." I wanted to give some realism to this experience and not have new people feel a disappointment that I now felt.

Zoe's assessment of the paradoxes of what it means to be part of a large donor sibling network reflects her own hurt feelings. She believes that choice—and being chosen—now prevails. And she does not feel that she is among the chosen.

Isabel's introduction to the group had some of the same elements. Everyone in the 7008er group knew that Isabel existed and lived in California. They also knew her birthday (a piece of information on the registry), and every year the group had written a message on their Facebook page saying, "Happy birthday to the oldest girl." They knew nothing else. And Isabel knew nothing about them. Two days before the California reunion was to happen, Isabel's mother, Amy, broke the news to her. She also showed her the kids' Facebook page, Jenna's note included, so Isabel could check it out. Isabel was clueless since she had never imagined donor siblings, even though she had realized that the donor might have children of his own. She didn't know how to react to the news that she had another kind of half-sisters and half-brothers.

A stunned Isabel, who barely had time to digest her mother's news, became "fueled up and interested" in the fact that she had donor siblings when she saw the posts wishing her a happy birthday "wherever in the universe" she was year after year. She figured that if they wanted to meet her, why not? Isabel, who was furious that her mother had kept this from her until now, barely spoke as they drove along the highway. When they arrived, Isabel rushed out of the car, leaving her mother behind. As Isabel looked at her donor siblings, she just stared in disbelief; her immediate reaction was, "I had a physical similarity to basically everyone in the group." These resemblances were a way for her to make a social connection. She stood there looking for the one person who would ground her and, as she put it, "explain the group process and help me accept it as fast as possible."

When Jenna saw that stunned look in Isabel's eyes, she verbalized what Isabel was feeling. And much along the lines of what Zoe had written to David, she provided Isabel with both the group's road map and a personal escape route. Isabel remembered both:

> Jenna was like, "It's a very bizarre thing that not a lot of people go through. We have a group that is able to support each other and we have a bond that's really abnormal and you don't have to be a part of it. You don't have to invest in it, but we're all here for you. We're all so excited about you. You don't even have to interpret it as siblings. We all acknowledge each other as family." I was like, "Whoa, that's crazy."

This reunion became another late-night "talk-a-thon," with everyone trying to make up for the years of not knowing the newcomers. Some of the members also ignored a few of the initial members. As much as the kids claimed they all enjoyed being together, they were beginning to assess each other as teenagers do. Some are more introverted and some are more charismatic. Who would become closer with whom? Is it possible to get to know eleven kids when you see each other only for a long weekend once a year? David and Isabel did not share the multiyear history of togetherness. Entering the group after the initial bonding among members made embracing everyone a more complicated task (as we discuss in the next section).

The warnings from Zoe and Jenna reflected an unraveling that began before this last reunion and escalated soon after; that unraveling was revealed in a series of incidents involving Facebook. Indeed, the public nature of Facebook—where a posting allows everyone to see details, such as which people are meeting together and which people are invited to someone's graduation—proved to be fertile ground for the emergence of a sense of exclusion and hurt feelings.

Different narratives circulate about why Zoe and Joseph decided to engage in the hostile act of "unfriending" the vast majority of the members of the 7008ers, but no one actually asked either Zoe or Joseph why they left.[11] For her part, Zoe told us that she was hurt when Jenna, who was preoccupied with a medical issue one of her parents was having, failed to post about the good time she had when she, Zoe, and Joseph had met together earlier that summer. Zoe has also said that the other kids were too busy with their own involvement with each other to get to know who she really is:

> I just kept getting angry and frustrated with them because they weren't really seeing me as a person, they were just seeing me as a number because our numbers [of donor siblings] I think were around twelve to fifteen. I'm not exactly sure. We have a lot of half-siblings. It's fun to say I have fifteen half-siblings, but you have to think, do you actually care about these people? I didn't feel like they cared enough about me. Even if I would just reach out and try to talk to them and try to get to know them, I didn't feel that being reciprocated.

The comments of other members suggest that she was right, that the siblings were *not* interested. The nonjudgmental kids—who thought Zoe and Joseph, with their love of Bronies, were adorable—had become more critical and more discriminating. They were also more willing to pick and choose among the siblings on the basis of whom they liked. And they liked those they perceived as being as cool as themselves. Coolness, it seems, is not about wealth or social status, but it is about being "hip." Zoe and Joseph, referred to by others as the "home-schooled kids" who "don't have social skills to know how to work things out with people their own age," were not hip. They didn't make the grade. When Zoe wrote her welcoming email to David and let him know that everyone would act like they cared about him when really this was not totally the case, she reflected the new reality in the group. As the kids continued to navigate relationships more on their own and the "coolness factor" had set in, donor siblinghood was no longer a sufficient basis for inclusion and closeness. Now some kids text more with each other, feel closer to one another, and see each other more frequently.

In general, teens become concerned with coolness and finding their "people"; many kids pick and choose among both friends and siblings. They turn to this one for advice about one thing and to another person for a different reason. In these larger donor sibling networks, this is also the case: they form pairs and triads.[12] Selectivity is inevitable, especially concerning invitations to graduations and other celebrations. When Nick from Massachusetts graduated high school, he had three extra tickets; he invited Jenna and Lizzie from Missouri and Chelsea from Texas. That same year, when Jenna graduated from high school, she invited only Chris from DC and Chelsea (and Lizzie, her sister she lives with). Not only have these girls attended each other's graduations, but they see each other every few months, usually flying between Texas and Missouri to spend time together. Most recently, Chelsea and her mom flew to Missouri to visit Jenna and Lizzie's family over Christmas for a few days.[13]

Jenna and Lizzie view Chelsea as a sister they always wanted. For her part, Chelsea identified Jenna, Lizzie, and Paul as the ones to whom she is closest; she added Nick and Chris as those with whom she has had a "decent amount of contact." She acknowledged, "It's a pretty large group and there are definitely some that I'm closer to than others." Another clustering occurred when Maureen invited everyone to her summer home in 2015, but only Chelsea (and her boyfriend), Lizzie, Paul, and Nick came, along with Oliver, one of the newer group members. Like late high schoolers and college kids do, they hung out themselves. Most of the parents of these kids were there as well, but they focused on renewing their own friendships.

In spite of their hurt feelings, Zoe and Joseph are not completely isolated. They remain close to David, to whom they refer as a "brother" they love. The three tease each other back and forth and enjoy a scheduled weekly Skype during which they usually watch TV together. Over the past couple of years the three have also visited a few times.

We Are Family but We Can Choose

In short, the original group of nine who bonded in Kansas City is now divided into a number of separate, smaller sets of relationships. The newer members of the group experience competing realities: shared genes as unifying forces *and* moments of choosing. Oliver provides a perfect example of these tensions. He joined the group at the end of his junior year in high school.

When Oliver, at age seventeen, first learned about the donor siblings from his mother, he thought that he needed to figure out where these people fit into his life before he would be ready to meet them. Oliver feared that adding "blood family" to his life would mean making a special kind of investment and that suddenly he would have new people with whom to celebrate a marriage or experience the trauma of loss:

> I don't know who these people are. Just because they have the same genetics, does that mean they're my family? I have blood family, but I also have friends who I consider more family than those people. I was just struggling with the definition of family, struggling with who I was and also struggling with how would I deal with these people. What did this mean? Is this a commitment?

Several months after his mother told him about the donor siblings, as he was finishing his junior year in high school, he decided he was ready to meet some members of the "preformed mega group" who were in Boston for Nick's high school graduation and had invited him to brunch the following day. He wondered how he would turn all these strangers into family, and he was anxious about whether he would fit into this group that already had its own history. Oliver drew on his own experiences of "chosen" family as he settled on the notion of selectivity: "I thought, 'I don't have to take on all of them. I can just choose the ones that I really relate to and I love and I can use my newly found skills of defining family to just set people at different levels of closeness to me.'" Even so, the first meeting was fraught. Oliver knew that his appearance at the brunch would prompt a two-way judgment: just as he had the option to make selective family out of the donor siblings, the others would have the same option regarding him. He hoped to present himself well, but as he approached the group all his rehearsed moves felt somehow foolish:

> I still remember it. They all waited in front of this restaurant. . . . I wasn't as confident at all. I looked kind of silly. I remember seeing them and being able to spot the crowd because they all had black hair and were kind of my height. Then, there was that awkward thing where you have to walk all the way towards each other. I very much felt like I was an outsider walking into this already formed clan or group or family. I had anxiety and I didn't know whether to hug them. I think I hugged some of them. I immediately identified Isabel as the one I would relate to the most, and that has come true.

When asked why he identified Isabel as "his person," the one he wanted to relate to the most, he explained: "We're like the boy-girl version of each other . . . we have the exact same eyes. I was disappointed that Isabel had to leave right after lunch as I wanted to talk more. I felt very close to her immediately." But it was more than being look-alikes that attracted him to Isabel. He felt that she is what he wants to be: "I always describe her as when I'm at my hundred percent, when I'm really killing life, and I'm getting a lot done and I just look great and feel great and I'm at a hundred percent, that's what Isabel is like all the time. Isabel is my hundred percent, all the time. When I'm with her, she brings out my best energy. She's like my evolved form."

Oliver added that he bonded somewhat with the others and once he decided they were just "other normal kids," he could let his defenses down. Everything he was concerned about—could they all be family?—gradually dissolved, and that day he felt included. For their part, the others posted on Facebook that "Oliver is cool," and this made him feel good, almost like a member. Oliver, who is gay, is not yet "out" to all of his old high school friends. He trusts the 7008ers as a group and he has told them. Yet he maintains his stance of selectivity and he is very impassioned about his favorite sibling: "I look up to Isabel and I want to impress her and I think she's really great."

Isabel, who is a year older than Oliver, reciprocates this admiration, saying she feels "fiercely protective" of Oliver, that they "love each other," and they are extremely close: "He reminds me a lot of myself. He also looks freakishly like me. We have very similar personalities. We can just connect over everything and he's just a ball of happiness and good energy and I adore him." Isabel includes others in her version of a newfound family. She thinks of Nick as her big brother, she said, and she considers Chris, whom she met at the California reunion, as another younger brother: "We hit it off in ten seconds because we knew we were cut from the same cloth."

Newcomers Isabel and Oliver do not try to connect with all the siblings. They do not have the time to get to know everyone, and they prefer some siblings to others. Since they do not have a broader history with the group, they only extend ideas about family to certain kids. The particular connections shared by these last kids may have to do with shared social capital more than they admit. Amid the diversity of the group, Isabel, Oliver, and Chris are the most artistic, into cutting-edge social media, and extremely politically engaged. Isabel and Oliver were selective from their start, and, believing it was impossible to get to know everyone, they chose people like themselves.

Still More Members

Since 2015, several additional members of the 7008ers have shown up on the registry and have contacted members of the already existing group. Interestingly, these new members appear to be less privileged in material and cultural capital than the early members. It could be that those with more affluent parents learned earlier about the option of the registry and of contacting genetic relatives, while other parents have only learned about these possibilities now that their children have become adept at using the internet and social media.

Scott, an only child from Arkansas, and the twins, Megan and Matt from Illinois, are the most recent arrivals to the group of 7008ers. All three discovered the registry on their own and were at least eighteen years old when they connected with their donor siblings. Their entrance was not greeted with the same level of fanfare that had accompanied news of David, whose appearance precipitated the 2013 reunion in California. There are many reasons for this shift, including the fact that the kids who were in college (over half of the group) were busy and spent their summer months working or being interns to advance their résumés. The new arrivals threw into relief the current state of the network, which has two important dimensions: the individuals' perspective on the network and the combined perspective of network members. As new arrivals, Scott and the twins were trying to figure out who everyone is, what the network is about, and what it means to each of them. For the older members, the entry of new donor siblings reinforces long-standing alliances and provides a unique opportunity to see how the network as a whole has evolved in a way that is different from the initial experience of those who created it.

Scott, who discovered the group during the summer of 2015 when he was nineteen years old, ignored the network divisions, focusing on individuals whom he could get to know. He did notice that the network's members come from different geographic locations and have significantly different personal histories, both individually and within the group. Scott imagined some of his donor siblings as possible templates for who he might have been had he been raised under different sets of circumstances, such as in a city rather than in a rural area, or with a nonreligious family rather than Mormon parents. These imaginings were fun, he said.

He has met some people in person. He and his parents, high school sweethearts Abigail and Don, featured in this book's opening, traveled from their hometown in Arkansas to meet the donor siblings in nearby Tennessee and Missouri. Scott said he would love to meet the others to deepen his connections to his newly found "brothers" and "sisters," but his family could not afford plane tickets while helping him pay for college. As an alternative to face-to-face meetings, he planned to have a Skype date once a month with each of the group members, hoping to learn about each individually this way. He has not formed alliances with anyone, and he might not.

Twins Megan and Matt, from Illinois, who are eighteen years old, have been in Skype contact and included on text messages with the others. But as they got ready to leave for their first year of college, they were hesitant about the commitment this group would entail, and it was unlikely that they would meet anyone in person. They are twins and have each other. After only two months in the group (they joined in spring of 2016), they did not know if they could fully embrace the "We love everyone and we are family" mantra. It sounded great, but was it practical? As much as they would have liked to meet more 7008ers in person, they were realistic about their situation: their single mom's paycheck was for college, and the summer was passing quickly.

* * *

This network is unique in the degree to which conventional ideas about families shape group dynamics. As the random families assembled from across the United States for the first reunion, the members of the group experimented with the idea that the children could be some sort of kin to each other.

When the teens were left to their own devices and had to figure out how to get along with each other, they structured themselves around a pecking order of birth—a surprising decision when the children are so close in age. In fact, they all told us that during the first evening they spent together, while watching a movie in the hotel's parlor room, the two oldest boys offered up the hotel adventure that included all of the donor siblings sneaking out of their rooms and wandering out to the pool. They told us as well that as they walked around in the dark the older boys watched out for the younger ones and that the older boys subsequently took the heat from the parents who were annoyed about their behavior.

The sibling pecking order adopted from conventional families was subject to constant revision. New joiners embraced this hierarchy as a crucial part of belonging to one big, new family. However, this structural arrangement did not determine how and when the children began to *feel* like siblings. Instead, they pointed to the "magic" of their connection at Lizzie's sports event, a moment that captured their attention and enabled them to establish an emotional bond. Certainly, this was a turning point. For some members of the group, that magic sense of bonding is re-created when they listen to the donor tape together. For some members of the group, observations of physical and temperamental similarities provide a different kind of magic.

Over time, however, it was not magic but more mundane actions that became the backbone of the network and structured what kind of siblings the members of the group became. In fact, notwithstanding the language of "family," the relationships among the 7008ers actually played out much the same way cliques of high school students play out. There were hurt feelings, active girls vying for control, and eventually a division into two competing camps. Left (again) to their own devices, the teenagers insulted one another and allowed popularity rather than the mantras of "love" and "We are family" to dictate interactions. As might siblings raised in the same households, when the 7008ers grew up, they changed their minds about their personal preferences, picking and choosing now this one and now another as their favorites. Because they have never lived under the same roof—and have many same-age peers—cousins might actually be a better parallel for how the relationships shifted and changed.

The parents in this network continue to say that they are bystanders even though they initiated the interaction among their children (who were then all under age eighteen). They did so for various reasons. These parents had selected an anonymous donor from a larger, national sperm bank in the mid-1990s when there were few identity-release donors. The parents knew they were choosing a donor who would never be known.

Whether or not they might have preferred an identity-release donor, none of them wanted a donor who might arrive to claim his offspring as his own children. In addition, only a few of these parents have found the relationships with the other parents to be especially meaningful. For most of them, the magic is watching how their children, who start out as strangers, become emotionally engaged with each other. The parents play minimal roles, not unlike those other kinds of family friends might occasionally provide. The *primary* ties are lateral—between and among the children themselves. If those bonds break, there is no group.

Network update: By 2016, the number of children within the group had increased from eleven kids (nine of whom attended the first reunion) to twenty. Donor 7008 still remains an anonymous donor; he did not respond when two of the older kids decided to write him a letter. The sperm bank reported nothing back to their inquiry.

In this network, the birth order of the children is extremely close: three were born in the last months of 1995, five were born in 1996, six were born in 1997, three were born in 1998, two were born in 1999, and one was born in 2001. The last four kids—born in 1998, 1999, and 2001—all have older siblings who share the same donor. Eighteen kids have made contact, and two kids from the same family remain on the registry. In the narrative we have featured the interviews with the first fifteen kids to make contact; we heard that the last three kids (a sibling pair ages seventeen and twenty and another girl age nineteen) had made contact with the group after we had stopped interviewing at the end of July 2016. These three children had not yet met any other member of the network in person.

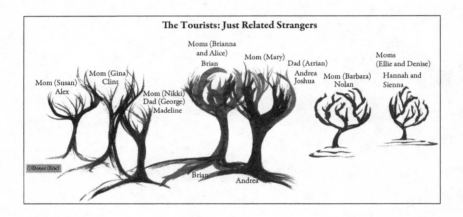

The Tourists: Just Related Strangers

7

The Tourists

Just Related Strangers

THE COHESION OF the 7008ers—at least in the early days—resulted from several factors, as we have seen. Yet what happens to a donor sibling network when the group members do not form deep connections, there is no magical bonding moment, and the mystique of the donor is lost or never present?

* * *

Stalled Connections, but Curious

The outcome, as the Tourists demonstrate, is a group of related strangers who navigate the land of donor siblings as if they were curious travelers, stopping briefly to discover who shares their DNA before moving along.[1] But unlike people who take the same flight, these "tourists" often seem to be moving in multiple directions at once. They also reject, for a variety of reasons, the "We are family" narrative that acts like glue in other networks. The result is that the members of this group—both the children and their parents—view donor siblings only as a novelty and a source of excitement. And like tourists, they take photographs and leave. Subsequently, the children find that occasionally seeing Facebook photos, or meeting one another for a weekend, is enough to satisfy their curiosity about their origins.

As Alex, who was a college freshman when we interviewed him, explained, the five donor siblings he'd met three years earlier didn't leave much of an impression on him. While it was "fun" and "cool" to be with them, he didn't form strong emotional connections with anyone, in part because for him sharing DNA doesn't mean "putting a sibling label on them."

Since these kids never bonded with each other, a larger structure with ongoing contact could not be created. Examining the reasons significant bonds failed to emerge among the members of this network gives us broader insight into the factors that shape interest—or its converse—in contact with donor siblings.

Susan, a single mother who lives in Maryland with her son, Alex, believes that shared experience matters more than genetics for social connection: "I don't think it's our genes that connect us. I think we feel a sense of connection through shared experience." Susan also offered an explanation for why her son and his donor siblings did not really form strong ties. She continued:

> I think donor sibling groups that find each other when the kids are younger make stronger connections—the parents (probably moms for the most part) initiate and perpetuate get-togethers when the kids are still under their control, but the gatherings create a history of shared memories and experiences, which make the kids feel connected. I think at this age of fifteen and sixteen they've already differentiated too much and don't have enough shared experience to have that bond like you do with a cousin.

She might well have a point. At the time of their first large reunion, the kids were in high school. However, Susan's comments only revealed part of the story. Few families joined the network before their kids were age thirteen, and for good reason. Internal family dynamics created additional barriers, as with two heterosexual divorced moms who had initially decided with their husbands not to reveal donor conception to their children. Another family—a lesbian couple—felt that their child should decide whether to search for donor siblings or the donor, so they did not play an active role in facilitating contact with their daughter's genetic relatives. And, as we discuss below, their daughter had her own reasons for being uninterested in contact with her donor siblings, although she *was* interested in the donor.

Other obstacles emerged among the parents, including cultural differences and geographic distance, which may explain why the initial joiners—a group of women who became a resource for some of the other moms—sometimes excluded other parents. The first moms, who immediately clicked with one another, had much in common and could afford to travel to visit each other. Yet they had limited interest in really connecting with the other families, whose backgrounds and social status were not like theirs. Ultimately, they decided that they had no need for— or interest in—further contact with the newcomers, much like tourists who travel to a foreign country and only interact with people who look and dress as they do.

Additionally, and unique to this network among those we feature, the donor, who had been anonymous (rather than identity release), decided to reveal his identity without first being contacted by a child.[2] He posted on a registry website that anyone listed under his number could get in touch with him, and that he would share his personal email address. This offer seemed to promise kinship, and it coincided with plans for a first group weekend. But donor Eric, unlike Michael (in chapter 5), would not become the catalyst that drew that network together. Instead, his actions made it clear that he was a traveler motivated as much by curiosity about what became of his sperm donation as by moral or ethical convictions.

Moreover, while there is no road map to turning strangers into kin, most groups that cohere have someone who becomes the group facili- tator: in Michael's Clan it was the donor himself; among the 7008ers it was one of the donor siblings. But the Tourists never had such a facili- tator, so the kids never formed a coherent group. Once they satisfied their curiosity about the donor siblings and the donor himself, they could get on with their lives, and they did not feel much need to reach out to their genetic relatives. In the pages that follow, we provide more details about all of these situations. We also offer our interpretation for why two kids in this network have become good friends.

The First Tourists in This New Land

The initial members of a network can be like tour guides, setting a pos- itive tone for those who follow, or like arrogant, sightseer tourists who undermine—intentionally or unwittingly—the group dynamics. The Tourist network included both, as well as solo travelers who never connected with others.

The two mothers who initially found each other on the registry were thrilled to do so, as they told us later, but they were driven by curiosity, not a desire to expand their families. Gina registered on an internet website in 2003 when her son, Clint, was six. Almost two years later, Susan, whose son Alex was then nine, showed up. The two women exchanged a few pictures of the boys. They were struck by the physical resemblances, from hair and eye color to the fact that both wore glasses for near-sightedness. A few weeks later, the women exchanged whole albums and were amazed to see how much the boys looked alike at every age. That helped the moms create a strong connection, which became even stronger as they learned how much else they had in common.

Susan and Gina were both single parents by choice, and both were busy professionals who lived in suburbs of major fast-paced cities, albeit one on the East Coast and the other on the West Coast. Neither had grown up in the region where they lived but had moved there for career opportunities. Susan, a PR consultant, traveled all over the world as part of her job; Gina was an IT manager. The boys also were initially excited to learn they had genetic relatives, "a sibling that was part of their dad," as Gina described it. The mothers soon decided to meet for several days in Yosemite National Park; there the boys, who were eight and nine years old, played together and the mothers enjoyed each other's company.[3] The next year, Gina and Clint came east to stay with Susan and Alex over the Christmas vacation. But while this new relationship was fun, it was not central to anyone's daily life. It would be several years before they met again.

Nikki, the third mother to join the registry, did so on a lark. She was married at the time and had not told her husband that her curiosity led her to sign up for the registry. Initially doubtful about how important these ties might be, once she connected with Susan and Gina, she was surprised to find out how comfortable she felt with them:

> At first, I kind of thought, "Okay, it will be cool to see if there's anybody else out there. Maybe share an email." I really was very skeptical and felt that [the network] just wasn't going to be a part of my life. I am married. It was more like fun: "Oh, my gosh. Look at these pictures. They look just like my kid. That is so weird." I never really thought that I would be close with anybody or make friends through it. I didn't go into it with that intention. It was just really weird how it just naturally happened. . . . We all just hit it off.

Nikki kept her contact secret, and she continued to keep another se-cret as well: neither Nikki nor her husband had disclosed to anyone that she conceived her daughter, Madeline, using a sperm donor. To others, she said, "We were just a married couple that had a baby." She continued that ruse even with her parents and siblings, whom she visited frequently.

When the marriage fell apart, Madeline's dad remained in the area for a while, then moved to another state when Madeline was age eight. Nikki continued to raise Madeline in the East Coast city where she and her ex-husband, both professionals, had met. Even though neither parent attended church regularly, they believed that a religious upbringing would benefit Madeline, who attended the local Catholic elementary school. Because conceiving through donor conception was not an accept-able practice in the eyes of the church, Nikki kept up the pretense that Madeline had been "naturally" conceived.

Madeline, for her part, told us that she was not surprised to learn at age fifteen that she was donor conceived. She had overheard a dis-cussion between her parents about her dad's vasectomy, which he had after the birth of several children in his first marriage. When her mom finally used the phrase "donor conceived," Madeline felt relieved. She had feared that she was adopted and her birth parents did not want her. The secret of her conception, now out in the open, comforted Madeline. However, she was shocked to learn about her mom's online friendships with Susan and Gina. Even more unsettling, initially, was the news that these women had children who were genetically related to her. Madeline recalled, "We got home and she says, 'Actually, we know a bunch of your half-brothers and stuff.' I was like, 'What?' She got on Facebook and showed me pictures of all of them. And I'm like, 'Uh.' I didn't really know what to think." Madeline soon became excited to learn that that she had donor siblings.

Meanwhile, around that same time, four additional families joined the registry and became members of the Facebook page. For varying reasons the parents in each of these families had waited until their children were in high school to discover who also purchased the same donor sperm. The new members included a two-mom couple and their son, Brian, from Kansas; a girl named Sienna, from Massachusetts, whose moms helped her sign on to the registry; a divorced mom and her daughter, Andrea, from the Midwest; and finally a single mom and her son, Nolan, from

Massachusetts. Nolan and his mom are the only African Americans in the group.

Now that Madeline knew about her donor siblings and none of the three original mothers were holding secrets, Susan, Gina, and Nikki decided to have a larger gathering at a water park located near Nikki's home in North Carolina. They posted an announcement to the entire group on their Facebook page suggesting that there be a two-day get-together to take place several months later. Brian and his moms, Alice and Brianna, and Nolan and his mom, Barbara, accepted the invitation. What none of them knew was that Gina and Susan had no interest in being tour guides who would embrace these genetic strangers as family and set that tone for the group. Rather than helping the group develop a sense of kinship, the gathering would cement everyone's experience as solo travelers.

The other two families who were Facebook members at that point did not accept the invitation. Andrea's mother wrote that she could neither afford the travel costs nor easily leave Andrea's adopted younger brother at home. Sienna, whom we discuss further below, was not interested in attending.

The First—and Only—Gathering

Everyone who attended that first—and only—"reunion" in 2012 had different motivations, which were influenced to some degree by the varying levels of contact they had had prior to the big gathering. The last time Susan and Alex had met Gina and her son, Clint, was five years earlier, when the boys were about ten. Alex recalled this time with Clint as "really cool that we had the same sperm donor." In kid years (even adult ones) the five-year gap was enormous, and in the interim the boys had no independent contact with each other but had relied entirely on their moms' reports. Although Nikki had emailed back and forth with Susan and Gina, neither she nor her daughter, Madeline, had met anyone in person. The mothers and children in the other two families had had even more limited contact with the other families.

When these five families met, three of the kids (Alex, Brian, and Madeline) were fifteen years old, and two others (Clint and Nolan) were fourteen years old. Each kid acknowledged that the opportunity to meet a gaggle of half-siblings seemed "cool" in the abstract and that, in reality, the weekend together *was* "fun." They also remembered that they came to discover they have the same "quirky sense of humor," which they attributed to shared genes.

While the resemblances were certainly there, the kids were skeptical about whether their donor siblings meant anything to them. As one of the mothers suggested earlier, age matters. As kids meet at older ages, they need something more than the happy playtimes of seven-year-olds if they are going to coalesce as a group. And the fact that there was only one girl among them—girls tend to facilitate interaction—made it even more difficult to find common ground. No magical moment made them feel united, as had been the case for the 7008ers when they collectively cheered on donor sibling Lizzie at her tournament. Rather, throughout the weekend, this group of young high school students felt the pull of their other concerns: some were busy learning to drive, most would have preferred being with their own friends from home, and each was involved in lots of extracurricular activities. Moreover, none of them had been especially enthusiastic about getting together in the first place, even if they were willing to go to please their mothers. As they later reported, it was their moms who were excited about this meeting and who wanted to get to know one another. Even though they had all wanted siblings when they were younger, they had become accustomed to being solo children with close friendships outside the family. When the reunion ended, these curious tourists—both the kids and their parents—were left with little more than pleasant memories.

Relatives Maybe, but Not Siblings

Once the five kids returned home, they each resumed their separate busy lives. No one initiated any further communication. Only Madeline and Brian use sibling language. The rest do not think of one another as anything more than acquaintances with whom they happen to share their DNA.

Now that he was a teenager with his own opinions, Alex felt there would be limited value in meeting more of his donor siblings. Unlike many kids we interviewed, Alex felt deeply ambivalent about having some of the same DNA as a bunch of strangers: "We definitely had a lot of physical similarities. It was kind of creepy, actually. We all just kind of eerily looked alike, 'cause we were all about the same age and we all had similar facial structures." While he still wasn't sure whether nurture was more important than nature, he viewed the donor siblings as he would any other social relationship, judged on the basis of having interests in common:

> Personality-wise, I didn't feel similar to my siblings. I never felt like they would be the people who would be in my friend group. It seemed like we were all pretty different. But then again, I didn't get to know any of them at a very deep level. . . . I never really had any desire to keep up these relationships. I know if I wanted to, I could reach out. But it's just not something that's on my mind, it's not something that I really think about doing.

Clint, interviewed at age seventeen, admitted that he was unsure where donor siblings belonged in his family constellation, especially when he felt the pull of college, a time to leave family matters behind. While his mom might be friends with several of the other moms in this network, he was not willing to sustain relationships for himself in which the foundation is genes. He recognized that he might have felt "brotherly" toward Alex when they were younger, but that they did not have any further responsibility to each other: "I guess it was easier to connect with them because we have genes in common, and with friends you don't share something that close. But I don't really think genes are that important. I know Alex the best, but even with him, I think the relationship probably would die out over time if contact didn't happen. . . . I don't want them to feel obligated to me, or I to them. It's pretty casual." Clint mentioned that he has other people he considers to be part of his family. His mother married when he was eleven and he is close to his stepdad as well as to various cousins in his stepdad's family who live nearby. Certainly donor siblings did not unsettle his views of who is important to him.

Madeline, who was eighteen when we spoke with her, also summed up the gathering at the water park as a one-time event: "They're all really, really nice people and they're fun and stuff. The moms got a lot more emotional than the kids did [when they met for the first time]. We all hung out a lot, and I like all of them." Madeline does refer to the donor siblings as her "brothers" (and she refers to her stepsiblings from her father's first marriage as her "sisters").

She also follows the donor siblings on social media. But she does not have any contact with them she considers meaningful. As did the others, she added that it was her mother who sought to keep the relationships going:

> I haven't really *talked* talked to Clint, for instance. We don't really have contact. We don't really text. I'm pretty sure we're friends on Facebook, but I don't think he posts anything. It's more like his mom that we have contact with; my mom and his mom have a pretty good relationship, and they're friends. . . . Then I follow Nolan on Twitter. Yeah, so I see stuff like what he's doing. Most of his tweets I don't really understand because he is in a different state and goes to a different school, so I don't know who he's talking about. I don't feel obligated to have a relationship with any of them just because we're technically related.

Nolan, who was interviewed at age seventeen, wanted to attend the reunion, but once he got there, he realized that the donor siblings didn't mean as much to him as his cousin who lives down the street. He said the two of them are "like brothers" because they were cared for together by their grandparents for much of their lives. He summed up the water park weekend as being a positive one, but not one that led to any ongoing relationships:

> That was the first time that [my mother and I] had any contact with them when we were going to meet them. We haven't kept in touch too well since then. . . . They were all nice people, I guess. . . . I'm not too sure what I learned about myself, but I would say it's a good experience. Overall, it was definitely better for me to meet them instead of knowing that I had siblings out there and having no clue who they were.

Brian, from Kansas (who is discussed in more detail below), thought the gathering was "really cool." Even so, at age eighteen, he described it much as the others had—as something that involved sharing of information and congeniality, but without follow-up: "To some extent we kind of hit it off right at the beginning. There was, obviously, 'Who are you? What are you interested in?' We all just kind of got along immediately. . . .

Since then we haven't been in touch. We get occasional Christmas cards, but I haven't met any of them since then."

Many other kids in our broader study echo the casual disinterest of the kids in this network, whether or not they actually met their donor siblings. As with Milo and his donor sibling Annie—whom we discussed in chapter 4 and who belong to a network not featured—meeting once or having contact only on social media satisfied their curiosity about who these others were. After that, they felt no need to follow through with more face-to-face interaction.

Donor Eric Reveals Himself, Further Scattering the Solo Tourists

Coincidentally, as the five families were planning to get together, Eric—the previously anonymous sperm donor—decided to come forward. That could have helped solidify the network; instead, it further splintered this group of solo travelers. Gina was the first to find out about him. While looking at the registry, she discovered to her surprise that the donor had signed up. She immediately phoned Susan and then Nikki, but not the other mothers in the network, to let them know. The mothers in this network had selected an anonymous donor at a time when there were few identity-release donors. They had discussed their hopes that he might choose to reveal his identity. They were excited when they found him registered. Coincidentally, Eric, who had donated sperm while in graduate school in California, now lived close to Nikki and only a few hours from the water park where the reunion would be held in North Carolina.

By the time of the reunion, Nikki and her daughter, Madeline, had already met Eric once. Now, Nikki invited him to dinner at her house to meet the two other families—Gina and her son, Clint; Susan and her, son Alex—each of whom had decided to fly out a few days before the reunion so their boys could also meet the donor. Each of the three mothers claimed that arranging for the other mothers and children in the group to meet the donor was "not our place," because they didn't want to "overwhelm the donor" with so many kids, and the planned get-together was about the siblings, not the donor. As one mom put it, "We figured it was everyone else's responsibility to arrange a meeting [with the donor] and not ours. We didn't even tell the other donor people we were going to be meeting Eric ahead of time. The whole trip was a 'meet the siblings event.'"

This became the circulating narrative they later told the other two families—Brian's family and Nolan's family—who had not been invited. But once the truth came out, a few days later at the water park, those families felt hurt and excluded. As one mother said to us, "Our kids weren't even given the opportunity to meet the donor." However, they focused their weekend on the kids and chose not to hold grudges, even though the lack of inclusion seemed mean-spirited.

Nice Guy but Not a Dad

Like so many members of this network, Eric also was just a "curiosity traveler" in the land of donor relatives, interested in only a passing visit. His curiosity about the donor kids did not begin until he received a call from the sperm bank wanting his updated medical information.[4] One of "his" offspring had a possible genetic disease, which jolted him to acknowledge that at least one child had resulted from his donations. His wife had encouraged him to earn money by donating when he was a graduate student and they were expecting their first child. But, besides her, no one else knew about his extra source of income.

He mulled over the bank's call for almost ten years, finally deciding "kids have a right to a sense of who they are," and "if kids have funny things about themselves, they might see them there [through knowing their genetic relatives]." By that time, Eric admitted that he had become curious too. At the same time, he very quickly let the donor-conceived children know that he did not feel comfortable extending family membership beyond his own wife and two daughters. To make this point clear he brought one daughter, who was also curious, to the dinner. (The donor-conceived kids referred to those two girls as the donor's "real" family.) And when we spoke with him, he drew a sharp distinction between the donor kids and his own daughters:

I am emotionally invested as a father in my own kids, and these [donor kids] I feel like I have a responsibility to them to be available, but when my kids do something exciting, I'm proud of them, right?

When these kids do something exciting, I don't feel like that because it's like I didn't have anything to do with it. Anyways, I don't feel at all "fatherly." I am glad that they are all good people and that they are doing well and seem smart and all of that.

Just as he has created boundaries with the kids, Eric has also learned to do so with the parents, because often it is the parents (although we don't know which ones) who have sought contact and peppered him with questions. In some cases, he said, they do more of the asking and talking than the children, and in doing so they prevent the children from speaking on their own behalf and figuring out what they want to know from him. Eric feels no obligation to the parents, and he does not want exchanges with them. Once he made that clear, the initial flurry of emails from both parents and donor kids petered out.

The three donor-conceived kids who actually met Eric were unsure what to expect from that evening. But if they had harbored any fantasies about having a place in his life, they had to settle for what he offered them: some information and a chance to ask a few questions. Alex emphasized that he felt nature's claim but no nurture connection: "There was this moment where I was just like, 'Wow, I have half of this guy's DNA.' I guess it was significant for me to see that this is the person that a lot of me comes from, you know. Other than that, we just had dinner together. It was never a personal connection, I never felt like, 'Oh yeah, this guy totally feels like my dad.'"

Clint, who has a stepdad, emphasized the novelty aspect of the dinner: "We just talked a lot. There were a lot of us, so it wasn't very much a personal thing, which was fine. It was very cool to meet him though." Madeline reported that she "didn't have a whole lot of questions to ask him." Instead, she put herself in his daughters' shoes as a distancing mechanism, reiterating that the donor's genes she shared should not be confused with nurture: "I didn't want anyone to feel like I was taking their dad or anything, and I didn't want them to feel that I thought he was my dad and stuff, and I wanted a big relationship or anything. . . . I still think of my dad [who raised me] as my dad, because he is." After meeting Eric, these three kids did look at his Facebook page and the albums he posted there to try to get more of a sense of his life. They each "friended" him, and their updates appear in his news feed. (He is not on the Tourists' Facebook page.) They do not see him as a father. Brian and Nolan, who were not included at this meeting (although they were en route to the water park event), have neither met Eric in person nor exchanged emails with him. They said that they were not interested in him right now.

The Emotional Cost of Solo Traveling

Another member of this network, Sienna, attended neither the meeting with Eric nor the reunion. She might have become a committed traveler—someone who forms deep ties with donor relatives—if her email interactions with Eric had not been so disheartening. Instead, she was turned away.

Sienna, a senior in high school when we met her, had asked one of her mothers to help her sign on to the internet registry about two years earlier, hoping that she might find clues to her donor. Sienna's parents were only interested in facilitating what she wanted; they don't believe in interfering with her rights. That hands-off approach reflects the fact that both mothers view donors (and the donor siblings) as outsiders—neither "chosen" kin nor relatives from either mother's lineage. Quite simply, they saw no need to go beyond the relatives they know and whose company they enjoy.

Sienna, however, felt differently. As a young teen she was deeply invested in knowing her donor, and by the time she turned fifteen she had built him up in her mind to be something he was not—a father figure. In his first email, which arrived a month after she sent hers, Eric told her he was very busy and would answer her questions when he could. She was crushed. After several more weeks, Sienna received a message that she described as "just really lukewarm, and he seemed really disinterested." She tried to engage him by asking some silly personal questions, such as "If you were an animal, what kind of animal would you be?" Eric's response, once again, was slow in coming, brief, and offered just a few tepid details. "As a kid who was *so* interested in him and wanting him to feel the same way about me, that was really hurtful," she said. After a total of five exchanges, Sienna dropped the correspondence, but inside she seethed: "I felt really jealous at first that he had these two daughters who got to have that relationship with him." She decided to strike back at him by "stalking his Facebook page," she said—as if he and his daughters could feel her staring at their pictures.

What Sienna didn't realize—or could not articulate—was that Eric's rejection of her, as she perceived it, reflected his rejection of her version of the "We are family" narrative, a version that included her unknown donor (but not her donor siblings). Sienna had invested heavily in that narrative, and losing it meant giving up a potential father and facing some hard facts about the business of sperm donations. As Sienna told us, she had always imagined that Eric became a donor in order to help couples realize their dream of parenthood: "I sort of pictured a really giving person, like seeing a family in need and saying, 'Here, I'll give you a child.'" When she discovered that for him it was a matter of economic convenience, she rethought what a donor was (and who he was): "The way I see it now or think about it is that he might have donated at a point when he was young and in need of money and it was not so much about giving to a family, as jacking off and getting easy money."

Sienna found some comfort, she said, when she read on the network's Facebook page that Andrea, another member who also emailed him, had had the same experience: "I asked a couple other questions [on email] and he never responded, so I was definitely a little disappointed." That slowness, along with Eric's tepid, perfunctory responses, led both girls, as well as other donor kids, to say that correspondence with him was "lame." Even though she might have bonded with Andrea over shared disappointment, Sienna kept her distance from the "others." Apparently, she has her reasons. Sienna and her sister have the same genetic mother but different sperm donors. Still, Sienna believes that sisters are special people because the social dimensions of their life together create lasting bonds:

> Sisters share a life together and genes don't matter. It was weird to me to think that I'm the same amount related to these kids, who I have no interest in, as I am to this girl who I've grown up with. Hannah is my sister. Hannah is someone I know who supported me throughout my life and who[m] I feel I can talk to about things. The donor siblings don't feel like siblings at all. They're just people who happen to be related to me.

Sienna does glance at the group Facebook page occasionally, but like other solo travelers in this network, she expressed no interest in connecting with her donor siblings. Neither Sienna nor Nolan realizes that they live a few towns away from each other. She remains private about her life, and after her disappointing experience with the donor, she has made no effort to contact him again. Thus, she remains ambivalent at best about further travels in the land of donor siblings.

Traveling with Their Own Kind, and the Two Kids Who Are Meeting on Their Own

Everyone we've mentioned so far—the moms, the donor siblings, and even Eric himself—has entered the land of donor relations at their convenience and navigated the terrain without establishing strong ties or roots. Two of the donor siblings, however, did try to create a lasting connection. Brian, who has two mothers, and Andrea, whose mom was newly divorced from her husband, might have seemed an unlikely match when they met in December 2011, six months before the group reunion. Yet the two, who were both age sixteen and lived a few hours away from each other, immediately hit it off. Their parents clicked as well.

As Andrea recalls, their meeting was "really nice" and focused on the similarities in their background rather than on other genetic relatives: "We didn't really talk too much about the donor and everything like that, we just kind of talked about how we grew up and what he was doing next and where I was at in my life and it was good."

Brian, who had grown up in south central Kansas, and Andrea, from Missouri, are both from families that have been rooted in small, rural towns for several generations; they thus "belong" in their communities because they have lived on the land for so long. So while opinions run deep about whether the use of donors is the proper way to make babies, both the parents and their children are accepted as part of those communities.

Acceptance does not equal understanding, however, and donor-conceived children who live in rural areas often feel alone because none of their peers know what it's like to suddenly learn that they have genetic relatives spread across the country. When her mom revealed that she had genetic relatives, Andrea shared the news with friends in her small high school. "They were really surprised" and "didn't really say too much about it," she said. Translation: they didn't know what to say because the term "donor siblings" was something they could understand in the abstract but hadn't encountered in their daily lives.

When Andrea met Brian, she could finally talk to someone who knew how it felt to love the family she had lived with for years yet still want to know "the others" as well. In fact, she had learned the names of all of the donor siblings, even though she and her mother could not afford to attend the reunion. Brian, who did go, later said that his meeting with Andrea was far more meaningful than the larger gathering because she seemed to have a deep interest in him.

The enduring bond that developed between the pair demonstrates the importance of shared backgrounds; like the children in the 7008ers, they wanted to extend family status to donor siblings. Ironically, residents of "flyover states," as one of the East Coast moms referred to Middle America, seemed to be more inclusive and embracing than many "left-leaning" coastal families. The coastal families easily dismissed those who do not share their economic and social status, without trying to find common ground. They were also more exclusive about family membership: they did not view their children's genetic relatives as kin, even if they formed friendships with other mothers. In contrast, Andrea's mom and Brian's moms were open to extending kinship to their children's genetic relatives even as they let their kids decide how these relationships might develop.

Brian: Belonging, with Complications

Brian's mom Brianna had grown up in south central Kansas, in a small town where she and her sister were called "the Baker twins." Their dad, just like their grandfather before him, ran the general store, a hub where townspeople liked to hang out before work. On Sundays, Brian's family went to the Presbyterian church, like everyone else in town. Brian's mom Alice grew up in a small town nearby and was raised in the Mennonite church, which Alice said has a "progressive" orientation to the world. Alice's mom, who was born in Germany, wanted her children to practice the family religion. When Brianna, now a factory worker, and Alice, a social worker, fell in love and decided to start a family, they sought a donor who was German like Alice's mom, for shared heritage, and who was said to be smart, with a good sense of humor. Alice's mom cared most that her daughter was happy, and she was an excited grandmother-to-be. At first, Brianna told only her mom that Alice was pregnant and they were going to be mothers. She left it up to her mother to tell her dad this news. When Brian was born, the parents in both families fell in love with their grandson.

That love and acceptance gave Brian, who grew up Mennonite, a firm foundation. Brian described the town he grew up in this way: "There was a church on every block and religion was a huge part of my town's composition." He also said that the town is divided between those whom he thinks of as "conservatives against gay marriage, and lesbians having kids. It's a sin and all this kind of traditional stuff" and other people who are really supportive of his family. Brian did hear mean-spirited comments about having two moms, especially in middle school and early high school; those comments were painful to him. People who were more conservative would say, for example, "You are going to go to hell because your parents are gay." However, as someone who does not subscribe to this opinion, he rejected those claims and looked for friends who were more congenial. As he said: "After a period of time, I surrounded myself with people who were like-minded and really supportive and great. . . . Most of my friends knew I had two moms and they were perfectly fine with that and they were supportive."[5]

Having grown up in a nontraditional family, Brian found it fairly easy to extend the notion of kin to his donor siblings. When we spoke with him during his freshman year in college, Brian explained that he had always been told that he might have "siblings out there," but his moms did not register Brian's information and their willingness to be contacted until he was about thirteen years old. When his moms registered, he was more interested in meeting donor siblings than the donor.

Likewise, his mothers, despite their hurt feelings about Brian not being invited to meet the donor, put aside their disappointment and were still thrilled to meet his "family," whom they considered their family by extension. Yet Brian, who described himself as shy around new people, was the only kid who was interested in getting to know more of "his brothers and sisters" prior to the water park weekend.

Making Andrea: Losses That Lead to a Search for More Family

Andrea grew up in Pleasantville, Missouri, a rural community of three hundred people, where she was one of fourteen seniors in her high school graduating class. The nearest mall was two hours away and even a trip to Walmart, an hour's drive, was very inconvenient. Only a few months older than Brian, Andrea was a junior in college when we met her. When she was growing up, her mom was a Baptist and religious, but her dad, who was Native American, was not a believer in any religion. She and her mother stopped going to church when her adopted brother, who has a neurological disorder, deteriorated to the point that he could not sit still.

While Andrea's parents divorced when she was fourteen years old, their commitment to both children never wavered. Andrea and her mom moved in with her grandmother while her mom went to nursing school and worked part-time. On alternate weekends, Andrea visited her dad and brother, who lived in a nearby town. This arrangement continued until Andrea's dad died unexpectedly. Then her mother revealed that Andrea had been donor conceived, a secret the couple had kept both during and after their marriage.

The more Andrea thought about this startling news, the more it made sense. As she told us, "I have green eyes and long blond hair and I can't believe I didn't think of it before, but my dad . . . has the long thick black hair and brown eyes." She too has kept the secret from her extended family, out of respect and love for her father. Yet once she learned about the registry, she became interested in learning about donor siblings.

Andrea and Brian Form a Bond

Prior to the big reunion, Brian had reached out to some of the other donor siblings on Facebook but was unable to meet any of them because they all lived far away. Then Andrea showed up on the Facebook page: she lived a mere four hours away, and her mom was willing to drive her to meet up at a pizza place halfway between. Andrea's mom and Brian's moms sat at a separate table and they did a lot of talking, noting with awe the traits the kids shared—a quirky sense of humor, sarcasm, and similar expressions.

Both nervous and excited, Brian got over his jitters fast, and by the end of lunch with Andrea he declared that "it was good getting together." Andrea also recalled that first meeting: "We did look a lot alike, too, so I thought that was kind of cool. It was interesting. It was a little awkward at first because we weren't really sure what to talk about. It was different, but it was good." Brian added more detail to his account: "We kind of tried to find some facial features that were similar and stuff like that. I mean, back then, I think that she was in a band and played guitar. So we talked about that for a while—and music we liked—and just kind of tried to see all the similarities between us."

Andrea and Brian began meeting on their own by the time they were both in college, and they continue to see each other every few months, meeting halfway between their two universities. While Brian is delighted to say that Andrea is his sister, Andrea hesitates to call him her brother, out of respect for Joshua, the brother she grew up with: "I usually just call Brian a donor sibling; I don't really think of him as a brother quite yet because we've only met face to face a few times and we haven't been able to talk a whole lot."

Even though Andrea doesn't see Brian as family just yet, both kids have fluid definitions of kinship. They also share geographic proximity, which is important for contact among families that don't have a lot of money. Brian spoke of his strong attachment only to Andrea among the donor siblings: "I think a lot of the reason that the donor siblings don't interact as much together is because there's such a big discrepancy in distances. Andrea and I have always been a few hours away, so it was a little bit easier."

* * *

The Tourists illustrate both the voluntary character of kinship and the internal variation in attitudes toward donor siblings that can emerge within a network. Neither the parents nor the children are willing to put aside their differences. As is the case in some other networks, the Tourist parents share little more than having purchased the same donor's sperm. In this network, the existence of a set of random families with dissimilar backgrounds ended up dividing, rather than uniting, the group. This is not the case with the 7008er families, where dissimilarities do not stand in the way of nurturing bonds for the children. Indeed, unlike the 7008ers, from the very start, almost every parent in this network engaged in picking and choosing among the families to create social ties.

Some parents and children pointed to the age at which the children in this network met to help explain this pattern. But age alone cannot account for what happened. We do not know what will ultimately happen in groups where donor siblings meet when they are very young (chapters 8 and 9). But we do know that meeting at an older age does not preclude the possibility of forming strong, emotional ties. The brothers in Michael's Clan, who met in their twenties, established strong connections. The 7008ers were about the same age as the Tourists when they had their first big reunion; they certainly became engaged with each other. And within the Tourist network, at least one pair of children found a basis for a meaningful bond: their own isolation as donor-conceived children in rural, religious communities created a reason to get to know each other and to continue to meet. Yet we do not dismiss the issue of age altogether. Clearly, the members of this network could not get over the awkwardness of meeting donor siblings as high school students; clearly, these teens had their own compelling interests as they managed their daily lives.

Other factors, however, might have been even more significant. As noted, this group never experienced a "magic" bonding moment that transformed them from separate individuals into a cohesive whole. And while the first wave of 7008ers *initially* subsumed differences within their construction of themselves as family, the Tourists never made even a tentative leap in that direction; perhaps because they are so very close in age, they did not even try to squeeze themselves into ideas about a sibling pecking order that immediately informed the social interactions among the 7008ers. Shared resemblances—physical, similarities, a quirky sense of humor—momentarily thrilled them even if they were eerie. But they were insufficient to sustain social interactions among these teens for any length of time. Moreover, no girl stepped forward—as was the case among the 7008ers—to counteract the forces of division. With only one girl member at the water park and all five children being born either the same year or a year apart, they appeared to one another like school friends.

Another relevant factor was the behavior of some of the mothers. Rather than letting the children develop their own dynamics, they created a rift when they invited some—but not all—parents to meet the donor. The first moms who met bonded over *their* similarities and not over their children's shared genes. They made no effort to overcome their differences from the other mothers. Their children reflect these divisions. In contrast, the moms from the two rural families were entirely open to expanding kin to include their children's genetic relatives. Their children reflect those views.

Finally, we consider the role of the donor. Michael brought his clan together. Among the 7008ers the donor was imagined and invented; he became a point of discussion that reinvigorated the group each time a new member appeared. When donor Eric revealed his identity, he compromised the ability of these teens to use their shared unknown donor—and the bits and pieces they thought came from him—as a way to bond. The group is divided in part on the basis of who has met him and who has not. Even more importantly, Eric's cool response to his offspring turned some people away from the group. If the teens had been close before Eric appeared, his distancing mechanisms might not have mattered; but because the group was not solid, his actions exacerbated an already difficult situation.

The Unknown Future of the Tourists

While network dynamics can change at any time, in any kind of kinship group, donor Eric continues to maintain a firm boundary between his daughters and the donor kids. Unless that changes, he will never be a unifying figure in the Tourist network. Andrea, who remains interested in meeting more donor siblings, may fill that role one day. But she would have to become more actively involved in the group than she is now. Sienna may also emerge as a leader. So too could other girls or boys who are currently unknown. If any of them step forward, other members of the group may be able to overcome the obstacles of distance, social and class distinctions, and parents who care more about "checking out the landscape" than fostering kinship. Yet without such a catalyst, the network will continue to founder and relationships among the various travelers will exist only on Facebook.

Network update: The birth order for the fourteen children listed on the registry is the following: one child born in 1994, two children born in 1995, four children born in 1996, five children born in 1997, and two more children (twins) born in 2001. We interviewed seven children (and eight of their parents) who joined the Facebook group through which the members of this network communicate with one another. The remaining seven children, including twins who have an older sibling and four single children, are listed on the registry and have not had contact with the other families. These families remain anonymous, listing only basic information (such as birthdate and gender). The sperm donor, whom we also interviewed, could recall the children and their parents, whom he had met in person. He also told us that he had exchanged emails with other kids or their parents. He could not recall how many kids or parents (and which ones) he had exchanged emails with several years back.

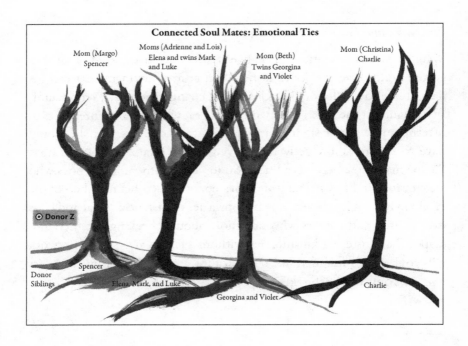

Connected Soul Mates: Emotional Ties

Mom (Margo)
Spencer

Moms (Adrienne and Lois)
Elena and twins Mark
and Luke

Mom (Beth)
Twins Georgina
and Violet

Mom (Christina)
Charlie

⊙ Donor Z

Donor
Siblings

Spencer

Elena, Mark, and Luke

Georgina and Violet

Charlie

8

Connected Soul Mates
Emotional Ties

EVERY DONOR NETWORK has distinctive features, and the Soul Mates are no exception. This group, which includes Margo and Spencer, whom we first met in the book's introduction, is one of the largest networks we have seen so far. With over twenty-two kids as of this writing, it is impossible for everyone to get together regularly, or even to coordinate one big reunion. Instead, subsets have formed to meet the specific needs of various members. The Soul Mates also represent a turning point in network creation: the initial group formed when all of the children were toddlers. At that time, the internet was booming and people-finding sites were emerging, including registries for locating donor siblings. Thus, these are among the first families in which the children have known about donor siblings for as long as they can remember.

* * *

When Margo met Adrienne and her then partner, Lois, for the first time in late 2005, all she could think about was the striking resemblances between their children. Margo is a single mom to son Spencer. Adrienne and Lois are parents to three children: Elena and twins Luke and Mark. The moms had shared photos of the children online and knew that Spencer has the same curly dark hair as Mark and Elena, and that Luke and Spencer have the same crooked smile and deep, piercing brown eyes. Still, that hadn't prepared them for the emotions they'd feel when Spencer and Elena, then three years old, and the twins, age two, got together. Adrienne recalls how the boys all tilted their heads at the same angle as they played with toys. Those uncanny resemblances set off tears of joy; the mothers loved seeing that their children now had others who shared their DNA.

Yet even as the mothers reveled in the excitement of their first meeting, Margo was troubled as she noticed that Adrienne and Lois's son, Mark, shared some disconcerting characteristics with her son, Spencer. When the mothers had first talked several months earlier, Adrienne, who did all the talking and arranging with Margo, had not mentioned that anything was wrong with her children: she had explained that the twins were preemies, but that even Mark, the smaller of the two, was a solid birth weight at four and a half pounds. For her part, Margo had told Adrienne that Spencer had been diagnosed with Asperger's. The day they met, as the kids chased one another around the dining room table and Adrienne videoed them playing, Margo noticed that Mark did not seem to make good eye contact, and that he was "up on his toes and flapping his hands." Since Spencer had previously shown the same behavior, Margo wrinkled her brow, concerned that little Mark might also be on the autism spectrum. She decided to ignore her unsettling thoughts and not mention them to Adrienne. Why upset the joy of the day?

Margo had two interwoven motivations for finding genetic relatives of her child. On the one hand, she wanted to know if others born from this donor's sperm shared her son's diagnosis. On the other hand, she was interested in pure sociability, eager to create what she saw as being more family for herself and her son. She had given a great deal of thought to her phone conversations with Adrienne, and she had decided to prioritize the social issue of family creation: "I don't have a lot of family around here. I think I was excited to make family for Spencer. He has automatic siblings. Why raise issues about my medical concerns? The twins and Elena are not my kids and we were just meeting." Her immediate reaction to Adrienne was positive: she liked that she was warm, embracing, and humorous. At the first meeting, the social attraction was reciprocated: Adrienne and Lois embraced Margo and Spencer, believing that they too could enlarge the sphere of people who cared about them while helping to create a "normal" situation for themselves and their children. Adrienne put it this way: "Our excitement was about the whole connection. We were very open to it, and we were both in agreement that the more people who love us and love our children, the better. It doesn't matter what they look like. I think, trying to take away the stigma and the shame, or whatever it is people have about donor conception. So many people, they'll say, 'It's weird.'" These mothers had shelved their concerns about their children for the sake of forming social bonds. However, each family was dealing privately with troubling issues.

Diagnosing Spencer and Mark

Although she was a first-time mom, Margo knew before an official medical diagnosis that something was not quite right with Spencer. He did not make clear eye contact. He was fascinated by spinning things to the degree that instead of playing with his car toys and making them move, he liked to turn them upside down and make the wheels spin. His language was slow to come in, and when he did start speaking, it was just nouns like "moon" or "tree." Most disheartening, Margo added, "He did not have a word for me. No Mommy. Nothing." His social skills were also a problem: when they went to the playground, he stuck close to the edges, walking around the fence. And, as he grew older, Spencer was "obsessed with numbers, especially pi," and with the subway maps that decorate his bedroom.

Margo was frightened when, at age two, Spencer was diagnosed with Asperger's, a diagnosis that is now referred to as an autism spectrum disorder. She did not know anything about this disorder. She expressed her acute pain bluntly: "I had to grieve for the child I had lost and accept the child I had." Her mother, a clinical psychologist, helped Margo figure out a strategy to find the kinds of help Spencer needed. She (along with Margo's stepfather) had already moved close to Margo when Spencer, her first grandson, was born. Now Margo had her mother there for support as her life revolved around trying to figure out how to deal with this diagnosis. Drawing on the multiple options of assistance provided by the city of Chicago, Margo made certain that Spencer had speech therapists, occupational therapists, and individual aides to go with him to preschool. As Margo explained, because autism is not a learning disability but a "social communication disorder," the support involved a great deal of emphasis on social skill development. By the time we met the family, Margo reported wonderful progress: "At age twelve Spencer is doing great and I'm not worried about him." She added that he had moved from a special education classroom to being mainstreamed, that he read at a level way above his grade, and that he loved stringing numbers together. Spencer, when interviewed, explained that advanced-level physics and astronomy were his other areas of interest.

In another part of Chicago, Adrienne was becoming aware that Mark, one of the twins, was not quite progressing the way the other two kids were, especially with respect to verbal skills: "He would never talk. He wouldn't speak, and he wouldn't respond to me, and I would call him, and he wouldn't even look at me, he would be so focused. One of [the others] would ask for a drink, and I'd give him a drink and Mark would just show up like waiting for the drink, too. He would never ask himself." Since he was the smaller of the twins, she figured his delays were caused by his premature birth and that things would straighten out once he got older. She thought maybe there was something wrong with his hearing because she'd call, " 'Mark, Mark, Mark,' and he wouldn't even turn to look."

Some weeks after the first meeting between the two families, Margo finally decided she needed to broach Mark's delays with Adrienne directly. She asked, "Have you had Mark tested?" Initially, Adrienne shrugged off the question. However, Margo's question stuck in her mind; she thought she might be "in denial and thinking this is about his being premature." She had him tested and discovered that he, too, was "on the spectrum," although defined as being "borderline." (He has a more fluid diagnosis of "pervasive developmental disorder non-specified.") Adrienne immediately called Margo, sobbing as she told her about the diagnosis. Margo, having been through the same emotional upheaval, was a major comfort to Adrienne, all the more important because Lois, who had decided not to be involved in the children's lives, was out of the picture.[1] Moreover, Margo was of practical help. Since they lived in the same city (albeit in different neighborhoods), Margo knew how to connect to useful social services. She also helped advise Adrienne about pushing for services. The psychologist had been hesitant to offer help for a child defined as borderline. At Margo's urging, Adrienne decided to insist: "I'd rather have him have services and not need them, than need them and not have them. The psychologist agreed with me, and we got him the services for two years until he was four."

Margo also called the sperm bank to notify them of the two diagnoses. The bank first made contact with the donor to find out if he knew of any members in his family with autism; reportedly neither he nor his brothers had that diagnosis. Even so, the bank acted as other banks have with respect to diseases and medical anomalies that have shown up among groups. It took the "suspect" donor out of the pool, making his sperm available only to families who already had a child from him and still wanted his sperm to create a genetic sibling. The bank did not inform previous users of the donor's sperm of the diagnosis of autism spectrum disorder; it only disclosed that issue when families asked for another vial of the donor's sperm. It thus decides about risk at one level (no new families can use that sperm), but at another level the bank allows families to make the decision for themselves (the families can try to create a sibling with the donor's sperm).

Even without actions on the part of the bank, the information about the diagnosis has spread as more families sign up either at the bank's private registry or through an independent registry. At the time of the interview, Margo and Adrienne had contact with twelve families who have nineteen children among them. They knew about several other families who were silent members on the registry. Among those families they knew, eight had children with a similar diagnosis. Margo continues to monitor the disorders showing up in this group. She also avoids judgment. Rather than blaming the donor, she wonders about other contributing factors: "Maybe there's something that all of us have in common, the women. Maybe it's environmental. Who knows what it is."

Developing Sisterly Bonds within a Growing Network of the Parents of Donor Siblings

When Adrienne signed up on the internet registry in 2004, the twins were around eight months old and Elena was a year older. Adrienne was excited by the idea of connecting with other people who shared the same donor and curious about what they would be like. As she waited to see whom she might meet, she thought about the donor. Adrienne and her former partner, Lois, had selected this donor because Lois was Puerto Rican and so was this donor. It was an easy choice. The kids would be Italian and German (her side) and Puerto Rican (Lois's side). While matching to Lois was most important, they also did not want one of these "superintelligent" donors; they wanted someone whom they saw as of "average" intelligence (they did not realize he had an advanced science degree). They also liked that he was musically inclined and athletic. They felt he was a good fit with the two of them.

A month after Adrienne signed up, Christina appeared on the registry. They were the very first to connect out of this group. Christina, an African American single mother from Ohio, had sent family photos to the sperm bank, which had a matching service. She cared most that her child would look like her family and she cared about skin tones—not race. The bank matched her with the donor, whom she described as "Italian and Spanish." When she swapped photos of her son Charlie with Adrienne, Adrienne thought that he looked like a darker version of Luke. The two mothers were excited to have found each other, and after emailing photos, they talked frequently on the phone, marveling at the likeness between their children: "They looked so much alike when they were babies, it was amazing. We were just like, 'Oh my God.'"

After college, Christina had returned to her hometown to enter the multigenerational plumbing business her grandfather had started. While her college-educated friends understood donor conception, her hometown friends teased her. How could there be a "real daddy" when she was ordering up sperm from an unknown man on the internet? Meeting Adrienne, whose children shared her child's donor, was a comfort. Adrienne was the exact antidote to the teasing she was putting up with in her home community. She felt that Adrienne, and later the other moms on the registry, understood that relying on a donor was a reasonable way to conceive. Christina did not want some man "bouncing back and forth in and out of her child's life." She preferred to know from "the start that it was just us two." Even though she lived far away, Adrienne provided Christina with a phone and email friend to discuss their babies, a friend who was especially important since she knew no one else who went to a bank for sperm.

Margo was the third family to sign on to the registry. After Margo met Adrienne in person, she also connected via email with Christina. To Margo and Christina, Spencer and Charlie also looked remarkably alike. They shared the same facial shape. Only their skin tones were different. Margo told Christina about Spencer's diagnosis. But since Christina had not perceived any developmental delays in her child, she could offer no further clues as to why Spencer and Mark were "on the spectrum." Busy running the family business in another state, Christina is limited to contact with the other two women through each other's Facebook feeds and infrequent phone calls. These are the "ground zero" parents in this network, or the first to connect with one another.

Several years later, when Beth's twins, Violet and Georgina, were eight and Spencer was nine, Beth, a photographer, met Margo, a media consultant, through a chance encounter at a fundraiser. Serendipitously they discovered their children had the same donor. Beth is a single mom who said if it had not been for this surprising meeting with Margo, she would not have sought out what she called "sperm siblings." She explained that she had flirted with the idea and then rejected it:

> One time I went on one of those registries. You know, I kind of looked, and I said, "Oh, wow, that's really interesting." . . . I was like, "Okay." I had zero desire to reach out to them, nor do I think I would have . . . because I think that I still held onto this idea that it's like *we're* the family and their biology doesn't really matter.

In fact, Beth has created a complex set of ties with many "moving parts of people" available to spend time with her and her daughters. When she met Margo, she told us, she felt that she "certainly didn't need more family." Yet when she saw Spencer's photo staring back at her, she thought "he looked so much like Violet that there is no question he is their sibling." She was stunned to learn from Margo about all the kids in the group on the autism spectrum. Eager to protect her children, Violet and Georgina, from what she feared might be a difficult encounter, she first met Spencer on her own before telling the girls about these new genetic relatives.

Ties within the Network

Because they live in three different parts of Chicago, Margo, Adrienne, and Beth usually see each other only for a daylong visit twice a year.[2] At the time we interviewed her, Beth was in a busy work phase as she got ready for a new showing of her photographs and had less time than usual for the donor siblings. Yet she recently had suggested that Adrienne's Elena sleep over so the twins and Elena could have some "girl time" together. Beth is less involved in the broader sibling network, so she relies

on Margo or Adrienne to tell her the news from Facebook or their meetings with other families.

Within that broader network, other families have met, and some continue to meet for weekends. Margo and Spencer visit another family
who live in Michigan with two boys on the autism spectrum; Adrienne's
family meets with another two-mom family that lives in the vicinity, especially during the summer when a stopover is on the route to a weekend
vacation at her sister's home. The members of the larger group monitor
one another on Facebook—more like parallel play than connection.
(When she is doing her own monitoring, Margo might call Spencer over
to see another child on Facebook. For the most part, as is the case for
the other kids in this network, he is less interested than his mother is.)
In addition, everyone is cordial. Margo connected us with Christina and
Charlie; Christina has told Charlie that someday she will satisfy his desire to meet his "siblings." Since people in the Midwest tend to come to
Chicago at some point, at least Adrienne and Margo have met various
families coming to see the city sights.

These meetings are more quick visits as part of vacations rather than
the central event like the reunions we discussed in the 7008er and
Tourist networks. Infrequent as they are, everyone agreed they are "fun."
Adrienne explained the failure of the group to spend more time together
this way: "Everybody kind of is just doing their life. I barely have time to
see my brother and sister and their kids." Margo noted as well that not all
the families wanted to be involved with everyone and that they "pick and
choose" whom to be involved with. Some make a quick appearance and
seem to disappear after a "Nice meeting you." Adrienne was "mystified"
that some people "didn't want to use the sibling words, and they were
very uncomfortable about telling the kids that they had half-siblings at
that time."

Within the larger group, the tie between Margo and Adrienne is ex-
ceptional. From the beginning, Margo and Adrienne both felt lucky to
have met and liked one another. If it were not for their donor-conceived
children, it is unlikely that their paths would have crossed. Margo, whose
desk was piled with reports she had to read, lives in a funky apartment in
a historic building located in a hip Chicago neighborhood. Spencer had
been in a public school but now attends an elite private school. Adrienne
and her current partner, Felicia, and the three children live forty minutes

away from Margo in a two-bedroom apartment in a predominately East Asian immigrant neighborhood dotted with small ethnic groceries. The kids' teachers in the public school they attend are sensitive to the fact that theirs is the only lesbian family in the school. Adrienne, who is an HR manager for a family care center, and Felicia, a purchasing manager in manufacturing, do not take work home. They make solid middle-class incomes that are hard to get by on in Chicago, but they are managing. These differences between Margo and Adrienne felt minor from the day they met and discovered how important they would be to the other, and how this connection could create intimacy between their families. This connection would also allow them to humanize an experience that otherwise would remain transactional. They agreed that they wanted their children to grow up knowing their genetic relatives.

Margo felt that she got the family she wanted, as not only Adrienne, but also Adrienne's entire extended family, embraced her: "You will see, when you meet her to interview her, that she's extremely warm, very loving, very effusive, Italian. Her whole extended family, her own siblings, they're just like they love everybody. It's just a very loving sort of environment, and so she's very welcoming." Margo, who is more "Zen- like and grounded," according to Adrienne, described the bond between the two as "sisterly," with Margo playing the part of an older sister to whom Adrienne feels she can always turn for advice. The instrumental exchanges around the shared medical diagnoses of their children bloomed into a simple and important ongoing social interaction: "In the beginning, we did a lot, just exchanging information, but after that, then we had Facebook, so we see what's up with each other." Now, ten years later, they still talk a few times a week by phone, send frequent text messages, and avidly follow each other on Facebook.

When we interviewed her, Adrienne was about to marry Felicia. She had been unable to legally marry her first partner, Lois, and they separated when their children were all under three years. Her second partner, whom the kids also referred to as their mom, died several years ago. Adrienne was grateful to Margo, who was there to console her. Now Adrienne and Felicia have formed a strong union. The ability for them to legally marry has been cause for great celebration. Among the members of the donor sibling network, Margo and Spencer were the only ones invited to the wedding. Adrienne was a bit defensive when she explained that she included only one of these families, noting that the room size limited the guest list and there were many other people they wanted to put on that list. She spoke her deeper feelings when she explained that although everyone within the donor sibling network may be part of her life, at bottom, she is "only really close with Margo."

Defining Donor Siblings and Finding a Soul Mate

Like their parents, the children in the donor sibling network tried to figure out what they meant to one another. As they did so, they drew on familiar concepts of friends and family in various combinations. Two of them—Spencer and Violet (one of the twins)—formed a special bond. Perhaps one reason they were able to do so is that they looked beyond fitting donor siblings into their ideas about friends and family.

As Georgina, Violet's fraternal twin, explained, half-siblings aren't very special:

> GEORGINA: I don't really see it as a huge deal. It's like another part of having a sperm donor or father. I think it's the sort of connection we have. That relationship—it's not friends, but it's also not siblings. It's not my sister. I think it's fun.
> INTERVIEWER: It's not super relevant that you share some DNA?
> GEORGINA: Not really. Like I said, I only see it as a result of having a sperm donor. You happen to have other siblings that you don't know very well.

For Georgina, the sperm donor siblings are *both* friend and family, another category that is separate from the members of her nuclear family, but also distinct from friends at school. Mark (one of Adrienne's twins) explained these connections similarly. On the one hand, he knows that the donor siblings are not "real" siblings: "To me you have to be more than related or biologically related for you to be a part of your actual family." On the other hand, he believes that they are different from friends "because they still are related to us." This difference carries with it special obligations: "We should be nicer to them and more caring for them." At another point in the interview, Mark struggled to explain these distinctions again: "They're not much family. They're *just* our half siblings. We're half related to them." For Mark, then, the boundary between friends and family is blurred.

Mark's twin, Luke, thinks of his half-siblings as being in a category similar to his friends from school, with the difference that he sees the latter far more often. When asked what it means to him to have donor siblings, Luke said, "It's kind of like having a billion different cousins," drawing an analogy to family that expresses relatedness and distance. However, shared DNA does not automatically create intimacy. His sister, Elena, has the same sense of distance but places a greater emphasis on sharing genes; she even considers how she will be related to her donor siblings' children and grandchildren in the future. "Even if they live on the other side of the world," she said, they will still share her "blood."

For the kids in these three families, donor siblings are both friends *and* family and neither friends *nor* family. This stance allows for the kind of intimacy that might be found in an extended family; the intimacy is limited as well, in part because the kids do not see—or even interact with—one another regularly enough to form close bonds. Their parents limit their use of iPhones and still control the time they spend together; none have their own Facebook page. The children really do not ask to see one another on their own, even though they are very aware of one another and each child can name something distinctive about the donor sibling with whom the child felt most connected.

With Spencer and Violet, however, something special happened. Violet felt an immediate connection with Spencer when she and her family spent time at his mom's beach house on Lake Michigan. She described a moment in which they both just seemed to be entirely on the exact same wavelength:

> When we first met, we were on a beach and we just stood there in the water telling each other random facts of trivia that we remembered off the top of our heads, [such as the fact that] the underskin of blueberries is actually green, so when they first sprout they look like limes, tiny little limes. I don't know why we know that, but we just do. When I'm with my family, I can't really do that as much. I know that does come from somewhere else. . . . We have a lot in common in specific ways that were just very factual, like going on random

tangents about random science and math and are very fascinated in certain ways.

Violet understands that Spencer has autism, but she looks past that diagnosis. "He's a pretty cool person," she said. "He just struggles with that a little bit and it's hard for him." The commonalities they share—including personality traits—have given her a better understanding of herself and of why she and her twin, Georgina, have often clashed.

> You could say that my sister is quiet and thoughtful and that I'm, as my mom puts it, very loud and thoughtful. I think we [Spencer and I] ever so slightly have a louder personality, less role oriented. I think we're a bit more stubborn and strong-willed than my sister. She's more go with the flow.

These discoveries answered some key questions for Violet, who had always wondered why she was so different from her sister and mother, neither of whom is interested in "random tangents about random science and math," as she referred to her own interests. "I'm happy that I know this big aspect with finality, and my loud ideas jumping all over the place, I know where that part comes from. I'm okay with that," she said.

The relationship between Spencer and Violet opened new possibilities for him as well, as his mother acknowledged: "I was always very open with Spencer about his diagnosis. 'You have a special brain that gives you special powers, but there's some other things that are harder for you.' He's memorized two thousand digits of pi, as of a few weeks ago, but making friends was harder for him at first." The friends Spencer made in elementary school shared an interest in video games, school subjects, and movies typical of boys that age. Their conversations never touched on deeply personal issues or delved into Spencer's interests in science and math. By the time they reached middle school, the group began to splinter. His mother's love and support remained unwavering: "I've really emphasized to him, be your own person, have your own voice," said Margo.

Yet when Spencer met Violet, Margo was stunned by the noticeable similarities, including the fact that Violet "is Spencer with a long set of curls." Margo noticed other affinities as well, including the fact that Violet understands science and math the way Spencer does:

> She's a very brainy girl. When we met, she was reading beyond her grade level. She and Spencer really connect, and they've hung out over summers, and she and Spencer just talk about all kinds of science. They bond.

Margo admires that connection but does not share it. "I'm awful at math," she explained, while Spencer "was seriously talking about astrophysics by the time he was about six or seven and was self-taught." Spencer was kinder in his assessment of his mother's aptitude: "If I'm trying to explain something in science or math to her, I might have to explain it multiple times for her to get it—[but] sometimes when she's trying to tell me about some stuff in philosophy, I might not get it at first either."

Spencer, who always speaks succinctly, described his relationship with Violet this way: "I'm closer to her than some of the [other donor siblings]. Sometimes we'll have deep conversations about politics, or I remember one time it was about sexism in the Bible. She knows random science and math facts I know. She gets me."

Violet, who is more vocal, said Spencer is another "quirky" kid who worries about existential questions, just as she does. He is her soul mate and understands her logic even if that logic makes no sense to anyone else in the world:

> I don't know if I consider him like, "This is a person who I'm half related to." I just think of him as my special person, like my special friend. We have a mind that's been slightly connected to each other, like traits that have been slightly connected to each other. Just think of it like that. Here's this friend that you know. We came from the same donor, so I know we have slightly the same eyes and slightly the same taste in stuff. It's just like that. It's when you've been with someone long enough that you have slightly the same things. It's just interesting.

* * *

This network began a new historical era for families with children whose births coincided with the startling media news that it was possible for families to find donor siblings. Among the many families for which this was the case, we chose to focus on the ones in this particular network because two sets of strong emotional ties emerged.

For most of the eleven- and twelve-year-olds in this group, donor siblings are a given; the children view these people as they might extended kin they receive from their parents. Like cousins, for example, they are there on social occasions. Children might still be trying to figure out who these people are, but for the most part they are blasé about these ties. They are thus quite different from the older children we interviewed for whom donor siblings were initially quite a shock (even if some of those older children later became uninterested in these relationships).[3] Within this younger group, Spencer and Violet stand out. They are not surprised by each other's existence, but they are surprised by how much they are drawn to one another. Larger nuclear and extended families might have provided this kind of special affiliation; now that families have shrunk and thinned, Spencer and Violet are "lucky" that they have the opportunity to find a soul mate within the donor sibling network. (In this strong attachment they resemble Oliver and Isabel in the 7008ers, although in that case each of the children was the only child in the family.)

Exclusive bonds have a tendency to cause jealousy among the 7008ers. They do not do so here, in part because there has never been a cohesive group within which fragmentation might create discord. Other factors also make a difference. All of the children, whether they articulate this or not, might understand that they too benefit from the connection formed with donor siblings. Elena and her brothers are the only children in their public school who have a lesbian mom (and a series of "step" moms); the donor sibling network gives them others who have the same experience they do. When Elena needs to get away from her brothers, her donor siblings provide her with "girl" time. Georgina might be relieved that the pressure is off her now that Violet has found someone to share her distinctive enthusiasms. Spencer's autism has made most interpersonal relationships difficult, but Violet is willing to look past that diagnosis. The donor siblings thus provide solutions to problems these children face in their daily lives.

The women at the helm of each family have created a flexible, kin-like arrangement. As do their children, they turn to one another for emotional and social support they do not find within their own extended families or their broader communities. Some of this support revolves around the diagnosis of autism spectrum disorder that might be traced to the donor. Margo and Adrienne exchange medical information and helpful tips about educational adaptations. But their support of one another extends beyond that shared concern. They offer each other sisterly advice over more personal matters. Even though Adrienne and her fiancée, Felicia, already have a complex set of extended family arrangements, Adrienne created room to assimilate Margo into her inner circle. Christina and Beth might not be as close to others as are these two women. Yet they also have found occasions to value this new set of ties.

Donor Siblings Create New Kinship Possibilities from Birth

For both the parents and children described in this chapter, the donor sibling network provides an important way to connect with others who understand the challenges they face and the common ties that bind. If in the past people sought connections through ethnic, religious, and geographic enclaves, today some people can add donor sibling networks to that list. In many ways, these networks become yet another "community" in which individuals can meet people who may profoundly change their lives. Unlike the kids in the earlier networks we described, Spencer and his crowd will share a long history of knowing one another. The same is true of the families we meet in the next chapter.

Network update: Spencer and Margo knew of twenty-two children in the network, between the ages of nine and twelve. They had recently been in touch with a new family with one child. Margo wondered also about the two children listed on the registry with only minimal identifying information.

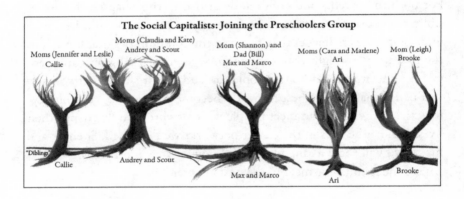

The Social Capitalists: Joining the Preschoolers Group

Moms (Jennifer and Leslie)
Callie

Moms (Claudia and Kate)
Audrey and Scout

Mom (Shannon) and
Dad (Bill)
Max and Marco

Moms (Cara and Marlene)
Ari

Mom (Leigh)
Brooke

"Dibling"
Callie

Audrey and Scout

Max and Marco

Ari

Brooke

9

The Social Capitalists
Joining the Preschoolers Group

THE PARENTS IN this network are creating a different narrative about the value of network membership than are those described in the previous four chapters. These parents introduce a set of new ideas about the meaning of these relationships. Rather than trying to squeeze themselves into any preexisting model, they actively negotiate their own rules for interaction and for language. They also introduce a set of ideas about the benefits the group can provide. These benefits include a large number of social ties they hope will advantage their children in the future; they include as well the anticipation of access to diverse experiences and kinds of knowledge individual parents cannot provide themselves. The parents scurry to become members early (while their children are under the age of five) because they want both to influence the group's formation and to secure the benefits they hope their children will receive in years to come. Because the children are so young, we hear only from the parents.

* * *

No Complete Reunion, Little Pods

When we met with parents in this network, much of the conversation had been about the ongoing plans for an event to take place the next summer. However, not everybody in the group was either interested in coming, or able to come, to that event. Five out of the fourteen families would be together in Minnesota. And aside from a single mother who had written the planning group to say that she could not afford the time or the money, we do not know why the other families would not be in attendance (although the fact that some of them live outside the United States in England, the Netherlands, and Australia might make travel too expensive). As in other networks, differences in social class might not have been significant obstacles to getting *along* within the group but were significant obstacles to getting *together* as a group.

In any case, by that time there had already been quite a few separate gatherings of group members who either lived within easy travel distance or could combine a visit with a business trip. Some of the families got together even before their children were walking. Leslie and Jennifer had met with a couple of parents on a vacation in Santa Fe; Kate and Claudia reported that they had traveled from Massachusetts to attend a birthday party for a single mother's child in Vermont; and Cara and Marlene had met with another family who happened to live near them in Connecticut. The one heterosexual couple within the network, Shannon and Bill from Virginia, feel closest to a two-mom family they had met in Alabama.

All of these meetings ended in goodwill and plans to get together in the future. Nevertheless, parents told us they are well aware that they might like some parents more than others. Shannon hedged, stopping short of explaining why she and her husband communicate less with the members of one same-sex couple than with the mothers in another same-sex couple, but acknowledged the fact: "We don't ever talk [one-to-one] to them." And Leslie and Jennifer were equally frank: "Who will become family? I imagine we'll have little pods. Not everyone is going to hit it off with everybody." For all that the parents are united in believing, as we will see further below, that there are some powerful connections among the children (based on genes) and some powerful connections among themselves (based on both having made the same series of choices and having children with shared genes), they know well that—as the members of other groups have already discovered—those claims will not *inevitably* supersede all other bases for sociability. These parents hope that over time their child will gain advantages from membership in this network. They enjoy as well the new Facebook friends they are acquiring for themselves. However, in this network the parents pick and choose from the very beginning which parents they want to get to know, and often these become their favorite families.

Finding Their Way to the Group

The members of the Social Capitalist network echo the motivations we have heard so often before. They are unique, however, in two ways. First, parents in this network are the only ones who scan network membership—and in one case join the group—very early. In Virginia, Shannon and Bill, parents of two-and-a-half-year-old twin boys, signed up for the registry on their bank's website as soon as they had a confirmed pregnancy. As Shannon explained, being open about the sperm conception—and what could be more open than joining a group for which that was the central unifying feature—signaled the absence of embarrassment:

> I think we actually signed up for the bank's registry pretty much after we got pregnant.... We always felt very strongly that if we did get pregnant, we would try to connect with other families because—just simply because this was never something we felt ashamed of.

Bill added, "We never felt like it is a secret."

For Cara and Marlene, who live in Connecticut, the possibility of a donor sibling group had actually guided the choice of a bank because originally they did *not* want to have their child's genetic relatives in the same community.[1] Although they did not mean to seek out genetic relatives at first, they were not bothered by the idea that donor siblings existed somewhere. In fact, Cara said that she had learned from reading the donor profile that there had been prior births; that knowledge gave her the security that the donor's sperm could work. Surprising herself, Cara began the search for the other relatives in the surfeit of adrenaline that accompanied her overwhelming love for her new baby while Marlene was still in the hospital recovering from her C-section. Cara suddenly felt that connecting with the other families who had conceived children with their same donor could even "humanize" an experience that had felt "transactional." And now that she had a real live child in her arms, she felt curious about who the other families were and what they could offer her son.

Second, a sense of urgency accompanied these early entries. Leslie and Jennifer were explicit about their reasons for signing on to the registry at their bank when their daughter was two years old. After they learned that friends of theirs had done it and had begun to meet with donor siblings, they discussed doing the same. Jennifer wondered what was happening with the offspring who shared her daughter's donor number:

> Friends of ours were going to gatherings with their donor sibs. [So I thought], "I'm just going to go see if there's any on our number." Then I looked and there were nine. I contacted one of them. You can message and then I got scared. I talked to her and then I was like, "I don't know if I'm ready to meet them."

In spite of her sudden fear, Jennifer wanted to ensure that her child would be one of the first members because she worried that it would be harder for both the parents and the children to connect with the others once the group had gelled.

From a Boston suburb, Kate signed up for the group because she wanted to sell their extra vials of sperm once her wife Claudia's pregnancy with their second child (Kate had carried the first) was well underway. Claudia shared Jennifer's feeling that they should rush to join because she did not want her children to be latecomers to whatever group was forming:

> If I were a donor-conceived child and I were interested in making this connection and I learned about and came into the group as an eighteen-, nineteen-, twenty-, thirty-year-old, but the group had been together and meeting each other in some way since they were two and three, that would feel really hard. So if it is an interest to [our daughters] Audrey and Scout, I don't want them to be left out of it. I want them to be able to be a part of it comfortably in whatever way in whatever level makes sense for them.

Cautious Entries

An eagerness to connect did not dispel all anxieties among the members of the Social Capitalist network. Although many of them are active on Facebook in multiple groups and forums, this network evoked the concerns we have heard from other parents with young children: What would the members want from each other? What language would they use? Would these other people disrupt the story they wanted to offer their children about who they were and where they came from? Unlike the members of networks created earlier, the parents in this network were not entirely taken by surprise by the possibility of making contact with the families of donor siblings. They knew these networks existed early in their own reproductive journeys. Yet they were recent entrants into their own network and they had their own concerns.

When Cara signed on to an independent registry, she found one parent, Leigh, to whom she sent an inquiry by email. A week later, Leigh, the group's founder, sent a welcoming note. As did one member of every other "successful" network, Leigh was not only a gatekeeper but also facilitated interaction. She told Cara that thirteen other families had already joined and that Cara and Marlene (and their son) would be the fourteenth family. The oldest donor sibling in this group would be four that summer; the youngest at the time was nine months old. Once they joined, Cara and Marlene's son would be the youngest. Cara was comforted by Leigh's response, and she became excited to join: "It does feel like this group is very important, and when you read how these other families communicate with each other, there is definitely a real sense of warmth, connection, kinship, and trust."

Kate also thought she and Claudia could trust the group members because they had a "shared understanding" that they would respect each other's privacy. Kate liked the summary Leigh gave with respect to this issue:

> She basically said something like, "Some of us choose to connect one on one through Facebook messaging. We never reveal in public forums how we know each other, but we like and support each other on Facebook." I thought in and of itself that statement in just a nice sort of way captures the spirit of "we are connected but we respect each other's privacy decisions" and are cognizant of that as we are in forums where people might be aware of that.

This statement about privacy was especially important to Jennifer and Leslie because Leslie, as a newscaster on a local television station, has become a recognizable figure in her community. She worried that information about their daughter Callie's origins will become too public:

> I just was very cautious. . . . I just feel like, still I'm very protective of Callie's privacy. I didn't want to have some fan somewhere telling everyone about Callie's history. We were processing on Facebook

and we were like, "You may not tell anyone who recognizes Leslie that you share donor sperm with your kid." The idea that some random person is going to come up to [our daughter] Callie and say, "I know your half-brother" is just not appropriate. We had to set some limits and that was interesting.

Jennifer especially liked the fact that the group discussed the issue of what language to use, saying, "We do a lot of processing on Facebook: 'How do we refer to our kids when we meet up? What language are you using? Well we use that language.'" Jennifer believed that the language should not assume siblingship, but leave that open for the children themselves to decide at a later date:[2]

We all decided only they can define it as a sibling relationship—we can't. They're too little to decide. We say, instead of the possessive, like, "That's your half-sibling," we say, "Oh, you share the same donor." The children can choose. Maybe they feel like siblings, maybe they don't. You know what I mean? They get to decide. That was the group decision and everyone was on board with that.

Kate also was reassured about the issue of language when she learned that the group has a shared understanding that they do not use the language of "donor siblings" or claim any kind of family affiliation:

At some point in talking with Leigh . . . we had talked about wouldn't it be nice if there was a more formal statement of the expectation of language within the group. She wanted to avoid the use of family language and really does not like the "donor sibling" term, doesn't like when people kind of crossed over into "brother," "sister," "family" kind of language.

Ultimately, the members of this network adopted a special language. The term they chose—"dibling"—indicates a donor connection (with the *d*) while dropping the *s* to indicate that the children are not conventional siblings. Like the parents who rely on the awkwardness of "children who share the same donor," the parents who embrace the lexicon of "diblings" want to acknowledge links among their children while avoiding assumptions about how important those links will be.

One other issue arose during these negotiations. One mother who was married to a man had joined the group briefly. She asked to join using a pseudonym instead of her real name because she wanted to protect her husband's anonymity. The group members discussed her request. They felt that everyone else put his or her identities on the line and that it would not be fair to allow an exception. Unhappy with this decision, the woman soon dropped out of the group.

Kate tried her hand at codifying these various norms to create a shared agreement about how the group would operate. When we spoke with her, she had still not found the time to write a formal statement.[3] Even so, Kate became comfortable enough: "It is a pretty thoughtful group of people, so it doesn't alarm me that there isn't a statement right at the beginning." Yet the prospect of an anticipated reunion made decisions about interactions among group members suddenly feel especially urgent again, particularly when some members asked if they could bring members of their extended families. Jennifer explained what happened:

> I am helping coordinate a meetup next month with five of the families in Minnesota, and . . . I did online surveys up the wazoo. Oh my God, is it okay to bring other family members? It's hard to make a group consensus decision with so many families. It's really hard.

As Jennifer indicated, group consensus takes a lot of work.

Shared Genes, Deep Connections

Whatever their motivations and reasons for caution, the Social Capitalists spoke in a shared language about the network's meaning. Given the historic moment in which these connections were formed—when genetic influences were heralded in the popular press—perhaps it is not surprising to hear parents talk as if the shared genes of the children have almost mystical importance. Cara said, "There is something very powerful about the fact that [my child] is genetically connected to these other kids." For others the connection simply exists and needs to be honored. Either way, shared genes—especially when they are interpreted as producing physical similarities so that other people's children resemble your own—become a reason parents offer for caring about children who are not their own. And this caring, the group members agree, must be a good thing. As Kate said, suggesting the potential utility of these new ties, "The more people out in the world who have a fondness for my kids and are fundamentally rooting for them in some ways, cheering them on, hoping for the best for them—that's not a bad thing." Kate and Cara had not met each other when we spoke with them, yet Cara used almost precisely the same language: "We're all rooting for each other."

As these parents talked about the group and why they invest in it, they focused on another set of benefits that extend beyond having a cheerleading team rooting for their children. They highlighted something that is simultaneously more amorphous *and* more tangible. Having already chosen what they believed to be the "best" genes they could for their family, they view the contacts available through a child's donor conception as an opportunity to further equip those children to venture out into the world. For example, although Kate from a Boston suburb and Marlene from Connecticut had also not yet met when we spoke with each of them in their separate homes, they spontaneously expressed themselves similarly when they explained why it was so important to nurture these connections. Kate suggested possible discrete opportunities for her child from these new social ties:

> It's too soon to know what that might mean in their lives. . . . Maybe there is something concrete about that. Maybe [our daughter] Audrey someday decides she is going to travel across the country; she will have a place to stay when she is in Chicago. A [genetic relative] in California opens the door for [our daughter] Scout to have an internship somewhere, I don't know. Maybe it means none of that concretely, maybe it just means that these people smile on them and think kind thoughts and hope good things for them. I feel fine about that.

Marlene did much the same when she compared the donor sibling group to a group of alumni from a high school organization that had had a powerful influence on her when she was sixteen:

> There are people all over the world. I felt this sense of connection. . . . I imagine [our son] Ari going to Australia . . . and being able to look [his donor siblings] up while he happens to be in Australia.

Although her wife, Cara, followed up with a tongue-in-cheek reference to the utility of "crashing on their couch," Marlene was suggesting something more substantial. Sure, Ari could find a berth on a genetic relative's bed in Australia, but the meaning of doing so would extend beyond that into a strong group of people who are "connected" through something important to each of them. As Leslie, yet another parent in the same group, said, "Well, hopefully [the donor siblings will] provide them with lifelong friendships and connections that will strengthen who they are in the world and how they feel about who they are in the world."

As the parents project into the future, they are aware that the developing network may provide all sorts of social and cultural capital. Cara predicted "more access, more knowledge, and more of a sense of shared community." Moreover, because her son Ari is one of the youngest ones, she imagined his having "these lovely little role models." Marlene agreed entirely, while suggesting, once again, that she is leaving the decision about whether to follow through on that advantage up to her son. This will be "something else he can choose to draw on or not."

Securing Other Benefits

These "friendships and connections" offer a range of additional benefits that parents want to secure right now and ensure are there for their children's future. One of the immediate benefits, curiously enough, is the cultural capital that attends interaction with a diverse group of people. Shannon, who lives with her husband in a heteronormative world, believes that the way her children came into being means that they "don't have the same story as everybody else." She turns the donor sibling network into a special advantage. She is enthusiastic about the opportunity for relationships that she believes would not have been possible if her husband's childhood illness had not left him infertile. The Social Capitalist network provides them with girl "siblings" for their sons (and many siblings at that). Even more importantly, it provides them with siblings attached to parents who might not otherwise be part of Shannon and Bill's world: "We love that they have siblings that we may never be able to have and . . . that [their siblings] have two moms, or that they have some single moms in the mix."

Leigh, a single mother in a rural suburb of Ohio, commented that having donor siblings gave her son the opportunity of seeing how another set of people live:

> The beauty of this kid being in New York City is, really, Brooke [my daughter] gets to see how another child lives, in a completely different part of the country. You know, city mouse versus country mouse. And I think that that is, sibling aside, a very good thing for her. And she can start thinking about who is this girl and who am I, in a different way, in terms of is this my sister?

The parents said that the diversity is fun for them too. Although many see themselves as sharing similar values, this group, like most, is varied enough to include lesbian couples, heterosexual couples, and single mothers. The members of the group are also scattered geographically, ranging from the Northeast (New York, Connecticut, Massachusetts, and Vermont), down to Virginia, across to the Midwest, down to Texas, and across national borders to England, the Netherlands, and Australia. In addition, the group includes those who define themselves as white and those who define themselves as African American; it also includes those who say they are Jewish and those who say they are Christian. Apparently, this wide variety is the result of the donor's having donated at a small midwestern bank that was subsequently bought by a larger bank in the East.

In addition to embracing diversity, at a far more utilitarian, daily level, parents acknowledged that knowing donor siblings enables them to compare how the children are developing. Through these comparisons, they believe, they are able to see what might be "genetic" and what might not be. Some even suggested that the donor sibling group provides an insurance policy in the sense that, should one of these children need matched blood or a matched organ, they might find that within the group. These straightforward reasons pale beside the more urgent sense that this is a group that offers something unique to their children—deep connections full of unexplored potential, a new form of social capital that can be trusted and counted on *because* it is based in a genetic connection.

A Safe Place for Parents to Share

Just as the parents see a connection between the children, so do they see a connection among themselves. The group feels like a safe place to share. Most of this sharing is not about material resources (although Shannon has shipped her twins' baby clothes to a two-mom family in the group). Most commonly, the sharing is about feelings and ideas. Marlene described this as a "community/family that we're going to be a part of." And if she hesitated ("Wait, I don't know any of these people"), she also relied on the fact, which she immediately prioritized, that they "all have kids that are genetically related." Suggesting now that this was a "random decision" for each of the parents involved, she still insisted that the "genetic piece" mattered: "I'd say it creates the conditions for us to be open to a level of intimacy and closeness with them that we wouldn't have with random people. It makes us want to prioritize these relationships because of a sense of what the potential can be."

Other parents prioritize the *choice* element rather than even mentioning randomness. Shannon and Bill talked about what they see as being a "different" story of how their twins came into being; for them the intentionality is especially important. That intentionality is something they see they have in common with the other members of the group, something that binds them together and makes them trust each other:

> And [our children] were—they were always wanted and we just needed some help to get there. . . . [All] these people [in the group], all of these kids, their commonality, is that they were very much wanted . . . and that people, because of love, created them, and because of that love and that bond that we have now, they have all these brothers and sisters.

Kate believes it was karma that the members chose the same donor:

> They seem like thoughtful parents, interesting people, kind, supportive—just nice, smart people. Somebody had speculated early on, "Is there something that links us in some sort of fundamental level in that we all chose the same donor?" There were some reasons there that we gravitated to him and maybe they suggest we might all have something in common. We might all gravitate towards each other in life.

Leslie focused her recognition of similarities among the people who have chosen the same donor less in their immediate personalities than in their similar orientation toward the world. The word "random"—competing with a sense of mystical importance—entered again:

> I feel like the folks that have chosen this particular donor are very similarly dedicated to their kiddos. They're similarly kind and open-hearted people. It's just really . . . interesting how similar we are in a sense. They're like-minded, like-hearted people. How cool is that to be connected through this almost, seemingly, almost random thing? But it feels very "aligned," I guess, is a good word.

The enthusiasm for these connections is especially interesting because almost all of the parents we interviewed in this network have their own rich sets of relationships with natal and extended family members. Unlike the families in Michael's Clan (some of whom were cut off from relatives who disapproved of their being lesbians), the members of this network retained ties with their blood or legal kin. Some, like Cara and Marlene, have relatives on both sides who have embraced their union. All also have rich professional lives and large friendship circles. Most also have numerous communities—the lesbian community; the synagogue; alumni organizations; their global work organizations—from which they can draw should they need companionship and support. Even so, they find the network of parents with children conceived from the same donor to be a special place of sharing. And for now, much of the group sharing revolves around how to handle donor conception issues and other subjects of parenting advice: "Someone will write, 'Today at preschool . . . one of the other kids said something to my kid and my kid said, I don't have a daddy! I have a donor!' And I was so happy that he had that language and said that." Group approval is instantaneous: "It gets ten 'likes' right away." Cara likes all those "likes." She described the Facebook page as a "happy place":

> There's humor, there's joy, it feels like a very happy place. I know that's silly to say, but if I'm feeling pissed about something at work, I will often go into the Facebook group and just stare at some of the photos of those kids and look at the comments and go, "Oh, yeah. This is a happy place."

The Disappearing Donor

The members of this group were all adamant about wanting to have an identity-release donor. And when speaking about why this had been their decision, they used the same language they used for group membership itself: they want to ensure that their children have every opportunity they might need—or simply desire. The ability to identify the donor and learn about their genetic origins becomes an additional privilege bestowed on children who should not be denied anything that might create advantage in a competitive world.[4] Claudia explained that both their egg donor and their sperm donor were identity-release donors and that this is impor- tant to Kate and her: "They were both willing to be contacted. . . . We wanted that . . . just to give our kids a choice. It's their story, and if they want to do something with it when they're old enough, they can pursue that. We didn't want to shut that off for them." Claudia added that she also wanted a donor who could "handle well" contact by a child, someone who "would be a thoughtful, nice person for a child to talk to or meet." In another family, Cara also spoke in the language of the benefit her son might derive from being able to know who the donor was:

> We made a conscious choice to use an identity-release donor to give our son that opportunity. I don't feel passionately about it one way or the other. It's not something I thought about. In an ideal world with ideal circumstances, sure, I think identity release is a good thing. I think it's good enabling kids to have the opportunity to seek contact with their donor when they're eighteen if that's some- thing that they want, especially when you're a teenager and when you head into young adult years, there's all these formative things that happen, and you start getting curious about your life.

Leslie and Jennifer said that they had the same interest in ensuring that the donor would be accessible to their daughter: "We were pretty com- mitted that we wanted someone who would be available at eighteen. That really narrowed our search." The parents in both the 7008 and the Tourist networks had limited options about kinds of donors. Even if they had wanted an identity-release donor, they might not have been able to find one who met their other criteria. Now that the banks entice their clients by offering more variety, parents actively imagine how the donor will interact with their children.

At the same time these families insisted on a donor who would be "nice" and "available" once their child was born, the donor was no longer very important to these adults; now that the child is *theirs*, the donor himself is pretty much irrelevant. That is, much as they want to secure all options for their children, they hope the donor might never be a very important person in their children's lives, even if he can supply his offspring with information they may want to have. The members of this group never refer to the donor as a "father," or even a "donor dad." They all applaud (with "likes") the fact that a child told her preschool classmates that she did not have a "daddy" but a donor. Unlike the members of Michael's Clan, who had no way to explain their family form to their children and to outsiders, for these contemporary parents, the donor is always "the donor." He needs to be a person and not just a "cell" because the child might meet him someday. But he is not meant to be an important person; he does not now have—nor do the parents anticipate that he will have in the future—a familial relationship to a child. We asked Claudia if their older daughter had asked about a "daddy" now that she was going to preschool. Her answer suggested that that word would carry no freight in their house: "We'll always be like, 'You have two mommies. And some families have two dads and others have a mom and a dad. We are a two-mom family." This new language is not unique to donor sibling networks but reflects a cultural shift that highlights parenting rather than biological reproduction.

Here Come the Diblings

As the donor recedes in importance, the donor siblings achieve pride of place. These parents share information about the "diblings" far and wide. Although extended kin are not included in dibling reunions, dibling families might be included at events with extended kin. The family for whom Cara and Marlene made the spinach frittata is regularly invited to their many parties along with their other family friends and their children. While the parents in the other networks remarked that the children's grandparents and uncles and aunts were not interested in getting to know donor siblings, diblings are commonplace within Cara and Marlene's crowd. As the landscape of families with donor-conceived children has changed, so has the inclusion of these genetic relatives who are not simply relegated to their own sets of donor sibling "reunions."

Perhaps even more significantly, Jennifer hopes that for her children, the donor siblings will be far more important than the donor. She noted that these children will have grown up together, shared memories, and understood the experience of being donor conceived. The donor, on the other hand, will remain unimportant—and an outsider to the family— even if the children have contact with him when they are eighteen. He will not really understand donor conception, and he will probably not know what it is like to have two mothers. Jennifer found comfort in a resource that suggested the priority donor siblings will have in her child's life:

> I don't know if it's anecdotal, or if there was a study that donor kids obviously have more in common with other donor kids than even with the donor. The donor didn't grow up in a donor family. These kids are living [my daughter's] exact experience. Do you know what I mean? Of growing up, most of them with lesbian moms. With no dad and not knowing who half their genetics are. Some of these kids are growing up with [both an] egg and [a] sperm donor.

Kate had the same wishful thought about the significance her daughters would give to the donor siblings relative to the donor:

> I do wonder if by knowing all of these kids . . . who used the same donor if that might lessen the curiosity and interest of the donor. I wonder if that is something that might happen, but not especially strongly—I don't feel here or there about it. That might be an out- come. They might feel, "I've got twenty-one people I am connected with and talking with all the time. I don't need one more!"

No one in this group cares particularly that there are already so many donor siblings and that it is likely more will come forward; they have not yet considered how so many children will form bonds as they get older. Because they view the members of these other families as an important resource for their children, they may hope that there are a sufficient number to provide contacts around the world.

Looking Forward

There is no way to know whether the children in this donor sibling group will express significant interest in the donor when they get older. In addition, there is no reason to believe that they will all—even if they come from the same family or from within the same family form—act in the same way. There is also no way to know how they will regard the relationships with their donor siblings as they mature. Because these children were too young for us to interview, what we know about them now comes from what their mothers said in describing both individual and group meetings. Kate, for example, wrote to us after the first reunion and said that she thought her daughter had a special bond with the other children, although she could not be sure that she was not reading something into the experience that she wanted to see:

> The children had a blast with each other. At one point, unprompted, Audrey told me, "I like these friends more better than my regular friends." No idea if that was just the joy of being on vacation with kids her age and getting to play endlessly and connect without some of the usual constraints of day-to-day life, or if there was some sort of "kindred spirits" thing happening, but either way, it was very, very fun.

Cara's emails to us sent from the same first reunion did not focus on her son's interactions with the other children, but she mentioned that the kids all seemed to trust all the other mothers, as if they sensed that there was something special in those relationships; she also mentioned how well the parents got along. She wrote, "It was interesting to watch how all of the [donor sibling] parents interacted with our respective kids. There was a lot of fluidity and trust in taking care of each other's kids throughout the weekend (i.e., I cooked French toast with Callie while Callie's moms hung out with Ari). At night after our kids went to sleep, we sat around drinking wine by the fireplace and talked about parenting, how/why we chose our donor, etc."

* * *

Within the Social Capitalist network, we were able to speak with parents as they were negotiating ground rules and figuring out just how they were going to conduct their relationships, both online and, especially importantly, at their first "reunion." These negotiations reveal just how far donor sibling families have moved from reliance on the model of a nuclear—or even of an extended—family. The donor is never a father figure. (The two-mom families do not ever think of their children as "missing" a dad. They provide two married parents; their children embrace that new model.) The different attempts to describe the relationships among their children—whether through roundabout phrasing or the cute tidiness of the term "dibling"—indicate that the parents want their children to appreciate a connection across families without making assumptions that these connections are the same as those defined by siblings who are raised in the same family. They want to reserve family language for their own nuclear families. Their discussions of other issues—how they should act in public, whether they can bring other relatives to "reunions"—illustrate that even if the social rules for interaction are not yet institutionalized, the parents are actively engaged in the process of creating something unique where they can feel more comfortable acknowledging donor siblings.

Whatever they are creating, the focus is on their children, not themselves. The parents who are now the active members of the Social Capitalists enjoy their social bonds with each other; they like having more friends, another online community in which they can indicate "likes," and another set of people they can visit across the United States and possibly abroad. But even more than that, the parents hope their children will be able in time to mine the relationships they (the parents) are now strategically creating. They want the donor to be a nice person who allows contact and acts as a resource for their children to learn about who they are and how their genes have shaped them. (They thus envision a donor who will act more like Eric did among the Tourists than Michael did among "his" clan.) They hope the diblings will do much more than that for their children. The parents are creating memories for their children; they expect that children who have known each other from early childhood will be there to help each other navigate an understanding of donor conception. They also see opportunities for their children to acquire cultural capital by interacting with, and learning from, others who are quite different from themselves. Above all, they are looking for people (and this includes *both* the diblings and their parents) who will take an interest in and be available to their children as they venture out into the world. As Leigh so frankly put it at the end of our interview, "I hope my daughter will say these connections with donor siblings deepen her Rolodex."

Network update: The birth order in this group includes five children born in 2011, six children born in 2012, three children born in 2013, and three children born in 2014. These seventeen children belong to fourteen families. Two of these families are expecting a second child. Members note that they know of four other children who are registered on the sperm bank's registry (conceived with their donor) whose parents have not opted to join their Facebook group. Two children are listed as single children, each with their own family. The other two children share the same parents.

Although the donor's sperm is no longer available at the sperm bank, the Social Capitalist network is likely to grow larger for two reasons. First, some of the members we interviewed said they plan to have additional children and they had sperm vials left to use; second, other families (who have conceived with the same donor but not registered) are likely to come forward in the future.

10

Donor Sibling Networks
Continuity and Change

Historical Moments and Children's Ages

Our five featured networks represent four different historical moments in network creation. At each of those moments, the children in the networks are at different developmental ages.

We began with the story of the network with the oldest children—Michael's Clan. Although the sheer act of having a child as a member of a same-sex couple may have been revolutionary in 1986, like other members of their generation, Celeste and Pamela still subscribed to a hegemonic notion of family as composed of both mothers and fathers (even if genetic "fathers" arrived after the child turned eighteen). This idea about the origin of male and female gametes residing in two opposite-sex parents reverberated through their family life and was critical to that historical moment.

The donor siblings came as an absolute shock to Justin and his mothers. Justin and his donor siblings took control here. They made their own decisions about contact with each other. The network belongs to them and not to their parents, even if the latter occasionally join in and derive pleasure from that joining. Justin sees similarities between himself, the donor, and his donor siblings. He embraces the influence of nature at both an intellectual and an emotional level. Now he believes he knows himself better and he finds comfort in that belief.

The second era began in the middle to late 1990s. As was the case in Michael's Clan, the existence of donor siblings came as a surprise to the members of the 7008ers and the Tourists. But unlike the parents in Michael's Clan, the parents in these two networks learned about donor siblings before the children were eighteen, and thus they were the ones to make the active choice to connect with donor-linked families. (Four children—Jenna, who was thirteen, and then later arrivals Scott, at age eighteen, and the twins Megan and Matt, also at age eighteen—in the 7008er network began to search online for information about their donor, found the possibility of connecting with donor siblings, and then involved their parents.) The parents in these networks unexpectedly became another set of pioneers. They engaged in an entirely new phenomenon, a phenomenon that required figuring out whether genetic strangers would become meaningful connections in their lives—as relatives, for example—or whether they would remain simply acquaintances who exist in the cosmos. The networks may have begun with parents, but children are key to their continuation. Indeed, as the kids grew older, the parents became appendages to their children's attitude toward the creation of meaningful bonds.

The children in these networks formed relationships with their donor siblings as adolescents. Broad questions about identity intersected with narrow concerns about popularity. Both bounced around within networks. At one point the teens were drawn to each other because they saw in those others the possibility for insight into the origin of their own physical traits and personalities; at other points, some teens rejected others because they could not provide the kind of interpersonal "capital" so important in social groups. And sometimes, being teens, donor siblings found their lives too busy to make room for each other. Even those teens who met when they were younger did not necessarily privilege those earlier interactions over their current sets of concerns.[1]

Around the turn of this century parents were still surprised to learn about donor siblings, but they were able to form those connections when their children were toddlers. By the time we met the members of the Soul Mates, the parents had long-established relationships with each other. Many of these donor siblings had also known each other for years; as preadolescents, they were old enough to try to make sense of their relationships with this new category of relatives who come from the "paternal" side. The bonds they formed at this age depended more on a sense of personal connection than on the attribution of any special meaning to shared genes.

The networks formed (since 2010) by the parents of preschool children—epitomized by the Social Capitalists—raised even newer possibilities. Parents like Cara and Marlene sought out genetic strangers without consulting their children because they did not want to miss out on any of the resources they believed these connections might provide. The children do not really know what donor siblings are. They engage with them as other children with whom to engage in cooperative play and, on occasion, to struggle over toys. Parents might think they see an extra spark here, but even the parents know they might be projecting.

Naming Conventions

Naming conventions within the networks reflect the changing models for relationships with genetic strangers and the changing rationales for pursuing them. Jocelyn, a recent entrant to Michael's Clan, was presented with preexisting definitions of both parentage and siblinghood. Michael signed group emails to his offspring with a declaration that he is "Pops"; Justin and Nathan claimed they are brothers. Jocelyn can accept or reject these definitions, but she cannot change them. At least for their understanding of donor siblings, the 7008ers also drew on the language of family—as well as on the most affirmative ideas about how family members interact (e.g., with love, trust, and harmony)—to serve as guideposts in the unscripted land of donor-linked families. They used these guideposts to socialize new group members. These same guideposts put people outside the network (e.g., their friends at home) on notice that these new connections are meaningful and deserve recognition.[2] However, none of the other groups fully adopted the language of family for either the donor or the donor siblings, although for the latter, some parents and children use variations like "diblings," "halfies," "sperm siblings," or—most humorously—"the besties of the testes."

Technology as Home Base for Connections

As naming conventions changed over the span of time our respondents represent, so too did the sheer possibilities for connection. The various members of Michael's Clan never established a Facebook group. They email and text, but they have not otherwise relied on the internet. The other groups all stand in sharp contrast.

Parents in the newer networks turned to Facebook (and earlier MySpace) to create private online communities; those online communities still exist today. The private Facebook pages for the 7008ers and the Tourist network became the spot in which the group interactions started and from which they grew to an interest in having a reunion. The kids in these networks also learned barebones information about each other through their Facebook group. They used that information to judge what they might share with these genetic strangers and whether they wanted to meet in person. Sienna, who chose not to meet others, suggested that the information she acquired made her believe that she would not have much in common with her donor siblings: "Most of them said they were into science, I'm not really a sciency person myself."

The private Facebook community transported kids to a world dissociated from the social demands of their local, teen peers.[3] Kids discovered "new acquaintances"; they looked through each other's Facebook photos and saw resemblances. Although these kids had been among the early users of Facebook, as they grew older, they reported shifting to other social media like Instagram (a favorite) and group texts. (Even so, it was a Facebook post that became the final step in the controversy that led to the fragmentation of the 7008ers.)

By way of contrast with the older children, Spencer and his crowd of preteens (featured in the Soul Mates) only use technology under parental supervision. But shared times, and early memories, make it likely that when the twelve-year-olds have access to text messages and other yet-to-be-invented technologies, they will make their own independent contact with each other.

The last network, with preschoolers, is entirely controlled by the parents; some form of "membership" occurred even before the children were born. Once the parents choose a donor (with a unique number), they could (and do) snoop online for information about, and pictures of, an intended child's donor siblings.

Interactions in Networks

Throughout the book, we have used the term "network" to characterize relationships between and among parents, children, and, occasionally, important others like donors. Sperm banks and independent donor registries may encourage network-building, but neither creates networks; parents and children do. Following Mario Small and others, we see networks as predicated on interaction. We may think of networks as being more or less active or more and less useful, but interaction is essential to sustaining a network.[4] Someone has to tend to the care and feeding of the group.

The two dominant kinds of interactions that take place in networks can be characterized as transactional and generative. The most obvious commercial transaction (after the purchase of gametes) is the exchange of membership fees (to the independent registry) in order to receive information about the other donor siblings (and, potentially, the donor).[5] It buys a ticket for admission. Revealing the identity of one's child (or a child revealing her own identity) is another transaction. It qualifies a new participant to ask questions of others in a network, and it provides the equivalent of an insurance policy for someone who might want to gather information about the children or the donor at a later time.

Generative interactions, on the other hand, are based on giving without expecting anything in return. These include unsolicited contributions, like posts, that can stimulate a conversation. Generative interactions often lead to new definitions of family, new feelings of belonging, and new occasions of intimacy. As an example of the first of these, a member of the 7008ers, David, who is an only child with a single mom, was asked by the interviewer, "Can you say what you learned by meeting them?" He responded: "Just a greater sense of the meaning of family. It's kind of expanded what I thought was family because growing up, it's like Mom was my family. . . . Now it's grown a lot. That's what it's taught me, for the most part." David, Zoe, and Joseph find a sense of belonging in their weekly Skype date, during which they watch a favorite TV program and joke around. Spencer and Violet described how as twelve-year-olds they came to think of themselves as soul mates. Violet explained that Spencer provided her with a sense of connection she could not get from her own sister. We repeat her comment from the narrative: "We just stood there . . . telling each other random facts of trivia that we remembered off the top of our heads. . . . When I'm with my family, I can't really do that as much."

Generative interactions thus represent a shift from simple transactional exchange to sociability and social support. When interactions transform the dynamics—enriching the network, altering participants' understanding of either the network itself or their particular position in it—we can think of them as catalytic moments. Catalytic moments are usually unscripted, but they may not be *entirely* unpredictable. Many events we observed in featured and other networks (in retrospect at least) could have been anticipated. Some of these events occur around the donor. For example, Annie (discussed in chapter 4 in relation to her donor sibling Milo) sent a letter to her sperm bank and asked the bank to pass it along to her anonymous donor. To her delight, he wrote back with answers to her questions even though he did not reveal his name. Annie felt she owed it to her sixteen donor siblings to share her discovery. She posted the donor's letter to their Facebook group knowing that the moms skimmed the posts regularly and they would see the letter and pass it along to their kids. Annie's generative act was unexpected, but the possibility of an anonymous donor coming forward was there all along. Even more predictable is the catalytic effect of the first sibling to reach eighteen years old in the case of identity-release donors. Even the act of writing a letter and not receiving a letter back—as happened in the 7008er group—can catalyze discussion about other ways to locate (or not) the donor.

Another set of predictable catalytic moments occur when new members show up. For example, when Scott appeared, the kids (and their parents) in the 7008ers were electrified. Before his arrival the kids had already formed ties and the network had fragmented into (two) separate sets of bonds. Scott does not feel as if he has to choose sides between the two subgroups that socialize (or text) together. He also carries information back and forth between the two segments.[6]

As we saw in an earlier chapter, networks made up of tourists rapidly dry up when new information is not contributed. Transactional interactions can keep a network alive, particularly when new members arrive seeking information. Generative interactions provide the most energy and catalyze deeper and more enriching relationships. In short, when there is renewal—whether it is transactional or generative—the network is active. Acts of renewal are essential to the vitality of the network. Absent any kind of renewal, networks stagnate even if at any future moment an online post can bring about a revival.

Interpersonal Dynamics among Kids in Networks

Donor siblings constitute an entirely new set of unscripted relationships, different from those with other relatives or friends where the social expectations might be relatively clear. Sometimes, as we saw in the featured networks, kids try to institutionalize their relationship by claiming one another as family. For those kids who never had siblings—or wanted more siblings—this new claim is immense and immensely meaningful. They show their delight and comfort in each other by acting "like puppies" in their rough-and-tumble physicality. Even if the kids do not consider each other to be siblings—but find a way to distance the relationship with a word like "cousins"—what might be a small family can be expanded through ties that are unexpected and can be unexpectedly rich. Kids also try to make sense of donor siblings by drawing on what they know about norms in friendship groups and in sibling relationships (whether or not they have siblings of their own). These understandings help them assemble a social order that informs them about how to act toward one another and shapes the consequences that can ensue.

ESTABLISHING SOCIAL ORDER

Kids look for ways to figure out how to be a new kind of sibling. Unsure about what this relationship might mean, they draw on the cultural narrative of birth order to establish rank. That is, they adopt age expectations from the oldest to youngest as measured in years, months, or even weeks. When Nick flew to Missouri for the first 7008 reunion, he was very aware that he would be the oldest of the donor siblings. Reflecting on this gathering, Nick wrote the following in a speech he gave to his class of schoolmates: "A comfortable group dynamic began to form. As the oldest I felt protective of the rest. Chris liked to give me a hard time, but it was nothing a short wrestling match couldn't fix." Nick thus willingly assumed and even embraced his new role, especially since he had no siblings who lived with him and his mom. For their part, not only did the other kids see Nick as their protector (he watched out for them at the pool), but the younger kids, such as Chris, knew that it was their "right" (and obligation) to challenge Nick's position. Of course, all of this could play a role in personality development in a conventional nuclear family with more than one child. But for donor siblings, even the kids themselves say that personality differences among members—these kids are shy and these kids are extroverts—are traits that kids bring to the group rather than traits that emerge out of group dynamics. Yet it makes sense that kids "line" themselves up by birth order simply because this is a script they know about (or have experienced if they have more siblings) and one that might fit an attempt to become like other families. Put differently, these expectations establish social patterns of interaction both when there are larger reunions and also between pairs of donor siblings as they text or talk about their lives with each other, institutionalizing an important aspect of siblinghood.[7]

However, birth order is also an unreliable guide to actions in these networks because membership is not fixed. Someone who is at one point the oldest can be "dethroned" (as a kid in the 7008ers put it) when a new member appears. We return to Nick, who was the oldest for a short while. But then David, who is a week older than Nick, showed up, and Nick responded with "Ack!" when he heard the news. David's arrival displaced him. The other kids also felt torn because Nick was not the oldest big brother anymore. Even the parents remarked that they wondered what would happen among the kids. Would Nick still be their protector?

Soon after David's arrival, Isabel showed up, and she is older than David by a few months. Now, however, birth order intersected with gender. Since Isabel is a girl, her arrival did not matter to Nick because she did not challenge his position but merely replaced Jenna as the oldest *sister*. Nick told us that he realized that he would still be an *older* brother, and in his opinion that still carried sway over other spots.

GENDER AMONG DONOR SIBLINGS

Once the group had become larger, the birth order was stated in terms of boys *and* girls: Isabel is the oldest girl and David the oldest boy. When children in a network discuss the donor siblings, they often suggest that it is a boy who looks (but not necessarily acts) most like the donor. In this way the group differentiates itself along both age *and* gender lines; boys and girls both scramble to find their place in these hierarchies.[8] Yet girls and boys often mix easily in the networks. As others have noticed among teens, groups of friends today often cross gender lines.[9]

Interestingly, however, we found that gender does play another, and even more important, role in the networks. Girls are more likely to play an active part in maintaining a large network itself. For example, both parents and children point to Jenna as being the "glue" that keeps the 7008er kids together. She prompts the others within the network to maintain ties, and she personally texts and tries to visit everyone in the group in college or in their hometown. She was the person who was on the registry greeting Scott when he showed up. The disagreement over leadership between Zoe (who created the Facebook group) and Jenna led to a rupture among the other kids and what felt like the necessity of choosing sides. Moreover, the boys in this group rarely communicate among themselves, and when they do, often there is a girl sibling in the mix. The fragmentation that did occur was not along gender lines but rather on the basis of other interests. Even the new joiners (Isabel, David, Oliver, and Scott) move freely between the girls and the boys in the network.

The Tourist network, on the other hand, lacks active girl leadership: when six kids finally met, Madeline is the only girl. The other girls in the network remained uninvolved with the broader group. We have pointed out many reasons why the Tourist members disengaged from their network and the network stagnated. We speculate also that the absence of girls who are active in this network (which is not the case in the parallel 7008er network) contributed to the lack of caring among its members and the failure of anyone to nurture the network itself.[10] It might also be possible that in the future a boy will come forward to revive this network through a generative interaction.

SIBLING VALUES

Even in thriving networks, interpersonal dynamics change constantly, just as they would with siblings raised together who might have favorites, shift alliances, and go to one sibling for this and another sibling for that. Young children (like Andy, discussed in chapter 4, or Spencer, discussed in chapter 8) are content to simply accept donor siblings as important people in their world. With growing maturity, however, they want their relationships to have more meaning. Take Alex in the Tourist network. He and Clint were eight and nine, respectively, when they met. They had fun simply hanging around together; Alex told us how much he had liked getting together with Clint. When we met the two boys, Alex was in college and Clint was completing his senior year in high school. As a first-year student, Alex was hoping that he would eventually continue his education and get a PhD in the sciences. Clint had chosen a different path, opting for a college where he could surf. The two boys now had little to talk about; neither felt he had much in common with the other.

Certainly they have fond memories of their younger selves, but at this point in their lives they want to be with people who are more similar to them. They distinguish between friendships formed on the basis of shared interest and the donor siblings, with whom the genetic connection is permanent but may not be meaningful at any particular moment.

SHIFTING ALLIANCES

In groups like the Tourists, different viewpoints about "donor siblinghood" matter little because no one seeks to unify the network members. In groups like the 7008ers, however, these different viewpoints cause trouble as the members try to impose a single definition of where on the spectrum between friends and family donor siblings reside. Trouble comes in other forms as well. Larger groups create the very real possibility of shifting allegiances. This year you latch onto and feel close to one donor sibling; next year you find another with whom you find greater comfort.[11] We saw these shifting dynamics most clearly within the 7008ers, a network that fragmented into competing sets of alliances.

Trouble like this can also have benefits for individuals, who now have more opportunities to assume leadership in at least one fragment. Large groups, whether fragmented or not, offer more specialization within the broader network (whether by geographic divides or by interests) and more opportunities for connecting with someone with a distinctive kind of understanding that does not exist at home. The kids in the Tourists have disbanded, but it is possible that, had they had more members, enough of them would have been interested in continued connection. At the time of our interviews, only the dyad of Brian and Andrea remained.

Interpersonal Dynamics among Parents in Networks

In the process of childrearing, parents are always thrown together with parents they might not already know: parents come to know each other on the sidelines as their children participate in day-care centers, schools, social relationships, and extracurricular activities.[12] Network membership offers these parents another set of opportunities for interaction. Like their children, parents have to figure out what it means to interact with people who both are—and are not—their relatives. If their interactions involve less of the jostling for position than the donor siblings themselves experience, they have their own problems and pleasures.

Parents often suggested that the social diversity in their groups constitutes a real and important benefit for themselves, a diversity more present in the networks that formed once sperm was shipped across the country. Some of the benefits of this diversity are simply the result of geographic dispersion: people find a way to travel to new places with local hosts (e.g., as we saw with the 7008ers). Although sometimes differences can impede the development of ties among parents, the diversity of values, social classes, races, ethnicities, religions, and family forms can also be a source of pleasure.

Parents was also delighted to find special friends among the parents of their children's donor sibling. For those parents in our featured networks, clicking with other parents on email or over the phone was a reason for parents and their children to decide to meet in person. Even when the kids become uninterested in one another, parents can (and do) remain friends. This was the case in the Tourists with the threesome—Susan, Gina, and Nikki—who kept Nikki's secret among themselves; it is also the case in the 7008ers with the ongoing relationship in which Greg messages Maureen when he reads something he thinks would interest her, even though their kids are not presently in close contact. An even more unlikely pairing in the same network is Iris and Tricia. Iris's husband thinks homosexuality is a sin, but he really likes Tricia and her new partner and he embraces the donor sibling kids as Chelsea's "siblings." Iris, who lives in Texas, talks or texts at least once a week with Tricia in Missouri. Moreover, they embrace each other's children, who recently started to add "Aunt" before their donor sibling's mother's first name. They came to care especially about these newfound connections. But these mothers also host other kids who live in nearby states (and they have become ambassadors for the parents of newcomers.)[13] In short, while parents saw their in-person gatherings as facilitating their kids' relationships (through creating memories of fun times in various places), parents also discovered their own set of emotional ties.

GENDER AMONG THE PARENTS

Although men occasionally are present at a gathering or engage in online postings, these networks are valued as women's spaces—spaces for women to bond in the experience of motherhood and delight in the perception of similarities (and differences) among their children. Drawing on her interviews with single mothers by choice over a decade ago, Hertz wrote that in the contemporary world "the core of family life is women and children."[14] Drawing on our interviews with parents in all types of family forms—and not just single mothers—we would argue similarly that when the donor sibling networks create a new kind of networked affiliations (whether thought of as kinship or something entirely different), here too the core consists of women and children.

We asked in the introduction whether conventional ideas about gender in kinship prevailed even when there are no men to divide or unite the women. What we found was that it is the women who take the lead in joining the networks. But they do more than that: they are the gatekeepers; they plan events; they welcome the random families as they appear and want to connect. Sometimes, especially when the children are young, the women in a group work together to facilitate relationships among the donor siblings. As convention might predict, the women are concerned about interpersonal relationships and about smooth dynamics. But the women do not always act in a cooperative way. They may not be antagonists, but they don't always like each other. And, at the end of the day, the particular needs of one's own children always take precedence over the needs of the other individual members or the group as a whole.

Social Resources and Costs in Networks

Parents become involved in donor sibling networks when they believe that these connections will add something important to their lives. The same is true of children old enough to make their own decisions about whether to become involved. For both groups, those beliefs are both confirmed and disconfirmed. Connecting to genetic strangers has some positive consequences that mirror those imagined. For example, the networks help satisfy curiosity about a child's genetic origins: by drawing comparisons among donor siblings, children and parents alike come to believe they can more easily sort out what came from the donor.

Connecting with donor siblings also has some more problematic consequences. Contact always initially heightens attention to genes. This new attention to genes can create difficulty for the nongenetic parent; it can also create difficulty within families where the children have different genetic origins. For the most part, these disturbances are fleeting. That is, although the initial moment of contact draws attention to something that divided a parent from their spouse or a child from their sibling, the long-term affiliations within the family quickly override those divisions. As we noted in chapter 4, no matter what kind of siblings one has at home, the children can differentiate between them and the donor siblings. Moreover, in the most inclusive donor sibling networks, a child's siblings are welcomed with open arms, even if they share no genes with anyone else in the group.[15] And parents do not form their attachments to other parents in the network on the basis of who holds a genetic tie to a child.[16]

Parents and older children alike experience some of the social costs of group dynamics such as the simple pattern of picking favorites. The basis for making these choices is pretty much the same among both parents and children: simple attraction and shared interests. For both parents and children, liking one another appears to transcend differences in gender, race/ethnicity, and sexual orientation. For both also, simple proximity (e.g., living close to one another, attending college in the same city) makes the chance of interacting regularly more likely.

The bases for disliking, however, differ somewhat between parents and children. The children appear to find it difficult to transcend differences in "coolness," especially once they reach high school. The emerging selectivity among the children in the 7008ers once the kids were older and the group was no longer facilitated by the parents led to feelings of disenchantment with embracing everyone in the network; some kids felt slighted or excluded. By way of contrast to the children, some parents find it difficult to transcend differences in social class and cultural capital. The emerging patterns of selectivity among the parents in the Tourist network and the hurt felt by Brian's mothers are yet other examples of social costs.

Even when the contact itself was not exclusionary, differences in social class meant that while some people could easily fly across the country or take off for a long weekend to participate in a "reunion," those with fewer resources could devote neither the time nor the money to these festivities. Some parents found the assumption that it would be easy to travel a long distance to spend a weekend at an expensive theme park offensive and classist, even if they did not express it in precisely those terms. Older teens also expressed disappointment when parents told them that they could not afford to attend a group gathering. These respondents did not want to be excluded from the developing relationships, but they could not find a way to be included, and they turned down invitations to attend gatherings. Even this kind of "voluntary" exclusion can be painful.

If social class differences occasionally become the basis for exclusion, they can also become the basis for sharing varied resources. The members of the newer networks used larger, commercial banks, and the sperm was shipped across the country (and even across national borders). Parents in these networks appreciated the fact that other parents sometimes became important sources of social and cultural capital for their children. For example, parents who knew about the world of colleges and universities helped kids with less knowledge (and less helpful guidance counselors) fill out financial aid forms and write college essays. Parents with more material wealth hosted small and large get-togethers, thereby sharing those resources with others in the network. Those parents with fewer financial resources offered what they could. They provided a bed away from home and (whether wittingly or not) insight into cultural and ethnic differences. Some of the less privileged parents became very active network participants. By way of contrast with professionals, many of these parents worked at jobs with hours that could be easily circumscribed; they could thus devote more time and energy to the network itself. When they were more used to sprawling extended family structures (as described in chapters 3 and 7), they could more easily integrate network members into their existing arrangements of kin, thus providing for children and parents alike new opportunities for emotional bonds.

As is the case for their parents, the social diversity of the group constitutes a benefit for children. In a world where neighborhoods and schools are increasingly segregated by both class and race/ethnicity, this diversity can be a novel experience. Because the shared genes in the group are viewed as the basis for social bonds, this diversity can be appreciated rather than becoming divisive. Indeed, the members believe they have reason to try to learn from each other and to try to get along. And, as noted, for some kids, access to another group of adults—who provide social, cultural, and even emotional capital—constitutes its own benefit.

Validation and Trust in Networks

The most important resources that participants can get are validation and trust. As our discussion has indicated, not all members of all networks get either or both of these resources. However, when they emerge within a network, they are critical resources for their members.

Validation

Validation takes the form of a realization, "I am not deviant, weird, or alone." Children learn from the network that other people share their identity and experiences of being donor conceived.[17] This is especially important to teenagers. For kids who have grown up in geographic isolation from other donor-conceived families, the donor network is an extraordinary gift that goes well beyond the narrowed notion of "normalization." As we saw in earlier chapters, kids struggle by themselves to make sense of the hollow concept of the donor and to find the concepts that will explain the donor and the meaning of donor conception to their school friends. Donor siblings offer kids words of advice and language to deflect teasing and questions about "dads." Most significantly, interactions with donor siblings support the conviction that one's feelings are real, understandable, and even appropriate.[18]

But the network also matters greatly to parents. Relationships within the network affirm their route to parenthood and their donor choice. Even with changing social attitudes toward single mothers, federal recognition of same-sex marriage, and early second-parent adoption in some states, parents still find comfort in encountering others who have made the same reproductive journey. The members of heterosexual couples, while not as vulnerable as single mothers or lesbian couples, might even feel more isolated in this respect, knowing fewer people who had relied on donor conception. The donor sibling group thus provides significant kinds of reassurance for people who use donors: there are other people out there who had a baby, so it must be a fine idea to have a child; there are other people who conceived using a donor, so that must be a reasonable thing to do; and finally, there are other people out there who conceived using the *same* donor, so that must also have been a reasonable—or even good—choice.

Trust

The other big resource that participants can get is trust: a sense that someone has my back; that no matter what else happens, this person will do the right thing and can be relied on to support me. Trust emerges more slowly than validation.

Among the children, trust is established through repeated interactions that occur both on- and offline. When kids report trust as the foundation of their relationships with donor siblings, they view their donor siblings as people who have a special spot in their lives. It's hard to underestimate the importance of this resource, particularly in an anonymous and sometimes hostile world.

Take the case of Isabel and Chris. Isabel described herself as very sociable at college and actively engages online with friends and a few members of the 7008er network. But her most frequent exchanges are with Chris, a younger donor sibling who is still in high school. Isabel explained, "I'm the person he comes to for advice on everything. I don't necessarily share my issues with him . . . 'cause he is younger and he's not going to have a handle on my relationship issues. He and I will be up at three in the morning having an insane philosophical debate and that's awesome." Chris said that he trusts Isabel because "if you need someone to talk to, you know she's there for you." Similarly, Isabel has frequent disagreements with Jenna, a donor sibling also in college, but Isabel deeply cares about her. Their bond, built on multiple visits and nightly texts, epitomizes trust. According to Isabel, Jenna "cares for me beyond belief, and I really have such a deep care for her as well. I think what defined family for me are people that have your back and you have theirs. It's more than just friendship. They're someone that you turn to in a time of trouble and nightly for conversation."

Parents too come to trust each other. This is especially the case among those who have children who share troubling issues. These parents find in the donor sibling network a resource for understanding their children's distinctive difficulties and for airing concerns about them. As one mother said, she felt comfortable discussing her child's ADHD with the other mothers: "Because there's this genetic connection, I felt a little more free to sort of ask them . . . what they were doing [for their child]." Two parents mentioned that they more easily discussed shared concerns with the parents of children who had the same donor than with other friends on- or offline:

CARA: All the kids have the same lisp, for example. And do we need to contact a speech therapist? That kind of thing. We talk about, "Your kid does that? God, all our kids do that! Isn't that amazing?"

MARLENE: We've had those exact conversations with friends in our community, but it's a different level when there's actually a genetic relationship.

Among the Soul Mates, as much as Margo and Adrienne call themselves "sisters" today, and both said their main reason for connecting when their kids were little was to expand family, Margo had an instrumental reason for locating other families: she was stunned to realize the first day they met that one of Adrienne's children also appeared to have an autism spectrum disorder. Margo and Spencer also visit other families who, Margo told us, have children on the autism spectrum. She monitors especially those kids with this diagnosis in the group. When the kids were toddlers, she tried to get the network into a research study that never materialized.

The Donor in the Network

We have talked about how genes are the start of a conversation. In fact, however, it is an absolute stranger, in the form of the donor himself, who is the point of intersection for every network. As we dug into the dynamics of the networks, we found a continuum of roles assigned to (or played by) the donor: from background figure, to conversation starter, to direct or indirect "convener" of the network. In this section, we explore these various roles and then turn to the question of what happens when the donor is revealed unexpectedly.

Absent Donors

We start with networks in which the donor is at best a background figure—not an active participant, but someone who made it possible for genetic strangers to find one another. (In truth, it is hard to imagine these networks getting started without an equally important [and equally faceless] enabler: Facebook.) For example, Shannon and Bill (in the Social Capitalist network) sought donor siblings while ignoring the donor. This is not to deny that they see shared traits among the children that logically lead back to a donor. In Shannon's words, "These kids are pretty similar, and it's pretty amazing to see their faces together." But when asked if she and Bill are curious about the donor's identity, they responded emphatically:

SHANNON: I never think about the donor—
BILL [INTERRUPTING]: The donor? No.
SHANNON: Not at all.

In other words, perceived physical similarities are sources of connection to donor siblings but *not* a reason why she and Bill should see the donor himself in their children or even think about him.

The donor can be a conversation starter that helps parents especially, but also children, through the awkward process of forming or entering a network. This was the case when Marlene and Cara joined a gathering of five families for the first time. Sitting around the campfire, the icebreaker that evening turned into sharing the reasons why they selected the donor. As each woman revealed her reasons, they realized that they had all chosen the donor for what they defined as "amazingly similar" reasons. Their individual answers resonated powerfully. The five families bonded immediately. From Cara's perspective, they were meant to be at that campfire together. Having the same reasons for choosing a donor became the foundation for the creation of a meaningful community. This was true in other groups as well where members told us, "We are Jewish and we all share the same cultural identity," or "We all loved the answer to the question 'Who do you aspire to be?' to which the donor responded, 'Be the person your dog thinks you are.'"[19] Even among the 7008ers and the Tourists, where the parents had chosen the donor for quite different reasons from one another, they also discussed the parts of the donor profile they found appealing. And this conversation starter enabled the formation of bonds within the network. Among children as well, the reference to common physical features helps transform a group of strangers into people who consider themselves to be some form of siblings.

As we have suggested above, the familiarity occasioned by reference to a common donor underscores the validation and trust that emerges, creating both greater sociability and even solidarity. Once connected on Facebook, network members share information relevant to raising children with the same genes. Questions about allergies, announcements of developmental milestones, birthday greetings, and adorable photographs of gap-toothed smiles are met with "likes" and cheery comments. Facebook acts as a repository and remembrance of face-to-face meetings. Take this post: "We love our extended family and [are] so glad Suri and Avery as well as Dylan and Dakota are here [on the shore] with us this week!!! Such a special few days and only the first of a lifetime of memories yet to come!" Other members post back: "Glad you got together"; "Awesome!!! I am sooo happy to see you all getting to experience this!!"

Perhaps most telling are the efforts to provide social support in trying times that link to the shared donor. When one child was diagnosed with type 1 diabetes, solidarity responses on Facebook were immediate: "Oh poor little guy. We will keep him close in our hearts. Keep us posted—and thank you for letting us know. We have a doctors appt in two weeks so we will certainly bring this up." Network members are grateful for information they did not have before, and they are also there (and "all in") in times of crisis.

Beyond being a mere conversation point, in networks with an identity-release donor, parents and children have an added reason for staying involved. Parents who select identity-release donors know that the donor will eventually become a human being. Even though they may have given great thought to this issue at the time of conception, as a child's eighteenth birthday approaches, they have to get comfortable with the notion that the donor is "real." Jennifer and Leslie, parents whose story we related at the opening of the book, are part of the active Social Capitalist network; they hope that the oldest child (out of seventeen kids) will share the donor's letter. And if he agrees to meet one of the children, they hope that he will meet everyone at once and not wait until the next child's turn. Here the order of age (even differences of a few days or weeks) among donor siblings can emerge as an important point of differentiation: the oldest child in the network might derive some measure of privilege by being the first to contact the donor.

Donors Appear

Whether anticipated or not, the appearance of a donor can shake up networks. For example, the parents in the Tourist network had chosen an anonymous donor. When donor Eric changed his mind about anonymity,

he did so in part to offer kids information and in part to satisfy his own curiosity about what had happened to his donation. When Eric posted that
he was willing to meet those who had used his sperm, registry parent Gina
was so excited that she sent a text message to another parent, Susan, who
was on a vacation with her son, Alex. Gina and Susan did not know how
the others who were not in their immediate friendship circle (but in their
network) would react; they left it to the other families to find out he had
posted and also to make their own plans to meet him instead of sharing
this information on the network Facebook page (or contacting other families they hardly knew). This action caused tension among the parents.

We have discussed Eric's sudden appearance in the narrative. We noted
that as much as the individual kids accepted Eric's position that he did not
want any role in their lives, some kids would have preferred someone more
likely to care about them. His careful boundaries—obvious even in email
correspondence with Sienna and Andrea—led both girls to decide he was
not worth meeting in person; the rejection, however, smarted. Interestingly,
although unknown donors are an important topic of conversation among
donor siblings (like the 7008ers) when they get together, because the kids
had different relations to Eric (some had met him and some had not), he
was not discussed among the kids at the one gathering they had.

Finally, as we saw with Michael's Clan, the donor not only can be an
indirect convener of a network but might, in fact, play an active role.
However, this is less likely in contemporary times when donor sibling
connections usually occur *before* connections with a donor and when the
networks are both larger and more geographically diverse than is the case
for Michael's Clan.

A Gendered Donor

Because the connection strategies that create networks are now only available with respect to "sperm siblings," the donor is always male. As an interesting consequence of these patterns of connection, sperm donors have
greater public recognition in donor sibling networks than do egg donors.
The networks trace their origins to a male progenitor (as have lineages in
the past). But this is a very different type of progenitor; the donor cannot
either control resources or dictate behavior. In fact, he may never know
any of his offspring at all.

We have introduced the readers to two donors who did appear; the other donors are *physically* absent (and usually entirely unknown). These other donors have no presence at the gatherings, and they do not have a voice in online postings. The donor's genes are significant *only* insofar as they are shared among the children—a basis for similarity, a possible source of some special ability or handicap. If the donor is imaginatively present (the reason for the network itself, the topic of a conversation), he is also *not present*. The male progenitor is thus both central to group formation and incidental to many of its dynamics, someone who simultaneously exists and disappears. As a person, the donor has limited power: he can appear or not appear. But whatever he does, he is always brought into a position of some kind of *symbolic* centrality by the sheer existence of the network.

Sleuthing the Donor

Some people do not want the donor fully present in a network, but they do not want him to entirely disappear either. Sleuthing—online detective work—is a way to track a donor to ensure that he can be found if desired when the child turns eighteen. For Adrienne in the Soul Mates, for example, the process of sleuthing was similar to tracking an important parcel in transit. The donor's profile contained unusual information that she uploaded and cross-checked to locate the donor on the internet.[20] She had done this initially when her three kids were in grade school; she continued the practice for years, and she made regular posts on the network's Facebook site to keep others up to date. Every few months she downloaded the donor's pictures and made them into online albums for her kids and the other families in their network. Her posts and albums were generative: they became occasions for conversations among the parents.[21] By way of contrast, the kids we interviewed in this network— between the ages of eleven and twelve—knew that the donor had been found, but they were uninterested because he was neither a person they could know immediately nor someone who could know them. The donor was "real," but to them he was invisible. Adrienne's familiarity with the donor's whereabouts blurred the border between her market transaction of purchasing this donor's sperm with her motherly wish to make sure he appeared when the network kids turned eighteen. By not actually making contact with the donor (such as would be the case if she "friended" him on Facebook), Adrienne had not broken any rules the industry set when it guaranteed the protection of anonymity.

As more identity-release donors come forward or are found through detective work, the issues of how to respond (and what constitutes breaking rules set by someone else) are likely to become part of the negotiations within the networks. For instance, the parents in the Soul Mates network have agreed that they should not contact the donor through Facebook (but that passive watching is fine). However, it is possible that one or more of the parents could change their minds down the line. It is possible as well that one or more of the kids who do not yet have Facebook pages of their own (shared or individual) will make a different decision and share that information within the network. As much as kids are all supposed to wait their turn until they individually turn eighteen, the network offers a way around this industry "agreement."

Within each network kids have very different stances with regard to whether they want to connect with their donor. At the time we spoke with them, they appeared to respect one another's different opinions rather than trying to convince each other that the entire group should believe or do this or that. For example, in the 7008ers, there were four kids who really wanted to meet the donor and a larger group of kids who really did not care much. But this latter group of kids said they might go along for the ride. The three who clearly did *not* want to meet the donor stuck to their views. If any of the kids could locate their donor, their discovery would be part of the conversation, and it could be hard to resist an available meeting.

* * *

This issue of different attitudes toward, and actions with respect to, donors reminds us that whatever the internal dynamics, the network itself has control neither over its membership (that is determined by the banks) nor over the actions of its individual members. The network is not a family with a conventional "head." Members who dislike the behavior of people in the network—or the people themselves—cannot appeal to a "higher" authority, such as a grandparent. They can form separate alignments within the whole or they can leave the network entirely.

Both parents and children have limited power over the dynamics in the networks they create.

Even so, at different moments in time, participants draw on different conventional models to try to influence network dynamics. The central actors in Michael's Clan effectively redesigned the preexisting, heterosexual model of a father and his children to suit their purposes. The "father" brought genetic relatives together and offered a limited kind of paternal support to his children. Those who did not buy into this model at that time remained peripheral. Among the networks formed with children who were younger and those that now have considerably larger memberships, attempts to use the model of any kind of family had less long-term success. The parents in the network of the youngest children actually talked about codifying norms for interaction in public and at get-togethers; the use of the term "diblings" suggests that they do not want to impose a traditional familial relationship. They have not completed the process of codification, and even if they had, they could only have an influence on people who chose to comply.

Codification might be especially difficult because within this network—as within all the others—neither among the children nor among the parents does everyone want the same things from the network itself. Some of what people want requires minimal interaction; this is even true of basic validation. But other benefits require more engagement; this is the case for the acquisition of social and cultural capital as well as the more profound resource of trust. Indeed, the network itself cannot survive without interaction.

Within all five of the networks we studied, some parents and some children found modes of interaction that embody the values of validation and trust. These values could emerge within a range of types of groups, ranging from families to online communities. When they emerge in donor sibling networks, they do so not because any one model has been created but because something else important has happened within connections that began with a conversation about genes and ended with choice.

Conclusion

Choice in Donor Sibling Networks

WHEN WE TALK with friends and colleagues about these networks of genetic relatives, they often ask whether these new connections heighten the significance of genes, and thereby make genes more important than sociability as the basis for the creation of kin across families. "Well," we say, paradoxically, "yes and no."[1]

Whatever the private intentions of the parents and children who pursue contacts with genetic relatives, the contacts themselves are made available (and even promoted) originally on the presumption that what are merely genetic ties are important because they will lead to expanding ideas about family to include donor siblings. Indeed, they are facilitated by online services that, by their very names, encourage this relationship: the Donor Sibling Registry or what California Cryobank simply calls its "Sibling Registry" and the Sperm Bank of California calls its "Family Contact List." Within these "family" connections, genes might even provide a willingness to open one's heart. As one parent said, she approached the family of her daughter's donor siblings with the orientation that "we're connected so they automatically get my love.... It's theirs to lose."

Over time, as we have seen, among children these shared genetic origins also provide excitement. They become the basis for sharing personal information and exchanging photographs; children take note of their similarities and differences. For their part, the parents experience a sense of instantaneous connection with the parents of children who look much like their own and, of course, at some level, with the children themselves. They start to trust the other parents and to "root" for their families.

In addition, shared genetic origins provide the "elasticity" in these relationships. Both parents and children say that they are willing to keep the network alive in some way even if they don't like particular individuals in the group. They acknowledge that these people are their—or their child's—genetic relatives even when they do not have much to do with each other.

Whatever the internal dynamics of an individual network, the addition of new members is always about a return to ideas about genes. The ongoing need to accommodate new members (and to transform genetic talk into sociability) occurs because the bank, and not the group itself, control the number of offspring; the final number remains unknown by the group. In some broader sense, the continued embrace of new members (even an exhausted embrace) stands in stark contrast to bank policies that derive from a profit motive rather than an interest in intimacy among real people. The two interests—those of an individual trying to create social ties out of shared genes and the commercialization of reproduction—are thus occasionally in direct conflict.

Yet even if the banks determine the number of donor siblings, parents and children are the actors who create intimate bonds. That is, there is no connection among these genetic relatives without volition, without a parent or a child choosing to make the connection happen.[2] These networks are not created through spontaneous combustion, although the bonds formed can seem spontaneous. For adults and older children, meeting online is voluntary. And the possibility of participating in subsequent face-to-face meetings depends heavily on issues like social class, geography, and familiarity with social media. Of course, for the younger children, these choices are made for them. Once they can exercise their own agency, they too will be able to determine what kinds of connections they want and what those connections will mean.

Interpreting Connection

If we could observe the concepts used by parents and children at the first moment they become aware of the possibility of these connections, we would probably find concepts that emphasize biology and therefore represent inevitability. The children are deemed half-siblings; they are thought to be of the same "blood"; they are related because they share genes. But among both children and parents, our evidence suggests, these concepts transmute over time; the stress on genetic ties recedes, to be replaced by an emphasis on the choice that the participation in these groups—and the dynamic affiliations that form within them—actually represents.

Choice and Biogenetic Connections among the Parents

The conceptual shifts among parents have features similar to those that occur among children and distinctive features of their own. Parents sometimes use concepts of kinship, referring to their child's genetic relatives as their children's half-siblings and donor siblings. Parents sometimes become more playful, simultaneously acknowledging biological ties and the necessity for a sperm donor, as they invent terms like "diblings," "halfies," and "sperm siblings" that distinguish between the children they are raising together and the donor siblings. Sometimes they rely on complex language that refers to the biological connection but makes no assumptions about sociability; they refer to the donor siblings as "children who have the same donor." Sometimes they, as do the children themselves, speak through analogies: these relationships are *like* those among cousins or in-laws. Whatever kinship terms they draw on, they suggest that the initial contacts are thrilling *because and only because they revolve around a child's genetic relatives*. However, as we hear the parents explain how they come to feel and what they come to believe, they make clear that these genetic relatives are important because they represent a number of discrete choices that in combination created the opportunity for them to connect with each other: the choice to conceive, the choice of the donor, the choice to be involved with donor siblings, and then—ultimately—the choice to like one another. The network that emerges embodies all of these choices.

In emphasizing the *choice to conceive* as part of what brings network members together, the parents place artifice above that which happens easily and without intervention. Upending the hierarchy of nature over artifice is of special interest because, as we noted in the introduction, donor gametes are usually—albeit not always—purchased in the market. In many ways they represent the ultimate occasion of merging markets and intimacy. As our respondents talk, the "transaction" part of the acquisition is subsumed within intentionality and thus given special status over other kinds of conception. Among the women with whom we spoke, many are choosing to become mothers from the margins (i.e., single women who use sperm donors, the members of same-sex couples); having done so, they find a place in a network in which women dominate, a network in which their route to motherhood is the most acceptable one because it is entirely intentional and avoids mistakes (or "oops" babies).

The usual privileging of heterosexual intercourse as the only method of conception is thus also denied.

Each parent we interviewed could offer an explanation for her or his particular donor choice, drawing on notions of privilege, fit, and likability. Having interviewed within a number of different donor sibling networks, we found that sometimes the donor was chosen for the same reason by several people in the network, and yet sometimes the people within the network had entirely different reasons for choosing that particular donor. Nevertheless, the parents assumed that they would have some commonalities with this random group of parents *because those other parents had also chosen the same donor*. Parents were not *just* drawn to any other people who were intentional; if that were the case, they might have been satisfied to be part of a group formed around being a single mother by choice, using a donor gamete to conceive, or having a same-sex partnership. That is, it was not just intentionality that made the donor sibling network a special community for them.

The parents make one more choice—to be involved with the donor sibling network—a choice they suggest they make not only for themselves but also for their children to create options and possibilities down the line. As noted already, they believe these relationships can benefit their children in a number of different ways, including normalization, insight into the unknown genetic line, and the creation of an extended family for their children. Especially among the parents with the youngest children, offering the *choice* to become involved with donor siblings (even as they took away that choice by making the contact themselves) is an important component of the social advantage with which they are providing their children. They want their children to "grow up in a world in which [they] will have more caring and more love and more compassion" because they are "in community with the diblings." The donor sibling network becomes one more community—this one primarily existing online—of people their children can rely on. The donor number is a passkey to social support. That is, although these networks might create an expanded family structure, they do so on a quite selective basis.

Choice and Biogenetic Connections among the Children

When we ask the children what their donor siblings mean to them, they try to find a way to make sense of biological realities in the context of their own origin stories and daily experience of kinship as something that is both social and especially meaningful. Sometimes kids do say that donor siblings are siblings, as we saw in Michael's Clan and in the original group of 7008ers. However, some kids say that the donor siblings are "related but are not family"; others say the opposite, that the donor siblings are "family but are not related." The two representations mean precisely the same thing: donor siblings share a genetic connection that initially has no given social meaning. As the kids struggle to define these relationships, some seek out other relational terms such as "cousin" or "distant cousin" to acknowledge the biological link without letting donor siblings get too close. They have no conceptual apparatus with which to distinguish the "merely" biological from the social; the understanding of kinship in the United States provides no lexicon. They also have no conceptual apparatus with which to describe the parents of their donor siblings; once again, language fails.

When donor siblings are in contact with each other (whether in person or online), they explore also the concept of friendship. The younger kids struggle to clarify how donor siblings are similar to—and different from—other friends that populate their worlds. What was once thought of as merely a biogenetic tie can become a relationship that incorporates people as unique individuals worthy of love. Some kids start with the premise that the donor is simply "a cell their parents needed." Some of these kids hold fast to the belief that although genes exist (as in biology), they carry little weight in social terms; these kids never imbue either the donor or donor siblinghood with special meaning. Other options exist. Some children dismiss the genetic importance of their donor siblings while embracing the donor. Some do the reverse: they privilege donor siblings as important people in their lives while dismissing the genetic importance of their donor. And, of course, some value both sets of ties. No matter where they start, the children we interviewed remind us that attitudes change over time. Feelings can grow weaker: for instance, those excited about the idea of having donor siblings as young children might be less interested in that possibility as teenagers; they may also discard one donor sibling in favor of another. Bonds among donor siblings can also strengthen over time. Ultimately what matter are likability and finding a basis for connection. Only then can a connection that emerges from shared genes extend well beyond the starting point. The significant relationships emerging from the meetings of donor siblings—whether called family or friendship—are those the kids choose to develop.

In short, the kids we interviewed are selective about donor siblings; they use the concept of "choice" to rationalize and justify that selectivity. Like other relatives—the great-aunt, the first cousins once removed—donor siblings exist in the cosmos, but the kids don't *have to* like them or have anything at all to do with them even if they recognize their (blood/genetic) connection; when the kids do like their donor siblings, they might even be thought of as being better than relatives given through traditional kinship formation. The concept of choice transforms the donor link into something voluntary. Put differently, the involuntariness (the biogenetic connections) disappears (even if it provides the basis for connection, the initial attraction, and perhaps some basis for continued attraction and elasticity). Donor siblings become all about choice.

The Question of Endurance

The question thus emerges of whether the chosen lateral bonds in a donor sibling network can create a lineage in the next generation. This question is especially pertinent given just how large, and random, some of these groups are. One mother addressed this issue, musing about whether these new connections would also become the stuff of conventional kinship once the donor siblings began to have children of their own:

> What's going to happen when [the donor siblings start] reproducing? Because you've got like twenty people on this Facebook page [of donor siblings]. Then, they're going to have another generation that they're all related to. That's a big-ass family. . . . I mean maybe it will be family, but I think family is something that you're in, you grow up in in the legends and traditions and oral histories. What's broken and what's whole and all of that is your family history. I don't know how these relationships [among the donor siblings] are going to fit in with that.

The children wonder about the future too. Take this twelve-year-old girl:

> And when the [donor siblings] grow up and they have kids, they're going to have a quarter of our blood. I thought that was kind of weird because we hardly know all of them and kind of interesting to think about. . . . Who will we be to them?

At bottom, then, as both the adult and the child implied, children will have to decide whether or not to count as relatives the generations their donor siblings create. And indeed, it is the kids we interviewed who will be left—sometimes long after their parents are gone—to ponder and maybe resolve this provocative question.

And so we end on the question of endurance. As active participants in donor sibling networks, parents and children construct individual and group narratives to guide their interactions. The narrative about the importance of shared genes ultimately gains strength by drawing on the powerful notion of choice. For some people—and within some networks—the social interactions that ensue are not sufficient to sustain connection; for others, those interactions provide the basis for what becomes a quite novel, and quite exciting, community. Those in this latter group can move into a world of thinning and shrinking families, secure in the notion that they too, have expanded the realm of useful connections in the present and, perhaps, in the years to come.

Appendix A

Respondent Characteristics

WE DESCRIBE OUR RESPONDENTS in three sections, starting with families (and how they located donor gametes), moving on to children, and then reporting on parents. Parents and children gave the same information about such vital issues as age, gender, and family form. We conducted interviews with the members of 152 different families; this sample includes 154 children and 212 parents.

Families with Donor-Conceived Children

Families Locate Gametes through Local and National Banks and Clinics

Our respondents are not limited to any one sperm bank or any one registry used to find donor siblings. Most of those who purchased sperm went to one of seven well-known banks: California Cryobank, Cryos International, Fairfax Cryobank, New England Cryogenic Center, Xytex Sperm Bank, Pacific Reproductive Services, and the Sperm Bank of California. Among our Minnesota respondents, Cryogenic Laboratories in Roseville, Minnesota, was a common choice; that bank is now listed as a "sister bank" of Fairfax Cryobank in Virginia. A few respondents followed the recommendation of their physician to use a smaller local bank affiliated with a particular university or clinic. Two families used the Known Donor Registry for free sperm. Regardless of the bank used, our respondents who wanted to find donor siblings were able to do so (with the exception of one family who used a small bank and is still searching for donor siblings).

The smaller number of respondents (13 percent of the total number of families) who conceived with the use of an egg donor or embryo relied on a wider range of clinics for those gametes. When respondents used *both* an egg donor and a sperm donor, they could select the sperm donor from any bank. These respondents were also able to connect with sperm donor siblings when they chose to do so. Those respondents who used only an anonymous egg donor have not made contact with egg donor siblings.

Fourteen families conceived with a known donor (e.g., a family friend, a relative, someone who they met through an advertisement). If the donor has children, the parents and children we interviewed know these children. Since the donor is raising these children, the children have different experiences than do the donor siblings in this study. Our respondents with this kind of known donor report that the donor only gave sperm or eggs to their family, so there are no donor siblings.

Type of Sperm Donors and Type of Gametes Used in Families

We show in table A.1 the frequency with which our respondents chose each kind of sperm donor. As we explained in the introduction, we interviewed in California, which is the home to two smaller banks that were established partly to serve the lesbian community and offered identity-release donors long before other banks were doing so. As a result, we have an unusual number of such donors among the children over nineteen years old (32 percent) and a smaller number of such donors among children between the ages of thirteen and nineteen (25 percent). However, the rates of identity-release donors are higher among children between the ages of six and thirteen (38 percent) and higher still (55 percent) among the parents with the youngest children (five or under).

The data in table A.1 reflect only the sperm donor used for the oldest child. Some families used more than one type of donor (i.e., anonymous, identity release, or known) if they had more than one child. Some families used more than one type of gamete (i.e., sperm alone, sperm and egg, egg alone, embryo) if they had more than one child.

TABLE A.1 Age of Oldest Child and Type of Sperm Donor Used in Families

Type of sperm donor used in families*	Age of oldest child				
	0 to 5	6 to 12	13 to 18	19 or older	All respondents
Unknown but identity release	55%	38%	25%	32%	36%
Known	16%	10%	0%	11%	8%
Unknown will remain anonymous	29%	52%	75%	57%	56%
Total	100%	100%	100%	100%	100%
N	31	29	52	28	140

*In nine families the oldest child was conceived using only a donated egg and not do-nated sperm; data about type of sperm is missing for three families.

Family Composition

In table A.2 we show family composition at the time the oldest donor-conceived child was born and at the time of the interview. In both time periods the majority of families were headed by a single mother.

TABLE A.2 Family Composition

Family	At time child was born		At time of interview	
	Number of families	Percentage of families	Number of families	Percentage of families
Single mother	79	52	88	58
Opposite-sex couple	25	16	30	20
Same-sex couple	48	32	34	23
Total	152	100	152	101*

*Total rounded up.

In ten of the thirty-four same-sex families (as constructed at the time of the interview) each of the two parents carried a child. In thirty-four of the families (out of a total of sixty-four coupled families) there had been a partner change; that is, slightly over half of the families (53 percent) had changed partners between the time when the oldest child was born and the time of the interview.

Racial Composition of Couples and Single Mothers

In all but six couples, both parents were white. In two couples, both parents were African American; in three couples, one parent was white and one was Hispanic. In addition, in two couples an original partner, who was deceased at the time of the interview, was Latina. The sample also included single mothers of African American, Indian, Persian, and Caribbean backgrounds.

Number of Children in Families

In 57 percent of the families, the parent(s) had only one child (table A.3). Two children were next most common. Only 5 percent of the families had three or more children.

TABLE A.3 Number of Children in Family

Number of children in family	Number of families	Percentage of families
1	86	57
2	59	39
3	4	3
4 or more	3	2
Total	152	101*

*Total rounded up.

Age of Children

The oldest children (i.e., the first child in the family) ranged in age from less than one to twenty-eight (table A.4). (By contrast, in table A.9 we include only those children we interviewed, none of whom were under the age of ten.)

TABLE A.4 Age of Oldest Child in Family

Age of oldest child in family	Number of families	Percentage of families
Under 5	28	18
5 to 9	16	11
10 to 14	45	30
15 to 19	42	28
20 or older	21	14
Total	152	101*

*Total rounded up.

Income

Because we were able to draw on networks to identify respondents, our sample is somewhat more diverse than the upper-middle-class respondents who typically populate research on donor conception. As we show in table A.5, among the families for whom we have data, 15 percent had family incomes of less than $50,000; 36 percent had family incomes between $50,000 and $100,000; 40 percent had family incomes between $100,000 and $200,000; and 9 percent had family incomes of $200,000 or more. We note that the same family income has a different meaning for families with one parent than for families with two parents and for families with only one child than for larger families. We note also that how far a household income can stretch will depend on the cost of living in any given geographic area.

TABLE A.5 Family Income

Family income*	Number of families	Percentage of families
Less than $50,000	22	15
$50,000–$99,999	53	36
$100,000–$199,999	58	40
$200,000 or more	13	9
Total	146	100

*Data is missing for six families.

Family income varied with family form: the single mothers had lower incomes than the two-parent couples (table A.6).

TABLE A.6 Family Income by Family Form

Family income*	Family form			
	Opposite-sex couples	Two mothers	Single mother	All families
Below $100,000	22%	26%	56%	43%
$100,000 or above	78%	74%	44%	57%
Total	100%	100%	100%	100%
N	18	43	85	146

*Data is missing for six families.

Type of Community

Almost two-fifths of the respondents said they lived in a city, and over half said they lived in a suburban area (table A.7). Very few came from small towns or rural areas. Eighty-six percent of the families owned their home rather than renting.

TABLE A.7 Type of Community in Which Family Lives

Type of community	Number of families	Percentage of families
Suburban area	83	55
City	59	39
Small town / rural area	10	7
Total	152	101*

*Total rounded up.

Donor-Conceived Children

The 154 children we interviewed lived in 115 different families. (The other 37 families did not have children we could interview.) Among the children are three sets of triplets and eight sets of twins. The data presented in tables A.8 through A.9 are reported by the children.

Children's Family Form

At the time when they were born, about two-fifths of the children we interviewed had a single mother, and almost half had two mothers (table A.8). Only 16 percent of the children had two opposite-sex parents.

TABLE A.8 Children's Family Form at Birth and at Time of Interview

Family form	At time of child's birth		At time of interview	
	Number of children	Percentage of children	Number of children	Percentage of children
Single mother	59	38	60	39
Two same-sex parents	71	46	49	32
Two opposite-sex parents	24	16	16	10
Same-sex parents separated			19	12
Opposite-sex parents separated			10	6
Total	154	100	154	99*

*Total rounded down.

At the time of the interview, about the same proportion of children were living with a single mother, but fewer were living with two parents.

TABLE A.9 Children's Age

Children's age	Number of children	Percentage of children
10 to 12	45	29
13 to 18	72	47
19 to 22	22	14
23 or older	14	9
Total	154	99*

*Total rounded down.

Age of Children at the Time of Interview

The median age of the children was fifteen; the mode was twelve. A quarter of the children were nineteen or older (table A.9).

Race of Children

Ninety-six percent of the children said that they were white/Caucasian; five of the remaining children gave some mixed race (e.g., black and white); one respondent identified as "Persian," and one was not sure.

Parents

Among the parents we interviewed were 195 women and 17 men.

Self-Reported Sexual Identity

Among the women we interviewed, equal proportions (47 percent) reported being heterosexual and lesbian (table A.10). Two women reported

TABLE A.10 Self-Reported Sexual Identity of Women

Sexual identity	Number of women	Percentage of women
Lesbian	91	47
Heterosexual	90	46
Bisexual	2	1
Other / no answer	12	6
Total	195	100

being bisexual, and ten women either gave some other answer or did not give an answer at all. All of the men we interviewed identified as heterosexual, and all of them were living in a relationship with a woman.

Religion of Parents

Among the parents we interviewed, 65 percent said that they were Christian, 25 percent Jewish, and 2 percent some other religious affiliation; 8 percent said they had no religious affiliation.

Education of Parents

The respondents were well educated; the majority of the sample (72 percent) had some education above a bachelor's (table A.11).

TABLE A.11 Highest Level of Education Achieved among Parents

Highest level of education*	Number of parents	Percentage of parents
High school or some college	17	8
BA or BS	55	26
MA or MS	96	46
JD, MD, PhD	42	20
Total	210	100

*Data is missing for 2 parents.

Employment of Parents

Most of the respondents were working full time when we interviewed them (table A.12). A few were either unemployed, retired, or on disability.

TABLE A.12 Employment Status of Parents

Employment status*	Number of parents	Percentage of parents
Employed full time	172	84
Employed less than full time	20	10
Retired	6	3
Unemployed / between jobs	5	2
On disability	2	1
Total	205	100

*Data is missing for 7 parents.

Appendix B

Interviews, Virtual Ethnography, and Language in the Book

WE BRIEFLY DISCUSSED our research methods for locating respondents in the book's introduction. Here we describe our two strategies for data collection—interviews and virtual ethnography—in more detail. We include in this discussion specific information about how we conducted our interviews and the strategies we used when interviewing parents and children in the same families and parents and families within the same networks. We then turn to a discussion of the decisions we made about what language to use in the book.

Interviews in Person and through Skype or Facetime

Altogether we conducted interviews with families in twenty-six states and two countries outside of the United States (totals are 212 parents and 154 children). We interviewed the majority of our respondents in person, and we always interviewed parents and children separately. The largest number of interviews were conducted within the states where we selected major metropolitan areas as our research sites: Massachusetts (36 families); California (29 families); Texas (18 families); Minnesota (10 families); the DC area, including Maryland and Virginia (24 families); and Illinois (4 families). (Kids who were in college or on their own after high school are listed under their parents' residences even though they might have been interviewed elsewhere.) We interviewed 12 donors related to the children in our research. They lived in an even wider range of states.

We reserved Skype interviews for the members of families who were part of a network in a state to which we were not traveling. We also used Skype when a member of one of these families—child or parent—was living away from home when we were in their state (e.g., parent was interviewed in her home state and the child was interviewed by Skype at college or the child was in college in the Boston area and we Skyped with the parent in Missouri). In addition, we used Skype to interview some parents in extremely hard-to-find categories of respondents who only make a brief appearance in this book (e.g., single mothers who conceived with both a sperm and an egg donor). We conducted Skype interviews with all the members of families in the following states: Arkansas, Arizona, Colorado, Connecticut, Florida, Georgia, Iowa, Kansas, Missouri, New York, New Jersey, Nevada, Ohio, Oregon, Pennsylvania, South Carolina, and Tennessee (and also with a few additional families in Texas, Illinois, and California whose networks connected us after we visited those research sites). Without Skype (or Facetime), technology that we have used for over a decade to talk frequently with our own friends and family, this research would not have been possible.

Hertz and Nelson conducted all of the in-person interviews with parents, either separately or as a team. If they were Skyped, Hertz conducted them (fifty-three interviews). Research assistants traveled with us to destination research sites to interview in person. Research assistants who were highly trained carried out in-person interviews with 105 kids. Hertz and/or a research assistant conducted thirty-nine Skype interviews with kids.

There is no difference for this kind of research between interviews conducted in person and those through Skype. Both sets of interviews are the same quality and the same length—between one hour and two hours; they were also coded identically. The interviews conducted by Skype were usually with respondents who were situated in a network or a familial context.

We were lucky to also receive Research Experiences for Undergraduates (REU) funds as part of the National Science Foundation grant that supported our research; these funds enabled us to hire and train the four research assistants—Jordan Parker, Chelsea Jerome, Jacqueline McGrath, and Rebecca Schwarz—who interviewed with us. We trained the research assistants in stages. They first listened to interviews we (or another, more experienced research assistant) conducted; they then conducted interviews with us. Gradually we faded into the background and simply observed them while they conducted an interview. Once they felt competent to conduct an interview on their own—and we agreed with their assessment—we allowed them to do so. At every stage we discussed each interview (as well as the field notes they wrote up after the interview), sharing ideas for improvement. As a team we also discussed all the interviews that had been conducted with the members of a given family, comparing notes about what we had learned and reading each other's field notes. Our research assistants eagerly participated in these conversations.

Virtual Ethnographic Fieldwork

In addition to interviewing respondents, we gathered data through "virtual" ethnography.[1] We joined several closed forums for Single Mothers by Choice members; groups for offspring, siblings, and parents; as well as sites for donors or those searching for embryos, eggs, or sperm (such as the Known Donor Registry). Members posted requests to participate in this research through their Facebook network after noting which area we would be traveling to and our timetable. During our visits, parents showed us their Facebook page, scrolling through the photos of their child's donor siblings and recent posts referenced in the interview. Their children also liked to show us their donor siblings, often from photos on their cell phones. Sometimes the Facebook page would become part of the interview, and other times it capped off the visit. We asked to join two Facebook groups to learn what members posted online and also to learn how the group might have changed from when we interviewed members (e.g., families getting together in person, discussion of developmental milestones). (All the members had to approve our joining, and we agreed not to download pictures.) We did not participate in the discussions or even "like" the posts. Other respondents "friended" us on Facebook and we accepted.[2] However, to ensure that all of our respondents had a chance to give us updates on their lives, we sent each family a separate New Year's email greeting about our progress and where we would be traveling next. We invited everyone to tell us what was going on in his or her life. We heard back from our interviewees with notes that sometimes included milestone events. The information we learned through monitoring these sites enriched the narratives and our analysis.

Conducting the Interviews

Our study is the first effort to interview both parents and children separately in the same family. The two sets of interviews give us an opportunity to *compare* experiences. They also give us the chance to shed light on critical processes like choosing a donor among parents and the formation of identity among children with an unknown donor.

We created two separate but parallel interview guides: one for parents and one for children. We asked both parents and children questions about their communities and family life in order to gather information about geographic context, family form, extended family members, and support systems. We asked both to discuss donor conception; we also asked them both to discuss the traits and characteristics kids and parents thought they held in common and what they thought came from the donor. We also asked both parents and children about the possibility of connecting with donor siblings and about issues that arose through the existing connections (e.g., kinds of connections, forms of communication, a parent's involvement with other parents and their children, a kid's involvement with other kids and their parents). And, where relevant, we asked both parents and children about connecting with the donor. We also asked separate questions of parents and children. We asked the parents additional questions about going to the banks or clinics and selecting donors. We asked children to tell us the stories their parents told them about their births and to talk about whether (and what) they told other people (e.g., friends and other family members) about donor conception.

When possible, we conducted the separate interviews with parents and their donor-conceived children in their homes and at the same time (i.e., we had separate interviews going on simultaneously in a home). If there were two parents in the family, they were also usually interviewed separately (and this was the case when parents were divorced or uncoupled). Those kids in college or living on their own were usually interviewed at a separate time.

In addition, we interviewed twelve donors who were connected to some of the families we interviewed. We created a separate interview guide for the donors that paralleled the interview guides for parents and children. Interviews for the donors also included specific questions related to becoming a donor as well their experiences with their donor offspring.

Complexities of Interviewing Children

When we began to interview children we tried to make the questions parallel to, and in the same order as, those we were asking of their parents. This strategy made some sense because we were trying to obtain information about the same issues from all members of a family. However, this strategy resulted in questions that, quite simply, did not work for our younger respondents. Instead, we developed a strategy that put kids at greater ease and brought about far better interviews. This new strategy involved two major changes. First, we opened the kids' interviews by emphasizing that it was fine to say "I don't know" or not answer a question. We also explicitly explained that not only were their answers anonymous and confidential but also that confidentiality extended to their parents. We demonstrated our commitment to this promise by spending no time during our visit talking privately with the parents after the children had been interviewed. Second, we revised the order of the questions and their phrasing with input from Jordan Parker, an undergraduate research assistant who then tested these questions and how they worked with youth. The revised interview format, which was developed after we piloted interviews with kids, involved opening with icebreakers (e.g., questions about hobbies and interests). The revised interview format involved also designing questions differently for different age groups and using age-appropriate language.

In the presence of their children, parents provided written consent for their children to participate in the research. Then children also signed the consent forms. The children in this study were excited to participate and almost none had ever signed a consent form before. The younger kids liked this grownup act of giving us permission to talk to them without their parents. Although, as noted, we made it clear that all communications with us were private, we also indicated that if family members wanted to talk together about the interview after we left, they could do this.

Parents were very helpful in introducing us to their kids. With the exception of one parent, all had checked with their kids (as young as ten) to make sure they wanted to be interviewed before they accepted our invitation. The majority of email invitations asking for interviews were sent to parents. Among the high school kids, parents often asked us to send a separate email or text message to their kid asking if the child would like to participate. No kids turned us down. Moreover, kids were extremely helpful in connecting us with members of their networks. Kids in some of the networks we featured contacted us asking to participate after they heard about the research from their donor siblings. They also then asked their parents to participate. In short, kids were active participants in agreeing to be interviewed and in helping us connect with members in their networks (including their donor siblings and in a few cases their donors.)

We interviewed children in a private space in their homes—setting the context for the fact that this was their interview and that it was confidential. We usually arrived for an interview as a group; we immediately let all the family members know who would be interviewing each person. We often overheard our research assistants establishing rapport in those first moments by starting a conversation with the kids they were going to interview. This preinterview conversation by our research assistants demonstrated their interest in knowing about the kids' ideas and opinions— what they thought and what was on their mind. For instance, they asked about recent activities. The research assistants were trained to understand that they had to communicate very quickly that the interview provided an opportunity for the young person to express herself.

We assessed levels of development among the younger kids early in the interview. As Chelsea Jerome, one of our undergraduate research assistants, noted, age alone does not always predict how a respondent will react. For example, one ten-year-old might interpret questions more like a typical thirteen-year-old and vice versa. Chelsea learned that how kids described their relationship with a parent (a question she asked early) could help her predict how complex a child's understanding was and how to design subsequent questions. Younger children, and those who were less sophisticated, often went directly to talking about similar interests, while older kids considered personality aspects first. When talking about relationships, younger kids often needed probing for similarities and differences. If coming up with answers became difficult, sometimes children needed a probe such as, "Are there things your mom likes that you don't?" However, older kids understood the question easily and did not need the same kind of probing.

We noted that the younger respondents enjoyed having someone who, like an older cousin or family friend, paid attention to them and took them seriously. High school kids saw our team as people who carried information about colleges; this became a major conversation after the interview. College kids liked the attention of faculty members or their college-age peers; they knew they were helping with research by sharing their stories.

Interviewing Adults

The authors conducted all of the interviews with parents. Initially we conducted these interviews with each individual parent separately whether they lived in one- or two-parent families. However, when we began to analyze the separate interviews with each member of a couple, we found they often contained similar accounts. We decided when we traveled to the last two sites (Minnesota and Texas) that we would interview together in both one-parent and two-parent families (and, in the latter case, with both parents at the same time); we chose the same strategy for several interviews in Boston with younger couples whose children were under ten years.[3]

Interviews among Network Members

When we interviewed families within a network, we (and our research assistants) were careful not to discuss interviews we had already conducted with other members of their network. We wanted each respondent to tell her own story of connecting with other donor-linked families. We also never initiated a conversation about any other families in their network. However, everyone brought up other members. We followed up with appropriate probes, letting respondents tell their own story without revealing the parts we had heard from others in their network.

Data Analysis

Qualified transcribers transcribed all the interviews. With a team of research assistants we coded the interviews using the software program HyperResearch. We started coding the data while we were still interviewing; doing so allowed us to create new questions. We coded the data using both descriptive and analytical codes that allowed us to generate reports using multiple variables. We worked extensively to train our coders. To ensure intercoder reliability, the majority of interviews were coded by two different research assistants. We discussed areas of disagreement as a team; our coders then recoded the conflicting items. We generated reports through HyperResearch that enabled us to analyze this large data set.

The Language We Use in the Book

One of the hardest parts of writing about these issues is finding appropriate language to describe the various actors who participate in donor conception. This quest is particularly difficult because some of that language already exists. Those who provide reproductive gametes are called donors even though in the United States sperm bank donors are not "donating" at all but rather are selling a product. Furthermore, although the word "donor" implies generosity toward intended recipients, sperm donors neither know who buys those gametes nor how much they pay.

Even more significantly, "donor sibling" is the term of art these days. However, donor sibling accurately describes only the biological closeness between children born from the same gametes; yet, the phrase itself also implies a social relationship that might not be present. A more appropriate language that makes no assumptions about relationships is also more complex. We could refer to a set of donor siblings as all "the individuals who were conceived from the same donor." The parents of these children then become "the group of individuals who used the same donor to conceive a child." Linguistic purity, it seems, would drive us (and our readers) crazy. And so we let the term "donor siblings" (and by extension the parents of a child's donor siblings) into our lexicon. We want to acknowledge, however, that we do so uneasily not only because some parents and some children object to this language but also because, as this study shows, the relationships among "donor siblings" assume so many different forms. "Genetic strangers" is a way of subsuming both the donor and the donor siblings as those people beyond the web of the immediate family who share one's genes (or one's child's genes) but do not have any recognizable kin tie.

One more note about language: whenever possible we use the language our respondents use. We decided to take our lead from the children in our research. Whether or not children know about the legal relations between their parents, children know who their parents are, and they know when their parents have split up. Children in a home with two parents do not distinguish between parents who are married and those who are not. Neither do we unless the parents themselves use the language of wife or husband or spouse; we note that neither marriage nor the language of marriage was available to all the respondents in this study at the time they conceived their children.[4] Children refer to their relationship with their parents as having "a mom," "two moms," or a "mom and a dad." Children, especially young children, do not identify their parents as heterosexual or lesbian. Children also rarely report the sexual identity of a single mother; therefore we do not make note of her sexual identity either unless she makes a point of it in her discussion with us. We do, however, talk about family form, and with that we imply the reported sexual identity in families with two parents—that is, those who live in a mom-and-dad family or in a two-mom family. With one exception, all of the adult respondents are cisgender. Similarly, we only identify the kids with their sexual identity when it is relevant.

We turn from using the "talk" of children when it comes to matters of the genetic parent or the gestational parent. This is particularly complicated, and when it is relevant we do let the reader know its relevance. To explain further: Among the two parent families there is usually one parent who has a genetic link. In two-mom families it is usually one of the two mothers, and in heterosexual families who used a sperm donor to conceive, this person is the mom. However, among a smaller group of parents in this study—whether a single mom, two moms, or a mom and a dad—there is no genetic link, but a mom did carry and give birth to the child. And among the two-mom families, sometimes each parent gave birth to a child who is genetically linked to a sibling through use of the same donor. We let the reader know when parents and children brought up these distinctions and when they are relevant to donor-linked families. When this issue is not relevant to the discussion, we simply refer to mothers as mothers and fathers as fathers.[5]

NOTES

Introduction

1. See Part II for illustrations that are renditions of this and other networks. Spencer and his mother Margo are featured in chapter 8, "Connected Soul Mates." Jennifer, Leslie, and Callie are part of chapter 9, "Social Capitalists." Scott, Abigail, and Don appear in chapter 6, "The 7008 Builders."
2. See the discussion in appendix B for the use of the term "donor siblings" and other language used in this analysis.
3. Curiously enough, no one keeps track of how many babies are born through the use of donated sperm. Various agencies do keep track of the number of babies born as a result of IVF and related technologies. That number has now reached an estimated 6.5 million worldwide. This estimate includes all babies created with IVF or related technologies regardless of whether or not donor gametes were used. See ESHRE, "6.5 Million IVF Babies since Louise Brown," *Focus on Reproduction, the Blog of ESHRE's Magazine*, July 5, 2016. Leena Nahata, Nathanael Stanley, and Gwendolyn Quinn ("Gamete Donation: Current Practices, Public Opinion, and Unanswered Questions," *Fertility and Sterility* 107, no. 6 [2017]: 1298) acknowledge that any numbers are "merely estimates and are likely to be poor estimates because there are few tracking systems." Evidence suggests that in the last thirty years, there has been an increase in the demand for sperm donors in the United States, and there is a large unmet demand in parts of the European Union and the United Kingdom. See Glenn Cohen, Travis Coan, Michelle Ottey, and Christina Boyd, "Sperm Donor Anonymity and Compensation: An

Experiment with American Sperm Donors," *Journal of Law and the Biosciences* 3, no. 3 (December 1, 2016): 468–88.

4. New techniques of IVF and intracytoplasmic sperm injection (ICSI) have reduced the need for heterosexual couples to turn to sperm donation. ICSI has a high rate of fertilization (75–85 percent of injected eggs). Since this procedure is more expensive than purchasing sperm, the use of these procedures is often associated with middle-class families or families located in states with fertility coverage. See Naomi R. Cahn, *The New Kinship: Constructing Donor-Conceived Families* (New York: New York University Press, 2013). The members of heterosexual couples in this study report that either this procedure was not available at the time the couple was trying to conceive or that, among the younger heterosexual couples, the male partner did not qualify for ICSI.

5. For discussions of changing clientele at sperm banks, see Laura Mamo and Eli Alston-Stepnitz, "Queer Intimacies and Structural Inequalities: New Directions in Stratified Reproduction," *Journal of Family Issues* 36, no. 4 (March 1, 2015): 519–40; for estimates that today 50 percent of the US recipients are single women and 33 percent are same-sex or transgender couples, see Nahata, Stanley, and Quinn, "Gamete Donation," 1298–99.

6. Norms surrounding disclosure have changed within the industry. Whereas people who received donor gametes were previously told to conceal that fact, in both the United States and the United Kingdom, disclosure to young children is now the "recommendation." Without disclosure there could be no contact between donors and offspring and no donor sibling networks. On these issues see Diane Ehrensaft, *Mommies, Daddies, Donors, Surrogates: Answering Tough Questions and Building Strong Families* (New York: Guilford Press, 2005); Tabitha Freeman and Susan Golombok, "Donor Insemination: A Follow-Up Study of Disclosure Decisions, Family Relationships and Child Adjustment at Adolescence," *Reproductive BioMedicine Online* 25, no. 2 (2012): 193–203; Susan Golombok, "Families Created by Reproductive Donation: Issues and Research," *Child Development Perspectives* 7, no. 1 (2013): 61–65; Susan Golombok, "Disclosure and Donor-Conceived Children," *Human Reproduction* 32, no. 7 (July 1, 2017): 1532–36; Susan Golombok et al., "Children Conceived by Gamete Donation: Psychological Adjustment and Mother-Child Relationships at Age 7," *Journal of Family Psychology* 25, no. 2 (2011): 230; Vasanti Jadva et al., "The Experiences of Adolescents and Adults Conceived by Sperm Donation: Comparisons by Age of Disclosure and Family Type," *Human Reproduction* 24 (2009): 1909–19; Sophie Zadeh, "Disclosure of Donor Conception in the Era of Non-anonymity: Safeguarding and Promoting the Interests of Donor-Conceived Individuals?," *Human Reproduction* 31, no. 11 (November 1, 2016): 2416–20.

7. For a discussion of the term "reunion," see chapter 6.

8. We have called the network members "genetic strangers." And before any form of interaction, they *are* strangers to one another. While a stranger can always be introduced to the members of a group (or community), the meaning of a stranger has changed over time. A stranger is now both more familiar and less threatening. A stranger is no longer a whole person who was an outsider to the village and therefore usually suspect. On these issues, see Georg Simmel, *The Sociology of Georg Simmel*, ed. Kurt Wolff (Glencoe, IL: Free Press, 1950); Anthony Giddens, *The Consequences of Modernity* (Palo Alto, CA: Stanford University Press, 1990). The members of donor sibling networks are modern strangers in a modern world, a world in which we often interact with people we do not know well and may never have met. The internet thus extends our acceptance of strangers who we believe can provide us with a sense of belonging, advice, and perhaps even intimacy. In the case of people relying on, or born by means of, sperm bank-donated gametes, some kinds of strangers might create special unease because they have in common something intensely intimate. Even so, donor siblings may also help parents and children counter the "strangeness" of the unknown donor.

9. No one with whom we spoke actually did DNA testing to find out if the other individuals who reported conception with the same donor number were actually genetic relatives. For a discussion, drawing on a UK sample, of searches conducted with the aid of DNA, see Marilyn Crawshaw, "Voluntary DNA-Based Information Exchange and Contact Services Following Donor Conception: An Analysis of Service Users' Needs," *New Genetics and Society* 35, no. 4 (October 2016): 372–92.

10. As sociologists, we know well that the normative obligations of kinship vary widely from social group to social group, as those groups are defined by class, gender, race, ethnicity, sexual identity, and immigration status. We also know well that those expectations are not always fulfilled: people desert, abandon, and otherwise turn their back on family members all the time; people choose selectively among their relatives when issuing wedding invitations or answering a summons to a Thanksgiving celebration. Indeed, we cannot and do not make any claims for the way people "usually" act in families—whether we are talking about what is sometimes called the "nuclear" or immediate family or the "extended" family structure.

11. An interest in genes occurs periodically in US history. The beginning of the twentieth century was a time when many people believed that genes alone determined individual outcomes; the beginning of the twenty-first century appears to be another such time. On these issues see Siddhartha Mukherjee, *The Gene: An Intimate History* (New York: Simon and Schuster, 2017).

12. 23andMe, "Our Health + Ancestry DNA Service—23andMe," 2017, https://www.23andme.com; AncestryDNA.com, "AncestryDNA US |

DNA Tests for Ethnicity & Genealogy DNA Test," 2017, https://www. ancestry.com/dna/.

13. D. O. Braithwaite et al., "Constructing Family: A Typology of Voluntary Kin," *Journal of Social and Personal Relationships* 27, no. 3 (April 22, 2010): 388–407; Margaret K. Nelson, "Fictive Kin," in *Encyclopedia of Family Studies*, ed. Constance L. Shehan (Hoboken, NJ: John Wiley and Sons, 2016), 1–3; Carol Stack, *All Our Kin: Strategies for Survival in a Black Community* (New York: Harper and Row, 1974); Jeffrey Weeks, Catherine Donovan, and Brian Heaphy, *Same Sex Intimacies: Families of Choice and Other Life-Experiments* (London: Routledge, 2001); Kath Weston, *Families We Choose: Lesbians, Gays, Kinship* (New York: Columbia University Press, 1991).

14. Known donors sometimes become more involved in the family and may also be involved in childrearing. See Martha M. Ertman, *Love's Promises: How Formal and Informal Contracts Shape All Kinds of Families* (Boston: Beacon Press, 2015).

15. See Rosanna Hertz, *Single by Chance, Mothers by Choice* (New York: Oxford University Press, 2006). Those single mothers who are lesbian and later find a same-sex partner become similar to two-mother families. The difference is that the new partner did not participate in donor selection. These complexities are beyond the scope of this book.

16. When couples split up (or legally divorce), the original parents still remain, and even if there are stepparents, the original equation of biological and social parenthood is retained. In effect the "links" between the two original parents determine the children's movement between households.

17. Now that problems of freezing and shipping sperm have been solved, people wanting to purchase sperm no longer need to go to a local bank but can order from anyplace where they find an attractive donor profile. FedEx or UPS will deliver. Indeed, in the United States, frozen sperm has become a major industry. See Deborah L. Spar, *The Baby Business: How Money, Science, and Politics Drive the Commerce of Conception* (Cambridge, MA: Harvard Business Review Press, 2006).

18. Frank F. Furstenberg Jr. discussed the distinction between "daddies" and "fathers" among the African American families he studied. See "Fathering in the Inner City: Paternal Participation and Public Policy," in *Fatherhood: Contemporary Theory, Research and Social Policy*, ed. William Marsiglio (Thousand Oaks, CA: Sage, 1995), 119–47. Carol Stack also observed the same distinction. See *All Our Kin*. Among these families (and also Native American families) caregiving, not biology, determines the child's "daddy."

19. See, for example, Linda M. Burton and Cecily R. Hardaway, "Low-Income Mothers as 'Othermothers' to Their Romantic Partners' Children: Women's Coparenting in Multiple Partner Fertility Relationships," *Family Process* 51, no. 3 (2012): 343–59; Kathryn Edin and Maria Kefalas, *Promises*

I Can Keep: Why Poor Women Put Motherhood before Marriage
(Berkeley: University of California Press, 2005).

20. Andrew Cherlin, "Remarriage as an Incomplete Institution," *American Journal of Sociology* 84, no. 3 (1978): 634–50.

21. Along with other changes, attitudes toward gamete use have changed dramatically in the past several decades. Something that was felt to be shameful and kept secret is now something that is openly discussed. Today *disclosure* about sperm donation to young children is almost universally the recommendation, at least for heterosexual couples and single mothers. For same-sex couples, of course, disclosure is more or less inevitable, whether it is a recommendation or not. This shift is also significant for our discussion because without disclosure there could be no contact across the separate families of donor siblings. And it is the interest in, and desire for, that contact that drives network formation. Within the world of adoption a similarly new interest in openness prevails. As a result, in that world as well, opportunities for contact now exist among people tied by genes alone. On this history, see Christine Jones, "Openness in Adoption: Challenging the Narrative of Historical Progress," *Child & Family Social Work* 21, no. 1 (February 1, 2016): 85–93; Samuel L. Perry, "Adoption in the United States: A Critical Synthesis of Literature and Directions for Sociological Research."

22. Of course, people do the same comparisons with other relatives (including siblings). The search for similarities and differences is not unique to donor siblings or people involved in adoption.

23. We note several further differences between the two practices. First is the simple fact that in the United States, eggs, sperm, and entire embryos are sold on an open market and a market decides a price for those products. The same is not the case for babies in the United States today. Second, children placed for adoption are not "body parts" but fully human people, whereas donor conception involves the transfer of individual gametes (or, at most, an embryo). Third, unlike birth parents, donors do not "place a child" for adoption; in fact donors do not know what (if anything) becomes of their donations. We note also that some embryos are not sold but given up for what is called "adoption." But this is still a different practice from placing a living child with another family.

24. Indeed, these may be more important comparisons than those made to friends and peers, both because the comparisons with siblings are "deeply embedded in family politics" (Katherine Davies, "Siblings, Stories and the Self: The Sociological Significance of Young People's Sibling Relationships," *Sociology* 49, no. 4 [2015]: 679–95) and because they are perpetuated by others (including, for example, teachers). Moreover, siblings can be important because of sheer longevity: siblings are among one's longest-lasting relationship, typically outlasting those of parents.

Sibling research is dominated by psychologists interested in theories of personality development. Among psychologists, Frank J. Sulloway looks at how siblings raised together are remarkably different (*Born to Rebel: Birth Order, Family Dynamics, and Creative Lives* [New York: Pantheon Books, 1996]). Various family dynamic factors, not simply birth order, affect personality. *Sociological* research on siblinghood is scant. For exceptions see Rosalind Edwards, Melanie Mauthner, and Lucy Hadfield, "Children's Sibling Relationships and Gendered Practices: Talk, Activity and Dealing with Change," *Gender and Education* 17, no. 5 (2005): 499–513; Melanie Mauthner, "Distant Lives, Still Voices: Sistering in Family Sociology," *Sociology* 39, no. 4 (2005): 623–42; Ian McIntosh and Samantha Punch, "'Barter,' 'Deals,' 'Bribes' and 'Threats': Exploring Sibling Interactions," *Childhood* 16, no. 1 (February 2009): 49–65; Janet Carsten, "The Substance of Kinship and the Heat of the Hearth: Feeding, Personhood, and Relatedness among Malays in Pulau Langkawi," *American Ethnologist* 22, no. 2 (1995): 223–41. For a review of sibling relationships in childhood and adolescence, see Susan M. McHale, Kimberly A. Updegraff, and Shawn D. Whiteman, "Sibling Relationships and Influences in Childhood and Adolescence," *Journal of Marriage and Family* 74, no. 5 (2012): 913–30. Among sociological theorists in the symbolic interactionist tradition, the emphasis has been on the role of parents in intergeneration transmission of identity. See, for example, Charles Horton Cooley, *Human Nature and the Social Order* (1902; New Brunswick, NJ: Transaction Books, 1983); George Herbert Mead, *Mind, Self and Society* (Chicago: University of Chicago Press, 1934), and later Herbert Blumer, *Symbolic Interactionism: Perspective and Method* (Berkeley: University of California Press, 1986) and Anselm L. Strauss, *Mirrors and Masks: The Search for Identity* (New Brunswick, NJ: Transaction Books, 1997).

25. For examples see Antti O. Tanskanen, Liviana Zanchettin, Giorgio Gronchi, and Valentina Morsan, "Sibling Conflicts in Full- and Half-Sibling Households in the UK," *Journal of Biosocial Science* 49, no. 1 (January 2017): 31–47, https://doi.org/10.1017/S0021932016000043; Kirby Deater-Deckard and Judy Dunn, "Sibling Relationships and Social-Emotional Adjustment in Different Family Contexts," *Social Development* 11, no. 4 (2002): 571–90; Susan J. T. Branje et al., "Perceived Support in Sibling Relationships and Adolescent Adjustment: Sibling Support and Adjustment," *Journal of Child Psychology and Psychiatry* 45, no. 8 (November 2004): 1385–96, https://doi.org/10.1111/j.1469-7610.2004.00332.x; Anne C. Bernstein, "Stepfamilies from Siblings' Perspectives," *Marriage & Family Review* 26, nos. 1–2 (1997): 153–75; Armeda Stevenson Wojciak, "'It's Complicated': Exploring the Meaning of Sibling Relationships of Youth in Foster Care," *Child and Family Social Work* 22 (2017): 1283–91.

26. Jens Manuel Krogstad, "5 Facts about the Modern American Family," *Pew Research Center* (blog), April 30, 2014, http://www.pewresearch.org/fact-tank/2014/04/30/5-facts-about-the-modern-american-family/; "Average

Size of Households in the U.S. 1960-2017 | Statistic," Statista, accessed April 25, 2018, https://www.statista.com/statistics/183648/average-size-of-households-in-the-us/.

27. National Center for Chronic Disease Prevention and Health Promotion, "ART 2010 National Summary Report," 2012. Isabel Sawhill predicts that single mothers by choice, who are older women and carefully plan their families, will continue to grow as both marriage and divorce are declining. See the discussion in Claire Cain Miller, "Egg Freezing as a Work Benefit? Some Women See Darker Message," *New York Times*, October 14, 2014, http://www.nytimes.com/2014/10/15/upshot/egg-freezing-as-a-work-benefit-some-women-see-darker-message.html.

28. Scholarly research finds that the more privileged are less likely to live near family. See, for example, Lillian Rubin, *Worlds of Pain* (New York: Basic Books, 1976). However, Claude Fisher finds that in the 2000s, Americans were less likely to move than in previous generations (*Made in America: A Social History of American Culture and Character* [Chicago: University of Chicago Press, 2010]). Those who do move away from their hometowns are likely to be those with higher incomes and those from rural areas. Our respondents usually settle down in a specific region of the country when their children are in middle school. Returning home (or never leaving the state where one of the parents had grown up) is common. Our point here is that regardless of family form, mobility also contributes to the sense of less family than in earlier generations.

29. This concept of a "thinned" family comes from Ross Douthat, "The Post-familial Election," *New York Times*, November 5, 2016, http://www.nytimes.com/2016/11/06/opinion/sunday/the-post-familial-election.html.

30. We called the Centers for Disease Control, the American Society for Reproductive Medicine, and the American Association of Tissue Banks. All reported that there is no centralized agency: no agency is responsible either for keeping track of the number of sperm banks in the United States or for any related information about what becomes of purchased vials of sperm. There are also no uniform regulations for accepting donors, limits on the number of offspring per donor, or the kinds of information that banks offer about sperm donors.

31. Laura Mamo, "Queering the Fertility Clinic," *Journal of Medical Humanity* 34 (2013): 227–39; Maureen Sullivan, *The Family of Woman: Lesbian Mothers, Their Children, and the Undoing of Gender* (Berkeley: University of California Press, 2004); Brian Powell, Catherine Blozendahl, Claudia Geist, and Lala Carr Steelman, *Counted Out: Same-Sex Relations and Americans' Definitions of Family* (New York: Russell Sage Foundation, 2010).

32. In order to limit the layers of complexity of our project we do not include gay or trans parents. We also did not include families who are coparenting (such as a gay couple and a lesbian couple who have a child together). For accounts of gay fathers and other modern families, see Judith Stacy,

"Cruising to Familyland: Gay Hypergamy and Rainbow Kinship," *Current Sociology* 52, no. 2 (March 1, 2004): 181–97; "The Families of Man: Gay Male Intimacy and Kinship in a Global Metropolis," *Signs* 30 (2005): 1911–35; "Gay Parenthood and the Decline of Paternity as We Knew It," *Sexualities* 9 (2006): 27–55; *Unhitched Love: Marriage, and Family Values from West Hollywood to Western China* (New York: New York University Press, 2011); and Joshua Gamson, *Modern Families: Stories of Extraordinary Journeys to Kinship* (New York: New York University Press, 2015). We also deliberately did not include families created through surrogacy. For a comparison of the surrogacy politics and policies that differ between New York and California, see Susan Markens, *Surrogate Motherhood and the Politics of Reproduction* (Berkeley: University of California Press, 2007). For a discussion of married women who become domestic surrogates, see Heather Jacobson, *Labor of Love: Gestational Surrogacy and the Work of Making Babies* (New Brunswick, NJ: Rutgers University Press, 2016). For a global perspective on surrogacy, see Amrita Pande, *Wombs in Labor: Transnational Commercial Surrogacy in India* (New York: Columbia University Press, 2014).

33. Although our group of respondents included a small number of families who used egg donors and an equally small number of families who used known sperm donors, we do not feature these families in this book. Egg donor families sometimes have the opportunities to meet donor siblings; this is rare right now. And while both known egg donors and known sperm donors might have their own children who are half-siblings to those conceived with their donated gametes, these sets of children are not socially the same as sperm or egg bank donor siblings. The families we interviewed who relied on egg donors are important to us as background information. We only mention them explicitly when the child has been conceived with *both* an egg and a sperm donor.

34. Spar, *Baby Business*.

35. Mamo, "Queering the Fertility Clinic"; Sullivan, *The Family of Woman*.

36. See Amy Agigian, *Baby Steps: How Lesbian Alternative Insemination Is Changing the World* (Middletown, CT: Wesleyan University Press, 2004). Her research was conducted through a Boston clinic.

37. The Single Mothers by Choice organization was founded in 1981. It has local chapters throughout the United States, Canada, and Europe. The organization has an online presence, including various private forums through its website.

38. This strategy also gave us a geographically diverse sample within the networks. In each network the readers will discover, as we did, the cultural diversity that characterizes the set of random families who happened to purchase the same donor sperm.

39. Because we made contact with children through their families, we had a more even distribution of boys and girls than is generally found in research

on donor-conceived children. For example, in an earlier survey of donor-conceived children, only a fifth of the respondents were boys. See Rosanna Hertz, Margaret K. Nelson, and Wendy Kramer, "Donor Conceived Offspring Conceive of the Donor: The Relevance of Age, Awareness, and Family Form," *Social Science & Medicine* 86 (June 2013): 52–65.

Chapter 1

1. Today the websites have built-in categories that clients can use as filters to help reduce the number of possible donors.

2. Donors might not have access to the information needed to be accurate about the family health history; they could also conceal information. The same is true with the representation of many of the other factors that become relevant to a particular individual's choice of one donor over another. Identity-release donors can break off contact with the bank, and the contract they signed is of little use if they can't be found; conversely, anonymous donors might come forward and agree to contact, even though they signed on as if they would not. Of course, genes themselves are always a gamble: a tall donor *might* help produce a tall kid but there is no certainty there any more than there is with respect to hair color or eye color. Moreover, the intending parents who impute genetic determination to traits like sense of humor or a passion for social justice may be flying on no more than a wish and a prayer. For a discussion of lawsuits against sperm banks for misrepresenting sperm, see Mary Anne Pazanowski, "Legal Checks on Fertility Clinics Lacking, as Cases against Industry Expected to Grow," Research Paper No. 17-284, Legal Studies Research Paper Series, University of San Diego School of Law, May 4, 2017.

3. Intending parents use SAT scores, GPAs, or graduate school attendance as proxies for intelligence; they might have more useful information if they knew about learning disabilities. See Liuyan Zhang et al., "ADHD Gene: A Genetic Database for Attention Deficit Hyperactivity Disorder," *Nucleic Acids Research* 40 (2012): D1003–9. On the issue of a desire for a "healthy" baby, see Ana Teresa Ortiz and Laura Briggs, "The Culture of Poverty, Crack Babies, and Welfare Cheats: The Making of the 'Healthy White Baby Crisis,'" *Social Text* 21, no. 3 (2003): 39–57. For a discussion of how filtering criteria such as hair color help create a white child without making a specific racial request, see Maura Ryan and Amanda Moras, "Race Matters in Lesbian Donor Insemination: Whiteness and Heteronormativity as Co-constituted Narratives," *Ethnic and Racial Studies* 40, no. 4 (March 16, 2017): 579–96. Parents choosing an egg donor sometimes included different criteria, suggesting a willingness to substitute attractiveness and similarity to the mother. Often those using eggs—and especially those using both eggs and sperm—had to make greater compromises about at least one, if not both, of their donors. For example, from her home in a Boston suburb, Kate explains that after years of trying to conceive—first with her own eggs

and then with those of her wife, Claudia—the two women were ready to
settle: "[The egg donor's] physical characteristics weren't a terribly good
match but at this point we had moved pretty far away from being too, too
focused on that." (We will meet these respondents again in chapter 9.) As
options dwindle, respondents do try to hold onto at least one ideal donor;
they are sometimes unsuccessful even at doing that.

4. See Rosanna Hertz, Margaret K. Nelson, and Wendy Kramer, "Gendering
Gametes: The Unequal Contributions of Sperm and Egg Donors,"
Social Science & Medicine 147 (December 2015): 10–19; Benno Torgler
and Stephen Whyte, "Selection Criteria in the Search for a Sperm
Donor: Internal versus External Attributes," Center for Research in
Economics, Management and the Arts, 2013; Joanna E. Scheib, "Sperm
Donor Selection and the Psychology of Female Mate Choice," *Ethology
and Sociobiology* 15, no. 3 (May 1994): 113–29; Iolanda S. Rodino, Peter J.
Burton, and Katherine A. Sanders, "Mating by Proxy: A Novel Perspective
to Donor Conception," *Fertility and Sterility* 96, no. 4 (2011): 998–1001;
Adrian Furnham, Natalie Salem, and David Lester, "Selecting Egg and
Sperm Donors: The Role of Age, Social Class, Ethnicity, Height and
Personality," *Psychology* 5, no. 3 (March 2014): 220–29; Mark D. Prokosch,
Richard G. Coss, Joanna E. Scheib, and Shelley A. Blozis, "Intelligence
and Mate Choice: Intelligent Men Are Always Appealing," *Evolution and
Human Behavior* 30, no. 1 (January 2009): 11–20.

5. In 2017, the average egg donor compensation was reported to be $5,890, and
the price for eggs ranged from $13,000 to $15,000, depending on various
factors. See Katherine M. Johnson, "The Price of an Egg: Oocyte Donor
Compensation in the US Fertility Industry," *New Genetics and Society*,
October 20, 2017, 10. In our research, embryo costs through banks and
clinics vary also. They are in the range of sperm vials. Two embryos usually
cost about $750. In addition, both sperm banks and embryo clinics charge
shipping and storage fees.

6. Viviana A. Zelizer, *Pricing the Priceless Child: The Changing Social Value of
Children* (New York: Basic Books, 1985).

7. We do not mean to say that low cost is the only reason for using the Known
Donor Registry. Some respondents wanted to be able to meet the donor
in person because it felt more "natural" than an anonymous stranger; some
wanted fresh sperm. For discussions of these kinds of registries, see Joyce
Harper, Emily Jackson, Laura Spoelstra-Witjens, and Dan Reisel, "Using an
Introduction Website to Start a Family: Implications for Users and Health
Practitioners," *Reproductive Biomedicine & Society Online* 4 (2017): 13–17;
Vasanti Jadva, Tabitha Freeman, Erika Tranfield, and Susan Golombok,
"Why Search for a Sperm Donor Online? The Experiences of Women
Searching for and Contacting Sperm Donors on the Internet," *Human
Fertility*, April 28, 2017, 1–8.

8. For further discussion of these issues, see appendix A. We interviewed twelve families where the parent(s) had conceived with a known donor for at least one of their children.

9. The oldest same-sex couples in this study also were concerned that having a known donor would be a problem for recognition of the nongenetic parent. Over thirty years ago, these early pioneers wanted to be able to petition their counties to grant second-parent adoption. For instance, Pamela, featured in chapter 5, told us, "The courts in California would have to treat a known donor as a parent" (see Ertman, *Love's Promises*). For other discussions of legal issues, see Susan Golombok and Stephen Wilkinson, *Regulating Reproductive Donation* (New York: Cambridge University Press, 2016).

10. Among the parents we interviewed, the majority of those with children under the age of six are now choosing an identity-release donor (see appendix A). However, most of the parents we interviewed did not oppose anonymity on principle. Over half (52 percent) said that anonymity should *not* be banned in this country as it is elsewhere; only 17 percent opposed it altogether; the remainder either gave conflicting answers or ambiguous answers. Parental support for anonymity in general is based in a belief that it is the donor's right to make that decision (32 percent) and that a large pool of donors is in everyone's best interest (33 percent). Those opposed to anonymity focused on children's rights (63 percent) and medical concerns (21 percent).

11. For discussion of the particular concerns of same-sex couples, see Laura Benkov, *Reinventing The Family: Lesbian and Gay Parents* (New York: Harmony, 1995); Sullivan, *The Family of Woman*; Caroline Jones, "Looking Like a Family: Negotiating Bio-genetic Continuity in British Lesbian Families Using Licensed Donor Insemination," *Sexualities* 8, no. 2 (May 1, 2005): 221–37; Elizabeth A. Suter, Karen L. Daas, and Karla Mason Bergen, "Negotiating Lesbian Family Identity via Symbols and Rituals," *Journal of Family Issues* 29 (2008): 26–47; Amy Hequembourg, "Unscripted Motherhood: Lesbian Mothers Negotiating Incompletely Institutionalized Family Relationships," *Journal of Social and Personal Relationships* 21, no. 6 (December 1, 2004): 739–62; Linda L. Layne, "'Creepy,' 'Freaky,' and 'Strange': How the 'Uncanny' Can Illuminate the Experience of Single Mothers by Choice and Lesbian Couples Who Buy 'Dad,'" *Journal of Consumer Culture* 13, no. 2 (July 1, 2013): 140–59; Karina Luzia, "Travelling in Your Backyard: The Unfamiliar Places of Parenting," *Social & Cultural Geography* 11, no. 4 (June 1, 2010): 359–75; Irene Padavic and J. Jonniann Butterfield, "Mothers, Fathers, and 'Mathers': Negotiating a Lesbian Co-parental Identity," *Gender & Society* 25, no. 2 (April 1, 2011): 176–96; Elizabeth Peel, "Moving beyond Heterosexism? The Good, the Bad and the Indifferent in Accounts of Others' Reactions to Important Life Events," *Psychology of Sexualities Review* 3, no. 1 (2012): 34–36; Margaret

K. Nelson and Rosanna Hertz, "Donor-Insemination Motherhood: How Three Types of Mothers Make Sense of Genes and Donors," *Journal of GLBT Family Studies*, December 15, 2016, 1–24.

12. For a discussion of the relationship between selecting a donor who looks like a parent and "passing," see Karen-Anne Wong, "Donor Conception and 'Passing,' or; Why Australian Parents of Donor-Conceived Children Want Donors Who Look Like Them," *Journal of Bioethical Inquiry* 14, no. 1 (2017): 77–86.

13. Jewish sperm is often a stand-in for being Eastern European; but whether Jewish sperm is a stand-in for whiteness is unclear. Yet, the use of Jewish sperm is also culturally specific. For a discussion of how Israel handles donor gametes and assisted reproduction technologies, see Susan Kahn, *Reproducing Jews: A Cultural Account of Assisted Conception in Israel* (Durham, NC: Duke University Press, 2000).

14. This is probably also the case among families who have adopted a child. Those families also have to claim "ownership" vis-à-vis the birth parents.

15. For discussions of these issues see Victoria M. Grace and Ken R. Daniels, "The (Ir)relevance of Genetics: Engendering Parallel Worlds of Procreation and Reproduction," *Sociology of Health & Illness* 29, no. 5 (June 6, 2007): 692–710; Victoria M. Grace, Ken R. Daniels, and Wayne Gillett, "The Donor, the Father, and the Imaginary Constitution of the Family: Parents' Constructions in the Case of Donor Insemination," *Social Science & Medicine* 66, no. 2 (January 2008): 301–14; Elia Wyverkens et al., "The Meaning of the Sperm Donor for Heterosexual Couples: Confirming the Position of the Father," *Family Process*, April 2015; Gay Becker, Anneliese Butler, and Robert D. Nachtigall, "Resemblance Talk: A Challenge for Parents Whose Children Were Conceived with Donor Gametes in the US," *Social Science & Medicine* 61, no. 6 (September 2005): 1300–309; K. Vanfraussen, I. Ponjaert-Kristoffersen, and A. Brewaeys, "An Attempt to Reconstruct Children's Donor Concept: A Comparison between Children's and Lesbian Parents' Attitudes towards Donor Anonymity," *Human Reproduction* 16 (2001): 2019–25; E. Wyverkens, V. Provoost, A. Ravelingien, P. De Sutter, G. Pennings, and A. Buysse, "Beyond Sperm Cells: A Qualitative Study on Constructed Meanings of the Sperm Donor in Lesbian Families," *Human Reproduction* 29, no. 6 (June 1, 2014): 1248–54; Abbie E. Goldberg and Katherine R. Allen, "Donor, Dad, Or . . . ? Young Adults with Lesbian Parents' Experiences with Known Donors," *Family Process* 52, no. 2 (June 2013): 338–50; Petra Nordqvist, "Out of Sight, out of Mind: Family Resemblances in Lesbian Donor Conception," *Sociology* 44, no. 6 (December 1, 2010): 1128–44; Petra Nordqvist, "Origins and Originators: Lesbian Couples Negotiating Parental Identities and Sperm Donor Conception," *Culture, Health & Sexuality* 14, no. 3 (March 2012): 297–311; Susanna Graham, "Stories of an Absent 'Father': Single Women Negotiating Relatedness through Donor Profiles," in *Relatedness*

in Assisted Reproduction, ed. Tabitha Freeman and Susanna Graham (Cambridge: Cambridge University Press, 2014), 212–31; Rosanna Hertz, "The Father as an Idea: A Challenge to Kinship Boundaries by Single Mothers," *Symbolic Interaction* 25 (2002): 1–31; R. Landau and R. Weissenberg, "Disclosure of Donor Conception in Single-Mother Families: Views and Concerns," *Human Reproduction* 25, no. 4 (2010): 942–48; Wyverkens et al., "Meaning of the Sperm Donor"; Ehrensaft, *Mommies, Daddies, Donors, Surrogates*.

Chapter 2

1. According to developmental psychologist Diane Ehrenshaft, by the time children have finished preschool they grasp that most children have mothers and fathers and that not having one or the other warrants an explanation. Ehrenshaft advises parents to provide an explanation by age two. See Ehrenshaft, *Mommies, Daddies, Donors, Surrogates*.

2. The parents had all disclosed one form of donor conception—either egg or sperm. This is an artifact of our sampling strategy. However, we interviewed some children who have both an egg and sperm donor; their parents say they disclosed both donors but that their children only picked up on the sperm donor. We agreed not to probe about the egg donor among children if (and usually it was when) they said they only had a sperm donor. We honored that agreement during our interviews, and we do not identify those children who only knew about the sperm donor. For a similar finding in Spain, where birth narratives mask two donors through a lack of specificity, see María Isabel Jociles, Ana María Rivas, and Consuelo Alvarez, "Strategies to Personalize and to Depersonalize." For research on the impact of disclosure and age of disclosure, see Marilyn Crawshaw et al., "Disclosure and Donor-Conceived Children," *Human Reproduction* 32, no. 7 (May 2017): 1–2; and Maggie Kirkman, "Parents' Contributions to the Narrative Identity of Offspring of Donor-Assisted Conception," *Social Science & Medicine* 57, no. 11 (December 2003): 2229–42. On the topic of when and whether to disclose, see Kirstin Mac Dougall, Gay Becker, Joanna E. Scheib, and Robert D. Nachtigall, "Strategies for Disclosure: How Parents Approach Telling Their Children That They Were Conceived with Donor Gametes," *Fertility and Sterility* 87, no. 3 (March 2007): 524–33; Jadva et al., "Experiences of Adolescents and Adults"; Freeman and Golombok, "Donor Insemination"; Petra Nordqvist, "The Drive for Openness in Donor Conception: Disclosure and the Trouble with Real Life," *International Journal of Law, Policy and the Family* 28, no. 3 (December 1, 2014): 321–38; Dorothy A. Greenfeld, "The Impact of Disclosure on Donor Gamete Participants: Donors, Intended Parents and Offspring," *Current Opinion in Obstetrics and Gynecology* 20, no. 3 (2008): 265–68; Gabor Thomas Kovacs, Sarah Wise, and Sue Finch, "Keeping a Child's Donor Sperm Conception Secret Is Not Linked to Family and Child Functioning during

Middle Childhood: An Australian Comparative Study," *Australian and New Zealand Journal of Obstetrics and Gynaecology* 55, no. 4 (2015): 390–96; Nuffield Council on Bioethics, "Donor Conception: Ethical Aspects of Information Sharing," 2013. For disclosure issues among single parents see Landau and Weissenberg, "Disclosure of Donor Conception"; Sophie Zadeh, Tabitha Freeman, and Susan Golombok, "Absence or Presence? Complexities in the Donor Narratives of Single Mothers Using Sperm Donation," *Human Reproduction* 31, no. 1 (January 2016): 117–24. For a comparison of disclosure in single- and two-parent families, see Tabitha Freeman, Sophie Zadeh, Venessa Smith, and Susan Golombok, "Disclosure of Sperm Donation: A Comparison between Solo Mother and Two-Parent Families with Identifiable Donors," *Reproductive BioMedicine Online* 33, no. 5 (November 2016): 592–600. For arguments that secrecy surrounding donor use is problematic given the rise of DNA testing, see Joyce C. Harper, Debbie Kennett, and Dan Reisel, "The End of Donor Anonymity: How Genetic Testing Is Likely to Drive Anonymous Gamete Donation out of Business," *Human Reproduction* 31, no. 6 (June 1, 2016): 1135–40. Finally, for an overview of studies on disclosure, see Maria Anna Tallandini, Liviana Zanchettin, Giorgio Gronchi, and Valentina Morsan, "Parental Disclosure of Assisted Reproductive Technology (ART) Conception to Their Children: A Systematic and Meta-analytic Review," *Human Reproduction* 31, no. 6 (2016): 1275–87.

3. For other discussions of the idea of the donor among children (including those under the age of ten), see Zadeh, Freeman, and Golombok, "Absence or Presence"; L. Blake, P. Casey, J. Readings, V. Jadva, and S. Golombok, "'Daddy Ran out of Tadpoles': How Parents Tell Their Children That They Are Donor Conceived, and What Their 7-Year-Olds Understand," *Human Reproduction* 25, no. 10 (October 1, 2010): 2527–34; Zadeh, "Disclosure of Donor Conception"; Vanfraussen, Ponjaert-Kristoffersen, and Brewaeys, "Attempt to Reconstruct"; and L. Blake, V. Jadva, and S. Golombok, "Parent Psychological Adjustment, Donor Conception and Disclosure: A Follow-Up over 10 Years," *Human Reproduction* 29, no. 11 (November 1, 2014): 2487–96, S. Zadeh, C. M. Jones, T. Basi, and S. Golombok, "Children's Thoughts and Feelings about Their Donor and Security of Attachment to Their Solo Mothers in Middle Childhood," *Human Reproduction* 32, no. 4 (2017): 868–75.

4. Heterosexual parents were less likely to introduce the donor until their children were between the ages of four and six prior to kindergarten.

5. The sex education curriculum also is most interested in preventing heterosexual intercourse. The cultural narrative reinforces the idea that only this kind of sex makes a baby, which is the "natural" way" to do so. By ignoring other kinds of conception narratives, this narrative marginalizes donor-conceived children, an issue that is beyond the scope of this book. For critiques of sex education programs and the promotion

of heteronormative families and heteronormative teen sex, see Tanya
McNeill, "Sex Education and the Promotion of Heteronormativity,"
Sexualities 16, no. 7 (2013): 826–46; Laina Y. Bay-Cheng, "The Trouble of
Teen Sex: The Construction of Adolescent Sexuality through School-Based
Sexuality Education," *Sex Education: Sexuality, Society and Learning* 3, no. 1
(2003): 61–74.

6. See Hertz, *Single by Chance*, chap. 4, for a comparison between anonymous
and known donors that examines the likable "fantasy father" versus the
"concrete" known donor. In either case, mothers present a positive image of
the donor important to their child's identity.

7. We deliberately did not ask kids (or their parents) to prepare for the
interview in any way. No one told us that she had looked at the donor
profile before we talked with her. Therefore, what we learn is what children
remembered from what their parents told them. Young children usually did
not read the donor profile. As they became older teens (fourteen to sixteen),
they might have read the profile on their own. Parents were the keepers
of the donor profile. On a few occasions kids told us they had their own
copies. None of the children read their donor's profile regularly; they simply
referred to it when they were curious.

8. As noted in chapter 1, some banks provide audiotapes. Whether a child had
heard the donor audiotape depends on the following: (1) whether the bank
offered it, (2) whether parents purchased the audiotape, (3) whether the child
met donor siblings who had a tape that they shared within the network, and
4) whether the child wanted to listen to the tape. The audiotape is also a
product that becomes important within the 7008ers (see chapter 6).

9. For research on adolescents and donor conception, see especially Joanna
E. Scheib, Alice Ruby, and Jean Benward, "Who Requests Their Sperm
Donor's Identity? The First Ten Years of Information Releases to Adults
with Open-Identity Donors," *Fertility and Sterility* 107, no. 2 (February
2017): 483–93; O. B. A. van den Akker, M. A. Crawshaw, E. D. Blyth, and
L. J. Frith, "Expectations and Experiences of Gamete Donors and Donor-
Conceived Adults Searching for Genetic Relatives Using DNA Linking
through a Voluntary Register," *Human Reproduction* 30, no. 1 (January 1,
2015): 111–21; J. E. Scheib, M. Riordan, and S. Rubin, "Adolescents with
Open-Identity Sperm Donors: Reports from 12–17 Year Olds," *Human
Reproduction* 20, no. 1 (2005): 239–52; Marilyn Crawshaw, "Lessons from
a Recent Adoption Study to Identify Some of the Service Needs of, and
Issues for, Donor Offspring Wanting to Know about Their Donors," *Human
Fertility* 5, no. 1 (2002): 6–12.

10. Andy's idea about claiming roots through connecting with a country
is similar to ideas about how African Americans might be claiming an
ancestral home through DNA testing. See Alondra Nelson, *The Social
Life of DNA: Race, Reparations, and Reconciliation after the Genome*
(Boston: Beacon Press, 2016).

11. Children who have known sperm or egg donors do not invent the donor in these ways. In this research, among those cases of a known donor, all the children's parents had contracts with the donor specifying some contact in the company of their parent(s) when the child was young. The few teens in high school or older with known donors determined their own contact (if any) with them.

12. In spite of how important the donor is to so many children, in response to a question about anonymity, almost three-quarters (72 percent) of those who gave a clear yes or no opinion (rather than expressing no opinion or ambiguous views) say anonymity should be allowed. Those with anonymous donors are (significantly) more likely to believe that anonymity should be allowed (82 percent) than those who have an identity-release donor (54 percent). But interestingly, even half of those with an identity-release donor believe that donors should be allowed to remain anonymous. The minority group of children we interviewed who wanted to ban anonymity gave reasons that focused on the needs and rights of children: equal proportions said that it was *good* for children to know their donor (42 percent) and said that it was children's *right* to know their donor (38 percent). By way of contrast, the larger group of children we interviewed who believed that anonymity *should* be allowed gave a variety of reasons for doing so: a third thought that donors should be protected from offspring; another third believed that it was the donor's right to remain anonymous. We discuss the range of these attitudes within a single network in the 7008er network. For other discussions of this issue, see Margaret K. Nelson, Rosanna Hertz, and Wendy Kramer, "Gamete Donor Anonymity and Limits on Numbers of Offspring: The Views of Three Stakeholders," *Journal of Law and the Biosciences*, October 29, 2015, 1–29; Margaret K. Nelson and Rosanna Hertz, "As Anonymity Disappears the Focus Becomes Limits on Donor Offspring," *Journal of Law and the Biosciences*, October 20, 2016.

Chapter 3

1. Founded in 2000, the Donor Sibling Registry proclaims that it will ensure "that the donor-conceived have a safe place to search for their biological identities and to make these connections with their half-siblings and where possible, their donors as well" (https://www.donorsiblingregistry.com/). Other websites soon followed, including those sponsored by sperm banks. While today the Donor Sibling Registry charges a fee, most of these other registries remain free to those who sign on. California Cryobank, a large commercial bank in the United States, offers this statement as to its intent: "In anticipating a child's need for information, as well as the desire of families to stay connected, we created the CCB Sibling Registry—allowing siblings and extended families to find each other." As the statements from the Donor Sibling Registry and California Cryobank suggest, the registries promise to create opportunities for the emergence of relationships among

genetic strangers—the family members of children who are "half-siblings" and occasionally the donor himself. We have no idea how many families have signed on to these sites.

Other independent websites, whose members continue to increase, include Donor Offspring, Parent & Siblings Registry (www.loricarangelo.com/DonorOffspring) and Donorchildren.com, both of which are free registries and websites for parents, offspring, and donors to find one other. Facebook groups that are closed groups include Donor Conceived Offspring, Siblings and Parents (Sperm, Egg and Embryo). Other sites are chatrooms that provide advice about searching for donors or donor siblings. In the late 1990s there was a registry connected with the national organization Single Mothers by Choice. Outside the United States there are other registries such as the UK Donor Conceived Registry (www.donorconceivedregister.org.uk).

2. The media's appetite for novelty and drama has fueled the growth of these registries. In the first decade of this century, people across the United States turned on their TVs to view the popular programs like *Oprah, 20/20, 60 Minutes, Good Morning America*, and the *Today Show*, among others, racing to arrange and then broadcast the first moments of encounters among donor siblings and their parents. The media especially loved the unusual (reporting that one donor has 150 children). Hollywood soon caught on: several of those we interviewed (both parents and children) learned about the possibility of donor siblings from the movie *The Delivery Man*, which highlights a single sperm donor discovering that he has more than five hundred offspring; others reported seeing the issue of contact with a sperm donor portrayed at length in the widely distributed movie *The Kids Are All Right*. See, for example, Amy Harmon, "Hello, I'm Your Sister. Our Father Is Donor 150," *New York Times*, November 20, 2005, sec. National; Jacqueline Mroz, "One Sperm Donor, 150 Sons and Daughters," *New York Times*, September 5, 2011, sec. Health; and Margaret K. Nelson, "Hollywood Sperm Donors," *Contexts*, Winter 2014.

3. Groups, especially those that have the older children we interviewed, might only use a group listserv on their email account. This could also be the case if only two or three families have come forward. The majority of families we talked with did have private Facebook groups. By September 2006, Facebook became open to everyone thirteen years old or older with a valid email address. October 6, 2010, was the launch of "New Groups," which allowed members to create both "closed" and "secret" groups. Group Chat also was launched as a feature. (Matt Hicks posted a public note to the company Facebook page available to all users on October 6, 2010 ["New Groups: Stay Closer to People in Your Life" www.facebook.com/notes/facebook/new-groups-stay-closer-to-groups-of-people-in-your-life/434700832130/]). Some groups of families we interviewed migrated from MySpace or other earlier online sites.

4. For other research on motivations and the experience of contact—most of which derives from surveys rather than in-depth interviews—see, for example, Tabitha Freeman et al., "Gamete Donation: Parents' Experiences of Searching for Their Child's Donor Siblings and Donor," *Human Reproduction* 24 (2009): 505–16; A. E. Goldberg and J. E. Scheib, "Female-Partnered and Single Women's Contact Motivations and Experiences with Donor-Linked Families," *Human Reproduction* 30, no. 6 (June 1, 2015): 1375–85; Rosanna Hertz and Jane Mattes, "Donor-Shared Siblings or Genetic Strangers: New Families, Clans, and the Internet," *Journal of Family Issues* 32 (2011): 1129–55; Rosanna Hertz, Margaret K. Nelson, and Wendy Kramer, "Donor Sibling Networks as a Vehicle for Expanding Kinship: A Replication and Extension," *Journal of Family Issues* 38, no. 2 (February 24, 2017): 248–84; Jenni Millbank, "Numerical Limits in Donor Conception Regimes: Genetic Links and 'Extended Family' in the Era of Identity Disclosure," *Medical Law Review*, January 28, 2014: 325–56; Joanna E. Scheib and Alice Ruby, "Contact among Families Who Share the Same Sperm Donor," *Fertility and Sterility* 90, no. 1 (July 2008): 33–43, https://doi.org/10.1016/j.fertnstert.2007.05.058. See also Lucy Frith, Eric Blyth, Marilyn Crawshaw, and Olga Van den Akker, "Searching for 'Relations' Using a DNA Linking Register by Adults Conceived Following Sperm Donation," *BioSocieties*, 2017, 1–20, DOI: 10.1057/s41292-017-0063-2; Joanna E. Scheib, Alice Ruby, and Stephen Lee, "Relationships with Families Who Share the Same Donor," in *Encyclopedia of LGBTQ Studies*, ed. Abbie Goldberg (Thousand Oaks, CA: Sage, 2016), 1108–13. An exception is an earlier qualitative, exploratory case study of two families who met. See Rosanna Hertz, "Turning Strangers into Kin," in *Who's Watching? Daily Practices of Surveillance among Contemporary Families*, ed. Margaret K. Nelson and Anita Ilta Garey (Nashville: Vanderbilt University Press, 2009), 156–74.

5. This was not part of our sampling strategy. However, we do have in our sample one single mother who intentionally gave a friend her child's donor number so their children would be relatives. But the mothers do not coparent. On the "collective effort" of Jo and Tess to make a genetic child with Michael and Joaquin, see Gamson, *Modern Families*, chap. 4. For a personal narrative about how her son came to have three parents, see Ertman, *Love's Promises*.

6. See discussion of this issue among the children in chapter 4.

7. Other scholars have talked in analogous language when they write about creating a choreography for the new relationships that emerge with donor conception. See, for example, Petra Nordqvist, "Choreographies of Sperm Donations: Dilemmas of Intimacy in Lesbian Couple Donor Conception," *Social Science & Medicine* 73 (2011): 1661–68; Petra Nordqvist and Carol Smart, *Relative Strangers: Family Life, Genes and Donor Conception*

(New York: Palgrave Macmillan, 2014); Janet Carsten, *After Kinship*
(Cambridge: Cambridge University Press, 2004); Charis Thompson,
Making Parents: The Ontological Choreography of Reproductive Technologies
(Cambridge, MA: MIT Press, 2007).

8. We will see in chapter 9 how parents in the youngest network—all of whom
   have children under the age of five—collectively try to form rules on their
   Facebook page before they meet in person.

9. We sought to create a sample of people who had connected with donor
   siblings in some way. We were not trying to find a sample of people who
   had met in person. However, parents who decide to register to connect
   with donor siblings are more likely to meet today than they were even
   five years ago. In a study using the Single Mothers by Choice organization
   conducted in 2009, all parents who registered were likely to exchange
   emails and photos, but only 21 percent had met another family (Hertz and
   Mattes, "Donor-Shared Siblings," 1129–55). However, in a more expansive
   survey that included a broader range of families in 2014, not only were
   more families located than in the Hertz and Mattes research, but in the
   course of this five-year period, twice as many (43 percent) had met in
   person. And once they met, they were more likely to meet again. See Hertz,
   Nelson, and Kramer, "Donor Sibling Networks."

10. We borrow Turner's term "liminality" to refer to entering a new stage,
    although in our case it is not a passage marked by known rituals (Victor
    W. Turner, *Ritual Process: Structure and Anti-Structure* [Chicago: Aldine,
    1969]). We use it to indicate that our respondents are on the brink of
    entering unfamiliar territory. This land of genetic strangers does not have
    accepted social meanings or established norms (as would "ordinary"
    kinship).

11. Interestingly, the different approaches we have defined here do not
    appear to be associated with family form: single mothers, the parents
    in heterosexual couples, and the mothers in same-sex couples could be
    eager for participation in a donor sibling network, but they could just
    as easily hang back. Family position, however, does seem to matter: the
    genetic parent is usually the one more interested in these networks,
    although as we will show with Brad in the 7008ers (chapter 6), that is
    not invariably the case. Because we focus on families who had contact
    with genetic strangers, we cannot discuss more broadly issues such as
    what type of family is most likely to make these connections or whether
    the number of children in a family affects the likelihood of making
    contact.

12. As noted in the introduction, in Part II we focus on respondents who
    became part of donor sibling networks; we therefore interviewed fewer
    people who decided not to move forward or who moved forward and then
    dropped out of contact with genetic relatives.

13. Most parents in this study initiated conversations about donor siblings. A smaller group knew about donor siblings but chose not to tell their children because they believed it was their children's decision whether to acknowledge those people. Parents tend to believe that the donor is *their* story but that the donor siblings belong to their children.

Chapter 4

1. Similar questions might emerge among children who are adopted and who meet members of their birth families for the first time.

2. This chapter is about children who were conceived with sperm purchased from a sperm bank. Children conceived with known sperm donors might have contact with the children their donor is raising. While these children are also genetically half-siblings, they are not socially in the same position as children born from purchased sperm. In effect, the donor's relationship to the two distinct groups of children sets the children apart. The donor is a dad to the children who live with him and he is raising; he is usually not a dad to his donor offspring.

3. They often refer to this as the donor's "real" family; they thus make themselves "shadows" or abstractions vis-à-vis the donor. (See chapter 7.)

4. For other studies that explore attitudes toward, and the experience of contact among, donor siblings, see Margaret K. Nelson, Rosanna Hertz, and Wendy Kramer, "Making Sense of Donors and Donor Siblings: A Comparison of Donor-Conceived Offspring in Lesbian-Parent and Heterosexual-Parent Families," *Contemporary Perspectives in Family Research* 13 (2013); Hertz, Nelson, and Kramer, "Donor Sibling Networks"; Eric Blyth, "Genes r Us? Making Sense of Genetic and Non-genetic Relationships following Anonymous Donor Insemination," *Reproductive BioMedicine Online* 24, no. 7 (2012): 719–26; Sherina Persaud et al., "Adolescents Conceived through Donor Insemination in Mother-Headed Families: A Qualitative Study of Motivations and Experiences of Contacting and Meeting Same-Donor Offspring," *Children & Society* 31, no. 1 (January 1, 2017): 13–22; Vasanti Jadva et al., "Experiences of Offspring Searching for and Contacting Their Donor Siblings and Donor," *Reproductive BioMedicine Online* 20 (2010): 523–32.

5. We discuss the issue of gender more fully in chapter 10. We note here that gender operates in the realm of similarity; we do not know whether a group of egg-donor-conceived children would designate a girl as looking like the donor.

6. For discussions of how genes have become medicalized, see Kaja Finkler, "The Kin in the Gene: The Medicalization of Family and Kinship in American Society," *Current Anthropology* 42 (2001): 235–63; Kaja Finkler, "Family, Kinship, Memory and Temporality in the Age of the New Genetics," *Social Science & Medicine* 61, no. 5 (September 2005): 1059–71; Jenny Gunnarsson Payne, "Grammars of Kinship: Biological Motherhood

and Assisted Reproduction in an Age of Epigenetics," *Signs* 41, no. 3 (2016): 483–506.

7. We were surprised that even among children who live in major metropolitan areas of New York City, Boston, Los Angeles, and Chicago there were children we interviewed who did not know other donor-conceived children.

Chapter 5

1. Cara Bergstrom-Lynch, *Lesbians, Gays, and Bisexuals Becoming Parents or Remaining Childfree: Confronting Social Inequalities* (Lanham, MD: Lexington Books, 2015); Katrina Kimport, *Queering Marriage: Challenging Family Formation in the United States* (New Brunswick, NJ: Rutgers University Press, 2013).

2. The AIDS epidemic changed the way that lesbians chose known donors by precluding the choice of gay men. On this issue see Agigian, *Baby Steps*, 115; Laura Mamo, *Queering Reproduction: Achieving Pregnancy in the Age of Technoscience* (Durham, NC: Duke University Press, 2007), 106. Today, clinics require donor's sperm—straight or gay—to undergo tests before using it for any medical procedures.

3. Weston, *Families We Choose*.

4. See Sullivan, *The Family of Woman*, and Agigian, *Baby Steps*, for studies of this same time period.

5. This informal personal interaction between the staff at a bank and the clients is not found often in more recent times. Today some banks do offer matching services for an additional fee. Intending parents send in family photos and a list of other qualities and traits they are seeking in a donor, and the bank provides several choices. This is a fee service and not informal, as it was in those early days.

6. Scheib, Ruby, and Benward assess the final phase of an open-identity program at the Sperm Bank of California ("Who Requests Sperm Donor's Identity").

7. For other studies on contact between donors and offspring *from the perspective of the donors*, see Rosanna Hertz, Margaret K. Nelson, and Wendy Kramer, "Sperm Donors Describe the Experience of Contact with Their Donor-Conceived Offspring," *Facts, View & Visions in Gynecology and Obstetrics* 7, no. 2 (2015): 91–100; Jadva et al., "Experiences of Offspring Searching"; M. Visser, M. H. Mochtar, A. A. de Melker, F. van der Veen, S. Repping, and T. Gerrits, "Psychosocial Counselling of Identifiable Sperm Donors," *Human Reproduction* 31, no. 5 (May 1, 2016): 1066–74.

8. For the single mothers in our sample, members of the Single Mothers by Choice organization arranged unofficial trips to camp settings, and they became a tradition. They provided very much the same occasions for normalizing what was viewed as being an unusual form of family creation to which Celeste refers (correspondence with Jane Mattes, May 22, 2017).

9. As we see in chapter 9, this interest in having additional people who can care about a child is resolved among the youngest cohort of parents by the donor sibling group itself and decidedly *not* by the donor.

10. For research on the relationships of grandparents and donor offspring, see Diane Beeson, Patricia Jennings, and Wendy Kramer, "A New Path to Grandparenthood: Parents of Sperm and Egg Donors," *Journal of Family Issues* 34, no. 10 (May 27, 2013): 1295–316; Nordqvist and Smart, *Relative Strangers*.

Chapter 6

1. The parents are similar ages (from forty-seven to sixty with one older dad age seventy-four). Most of the parents grew up in the areas of the country in which they are presently raising their children. The geographic distances make it unusual that these families would meet casually (i.e., that a family from Texas would meet and become friendly with a family in Missouri or California). The parents may be somewhat less diverse in their political views. One parent volunteered the information that she considered the other parents in the group politically and socially liberal with the exception of those from one or two families. She added that even those parents were very warm and accepting of the different views of the others.

2. Religion is particularly interesting. When Scott, a newcomer to the 7008ers appeared, at age nineteen, he was worried that his "conservative, traditional Christian parents" would not be accepting of either the lesbian parents or the lack of religiosity among the network members. Everyone suggested that Iris, who is an active Baptist and talks freely about her beliefs, speak with his parents and make them feel welcome. This conversation was very reassuring for Scott's parents before they met other families in the group. Even though they neither knew about donor siblings nor would have initiated contact, when Scott discovered them, they realized their son needed these connections. They turned out to care most that the other families were "good people" who "welcomed" them and their son. Iris also made another point about Scott's parents that reflected how her own religiosity had been relevant to her experience of donor conception: "I think to be able to do this, though, you're a certain type of adult if you will do in vitro or use donors. That's one level because some people are against anything artificial. If you're real conservative religion, you've got issues about that. The fact that you would build a family in that way and then share it with your kid. The fact that we connected, they did it, they shared it. So they're going to have more flexible personalities."

3. Their occupations include several lawyers, a journalist, and a tax accountant; these are the wealthiest. Others are self-employed (e.g., writer, consultant, social worker). Still other parents are employed as an occupational therapist, bus driver, nurse, and several sales clerks. One mother talked about "opportunities" among some of the families that were her clue to social class

differences, such as the affordability of a private university education. She felt that as much as her son had some opportunities (e.g., to travel with her), some of the other children "came from families with *great* [emphasis added] opportunities." Moreover, she did not reveal to these other families that she was "struggling financially right now." The distinction she is making was between middle-class and upper-middle-class opportunities. No one in this group came from inherited wealth.

4. The Facebook group names are often the donor's number, symbolizing the link they share.

5. See, for example, Danah Boyd, *It's Complicated: The Social Lives of Networked Teens* (New Haven, CT: Yale University Press, 2014); Berkman Center, "Pew Research Center Release Findings on Teens, Social Media and Privacy," *Harvard Law Today*, July 15, 2013.

6. While the majority of the kids are straight, Paul is gay but not completely "out" to the group, and Molly recently transitioned to Micah. Later kids who joined the group include Oliver, who is gay (and "out"), and Scott, who is bisexual. Further, the kids do not share religious beliefs, and some are practicing while others are agnostic. Some see other kids as having more cultural opportunities because they live in urban areas; some know that other kids' parents earn more money than do theirs. This diversity is accepted.

7. We could also think of the tape as being a totem, a collective symbol that creates solidarity. See Emile Durkheim, *The Elementary Forms of the Religious Life*, trans. Joseph Ward Swain (1912; New York: Free Press, 1965).

8. Several children we interviewed told us that they had found these receipts and that they therefore knew that, in some sense, they had been "purchased."

9. See Scheib, Ruby, and Benward, "Who Requests Sperm Donor's Identity." These authors are affiliated with the Sperm Bank of California and conduct research through this bank. They find that even with identity-release donors, not all donor-conceived individuals have chosen to contact the bank to be put in touch with the donor. The 7008ers have varying views similar to the members of other donor-linked networks not featured in Part II. For instance, in chapter 2, we briefly discuss Milo and his donor sibling, Annie. They also have an anonymous donor. Given the opportunity, Milo, who has two moms, would like to meet their donor; Annie, who also has two moms, is ambivalent; and the third donor sibling interviewed from this network, who has heterosexual parents, is not interested.

10. Amy had been a silent member who listed only demographic information about her child on the registry. She did make brief contact with another parent and then disappeared. She never revealed her identity or her child's.

11. Kids remarked that they hoped Zoe and Joseph would decide to rejoin the larger group.

12. Donor-linked children come to realize that a large group can be unwieldy. On this issue of the geometry of numbers, see Simmel, "On the Significance of Numbers for Social Life," in *Sociology of Georg Simmel*, 87–104. He

focuses on dyads and triads but also suggests that group members can
benefit from larger numbers.

13. Meanwhile, everyone excused Molly, who was off the grid while
transitioning to Micah. However, he is now back and in touch with
members in the group.

Chapter 7

1. Tourism is used to indicate travel and associated with vacation and fun.
The term "tourism" is also used as part of the fertility industry in reference
to people who cross borders in their desire for children. "Reproductive
tourism" is a term popularized and used to frame "treatment travel" as
an expression of the activity of wealthy westerners who travel to acquire
reproductive services, gametes, or surrogates. The term does not capture
a burning desire to have a child. Feminist scholars have critiqued the
term both as a problematic framing and because it does not reveal that
border-crossing exiles individuals from their home countries (because of
the regulatory reproductive system in those countries). On these issues,
see especially Marcia C. Inhorn and Zeynep B. Gürtin, "Cross-Border
Reproductive Care: A Future Research Agenda," *Reproductive BioMedicine
Online* 23, no. 5 (November 2011): 665–76; Charlotte Kroløkke, "Eggs
and Euros: A Feminist Perspective on Reproductive Travel from Denmark
to Spain," *International Journal of Feminist Approaches to Bioethics* 7, no. 2
(2014): 144–63. Our use of the term "tourist" for this network indicates
border-crossing as a liminal movement. (On liminality, see Turner, *Ritual
Process*.) That is, individuals stand on the threshold of their everyday lives
in which social (and sometimes genetic) relationships are important, and
they have to decide to use the donor number as a passport to enter the
world of genetic strangers. Those who venture onto registries and connect
up (whether briefly or longer) acquire information not provided by the
US fertility industry. In some ways all families (parents and children alike
who search for genetic relatives) start as tourists, curious about the parents
who chose the same donor and the children that resulted. In all networks,
there are families who remain tourists: one visit or even brief contact is
enough.

2. Donors cannot make independent contact with offspring. The child-donor
contact flows from the child's wish to connect at age eighteen. None of the
banks presently has a registry to allow donors to express their interest in
connecting with their offspring. However, donors can register on a registry
or one of the Facebook groups so that parents and offspring can make
contact with them even before a child turns eighteen.

3. For further discussions of the importance of "clicking," see Goldberg and
Scheib, "Female-Partnered and Single"; Abbie E. Goldberg and Joanna E.
Scheib, "Female-Partnered Women Conceiving Kinship: Does Sharing
a Sperm Donor Mean We Are Family?," *Journal of Lesbian Studies* 20,

nos. 3–4 (October 1, 2016): 427–41; Hertz and Mattes, "Donor-Shared Siblings,"; and Hertz, Nelson, and Kramer, "Donor Sibling Networks."

4. The sperm bank where Eric donated did not provide information to donors about the number of live births that resulted from their sperm. Donors leave behind a profile and a promise never to lay claim to the children who result from insemination. Maureen Sullivan refers to the industry's legal protection as "a system of bilateral ignorance of paternity among donors and recipients" (*The Family of Woman*, 53). When Eric registered, he was surprised by how many kids his sperm had produced over the two years he was a donor (and he now knows there could be more children who have not registered). In his midtwenties, Eric needed extra cash to support his wife and children. He discovered sperm donation through an advertisement in the campus newspaper. He remembers earning approximately $35–$50 for each donation in the mid-1990s. At the time, he actually did not think many people would pick him because he had "lousy eyesight" and allergies. Eric, who was forty-seven years old, was the youngest sperm donor we interviewed. The sperm donors' ages ranged from forty-seven to sixty-three. The oldest egg donor we interviewed was forty-seven; the youngest was thirty-three.

5. We found several examples of same-sex couples returning to one partner's (rural or urban) community where they had extended family. Although these communities were not necessarily sympathetic to same-sex relationships, generations of family ties protected these couples. However, their children still went to school, played sports, and attended religious institutions; they often faced hostility from their peers. The message appears to be that love between people of the same sex is one thing but same-sex couples having children is quite another.

Chapter 8

1. Adrienne and Lois were together ten years, and together they picked the sperm donor. Adrienne became pregnant; the children were given Lois's last name, but the moms could not legally marry. Lois left when the twins were just over two. Margo only met her on that first visit. Adrienne met and married her second partner, Alice, when the children were five and six. When Adrienne and Alice married, Alice legally adopted the children. She died in 2014. Adrienne and Felicia, who is divorced from *her* first wife, were legally married in 2016. We were able to interview Felicia. We note that Lois's name is on the illustration as Adrienne's original partner as the other divorced or split couples (in chapters 6 and 7) are represented.

2. The members of this group were specific about their sexual identity. They recognized these differences with each other. Margo self-identifies as bisexual, Beth as bisexual leaning toward lesbian, Adrienne as lesbian, and Christina as straight. Sexual identity is not relevant in their story of network formation. Relevant is their involvement in each other's lives over the love,

loss, and legal changes that have occurred with their respective partners. Further discussion of the issue of sexual identity is outside the scope of this book.

3. Children who will join this group at later ages—such as the new eleven-year-old whose mom signed him on to the Facebook page recently—might still have an "aha" moment" of discovery.

Chapter 9

1. See Mignon Moore, who makes a similar point about black lesbians not wanting to have the same donor as their friends (*Invisible Families: Gay Identities, Relationships, and Motherhood among Black Women* [Berkeley: University of California Press, 2011], 143).

2. Of course, it is contradictory to claim (as these parents do) that the children have the right to "define [their ties to donor siblings] as a sibling relationship" or not when, for these children, the parents have already made the choice to connect.

3. Cherlin, "Remarriage as Incomplete Institution."

4. For references to "competitive" parenting, see Annette Lareau, *Unequal Childhoods: Class, Race, and Family Life* (Berkeley: University of California Press, 2003); Margaret K. Nelson, *Parenting Out of Control: Anxious Parents in Uncertain Times* (New York: New York University Press, 2012).

Chapter 10

1. However they handle their interactions with donor siblings, during adolescence, donor-conceived children might have a special interest in the unknown donor, as children who are adopted have in their birth parents. On this issue, see "Developmental Concerns in Adopted Children"; Gretchen Miller Wrobel, Harold D. Grotevant, Diana R. Samek, and Lynn Von Korff, "Adoptees' Curiosity and Information Seeking about Birth Parents in Emerging Adulthood: Context, Motivation, and Behavior," *International Journal of Behavioral Development* 37, no. 5 (September 1, 2013). As we noted in chapter 2, at the very least, donor-conceived children might use the donor to help them separate their identities from those of their parent(s).

2. For a discussion of legal recognition, see Cahn, *The New Kinship*; Naomi Cahn, "The Uncertain Legal Basis for the New Kinship," *Journal of Family Issues* 36, no. 4 (March 1, 2015): 501–18.

3. Giddens (*The Consequences of Modernity*, 21) uses the term "disembedding," which he explains as "the 'lifting out' of social relations from local contexts of interaction and their restructuring across indefinite spans of time-space." Facebook epitomizes ideas about modern transient strangers. (On other ideas about strangers, see Simmel, *The Sociology of Georg Simmel*.) Facebook "friends" and the informal rules governing posts hardly establish the trust that is part of "face work" (see Erving Goffman, "On Face-Work: An

Analysis of Ritual Elements in Social Interaction," *Psychiatry* 18, no. 3 [1955]: 213–31).

4. The term "network" is usually referenced with regard to neighborhoods, immigrants, and other institutions (such as day-care centers). Often scholars discuss social networks as a means of "getting ahead" or creating advantage (or social capital). See Douglas S. Massey, "The Age of Extremes: Concentrated Affluence and Poverty in the Twenty-First Century," *Demography* 33, no. 4 (1996): 395–412; and Deborah J. Warr, "Gender, Class, and the Art and Craft of Social Capital," *Sociological Quarterly* 47, no. 3 (2006): 497–520. In his classic article on this topic, Mark Granovetter demonstrates the importance of "weak ties" as important to building "bridges" between separate networks ("The Strength of Weak Ties," *American Journal of Sociology* 78, no. 6 [1973]: 1360–80). But as Mario L. Small (*Unanticipated Gains: Origins of Network Inequality in Everyday Life* [New York: Oxford University Press, 2009], 84–85) also argues, weak ties "are more likely to offer information that a person did not already know or resources from a network to which a person did not already have access." As much as we have avoided using the term "weak ties" to characterize donor siblings, they are in effect this kind of tie. At the very least donor siblings provide kids with a "bridge" to their paternal side. However, donor sibling networks are an attempt to create a "bond" that does not always materialize. See also Barry Wellman, "The Place of Kinfolk in Personal Community Networks," *Marriage & Family Review* 15, nos. 1–2 (1990): 195–228, for an overview of networks and family ties.

5. Today the purchase of sperm gives people access to the bank's registries. Banks expanded their offerings to clients to meet new market demands.

6. We observed that the donor sibling networks link people across time and space who may not have even met. Annie's generative act occurred among people who remain online members. Scott (and then the twins Megan and Matt) became an important "bridging link" between the two fragments (see Granovetter, "Strength of Weak Ties").

7. Among siblings who live together, birth order influences behavior on a day-to-day basis. See Michael E. Lamb and Brian Sutton-Smith, *Sibling Relationships* (Hillsdale, NJ: L. Erlbaum Associates, 1982); Michael E. Lamb and Brian Sutton-Smith, *Sibling Relationships: Their Nature and Significance across the Lifespan* (New York: Psychology Press, 2014); Sulloway, *Born to Rebel*. Donor siblings are not just competitive about who is the oldest. They too adopt behaviors that derive from the expectations surrounding birth order. Isabel put it this way, "I do have an insane protective instinct for my younger [donor sibling] brothers. If I catch them screwing around, I'll let them have it."

8. Sociologists rarely study children's understanding of age norms among themselves. An exception is Patricia M. Passuth's research ("Age Hierarchies

within Children's Groups," *Sociological Studies of Child Development* 2 [1987]: 185–203). She found that among young children in various settings the conception of age is used to develop a hierarchical and moral social order.

9. Hugo Schwyzer, "The Benefits of Men and Women Being Friends, Even If One Is Married," *The Atlantic*, May 1, 2013; Michael Kimmel, *Guyland: The Perilous World Where Boys Become Men* (2008; New York: Harper Perennial, 2009), 249, 280.

10. See Robert D. Putnam, *Bowling Alone: The Collapse and Revival of American Community* (New York: Simon and Schuster, 2001), 95. Putnam notes that "women are more avid social capitalists than men." Gender role expectations are notable for emphasizing that women are more inclined to acquire social skills that facilitate interaction. They take more responsibility for maintaining social relationships in the family and in communities. On the differences in carework between brothers and sisters, see especially Shelley Eriksen and Naomi Gerstel, "A Labor of Love or Labor Itself: Care Work among Adult Brothers and Sisters," *Journal of Family Issues* 23 (October 2002): 836–56. On gender differences in help to parents, see Naomi Gerstel and Natalia Sarkisian, "Explaining the Gender Gap in Help to Parents: The Importance of Employment," *Journal of Marriage and Family* 66 (May 2004): 431–51. In general on gender differences among family members, see Michela Di Leonardo, "The Female World of Cards and Holidays: Women, Families and the Work of Kinship," *Signs* 12 (1987): 440–53; and Karen V. Hansen, *Not-So-Nuclear Families: Class, Gender and Networks of Care* (New Brunswick, NJ: Rutgers University Press, 2004).

11. See Simmel, *The Sociology of Georg Simmel*, who suggests that large groups offer benefits that dyads and triads do not. Smaller groups might be more constraining, as there is less room for different perspectives. Groups that are larger and fragmented might increase people's freedom to figure out new goals or a different mission. See also Granovetter, "Strength of Weak Ties," on the dissemination of information that increases with "weak ties." The 7008ers do benefit from new members who increase the size of the subgroups.

12. Kids in areas with a large same-sex couple demographic often went to the same camps, where they met another community of families like themselves. In a few cases, kids discovered by themselves they shared the same donor, or through a camp friend's friend, they serendipitously found donor siblings. Of course other kinds of opportunities provide kids (and their parents) with ways to meet other families like themselves. See, for example, Peter Cookson and Caroline Persell on how prep schools connect wealthy families (*Preparing for Power* [New York: Basic Books, 1985]).

13. Donor siblings might make strange bedfellows, but they become people one cares about specifically rather than attending to the broader social polity.

14. Hertz, *Single by Chance*, 197.

15. Sometimes children in a nuclear family do not share the same donor, or one child was conceived with a sperm donor and another with an embryo; sometimes one child may be donor conceived and another child might be adopted or a stepchild from a former relationship.

16. Genetic issues sometimes resonated in surprising ways *within* a household. Some parents were surprised to discover that meeting a child's donor siblings actually equalized the position of two parents when only one has a genetic tie to the child. A nongestational mother made this point for us as she claimed her daughter's donor siblings and their parents were in a special category of people in her universe, even as she claimed that neither she nor her wife was central to their daughter's newfound relationships:

   > They don't feel like family but they're more than friends.... We're bonded through my daughter like in a way that a stepparent would be. Their children and my child will forge whatever they make of their relationships, and I'm honored to witness it as a stepparent. *Like I'm not in it and* [my wife] *isn't either.* (Emphasis added.)

17. Some of the kids in this research did know other kids who were donor conceived. Others reported they did not. However, meeting kids who share the same donor confirms kids' understanding of donor conception in a very different way than simple knowledge of a similar mode of conception. They discover that they have paternal kin like everyone else. They can also discuss their mutual connection to the sperm donor.

18. See Joshua Gamson, *Modern Families*, on how the creation and sharing of varied birth stories is an important part of the normalization process. Gamson writes that as long as the idea that the "One True Family" remains heterosexual coupling in marriage, all other ways of creating a family are "illegitimate or unnatural or shameful and they serve to justify the denial of equal respect . . ." to all families (209).

19. We might recall from chapter 3 that the parents enjoyed what they thought of as signs and portents (such as shared names) indicating that they were meant to know each other.

20. Women who inseminated at home sometimes had the donor's birthday on the vials of sperm they received. Several women entered that information, combined with other data supplied by the intake interview, to identify the donor. These women are monitoring the donor and mulling over what next steps they might want to take. No one we interviewed had yet contacted their child's donor.

21. See Karen E. C. Levy, "Intimate Surveillance," *Idaho Law Review* 51 (2014): 679–93, who surveyed types of online monitoring technologies across the "life cycle" from fertility to fidelity; she raises concerns about the legal and social challenges that are new and unresolved territory. See also Elizabeth Yardley, Adam G. T. Lynes, David Wilson, and Emma

Kelly, who discuss "websleuthing" by the criminal justice system and associated outcomes ("What's the Deal with 'Websleuthing'? News Media Representations of Amateur Detectives in Networked Spaces," *Crime, Media, Culture* 14, no. 1 [2018]: 81–109).

Conclusion

1. Other scholars writing about issues created through donor conception also rely on the concept of paradox. See, for example, Susan McKinnon, "Productive Paradoxes of the Assisted Reproductive Technologies in the Context of the New Kinship Studies," *Journal of Family Issues* 36, no. 4 (2015): 461–79; Nordqvist and Smart, *Relative Strangers*.
2. Of course we have examples of serendipity, as discussed in chapter 3. In many of those examples the parents opted to keep the information from the children for a long time.

Appendix B

1. Christine Hine, *Virtual Ethnography* (Thousand Oaks, CA: Sage, 2000); Daniel Miller and Don Slater, *The Internet: An Ethnographic Approach* (Oxford: Berg, 2000); Nelson, *Social Life of DNA*.
2. Jen Silva (*Coming Up Short: Working-Class Adulthood in an Age of Uncertainty* [New York: Oxford University Press, 2013]) suggested that Facebook is a fluid way to stay in touch with respondents.
3. For more information about the strategy we used for training research assistants, for joint interviewing, and for age-appropriate in-depth interview guides, see Rosanna Hertz and Margaret K. Nelson, "In-Depth Interviewing of Parents and Children: Lessons from Donor-Conceived Families about How to Conduct Research on Sensitive Topics," in SAGE Research Methods Cases (Health, Part 2), 2017. (London: Sage, 2017).
4. Children, especially our younger interviewees, rarely understood the legal circumstances of their families. Some of the older children, however, did remember their parents' marriage ceremonies. We discuss second-parent adoption in some of the narratives as a context. It is beyond the scope of this book to discuss the legal circumstances of our respondents except if relevant to reasons for connecting (or not) with donor-linked individuals and their families.
5. For discussions of differences between non-birth mothers and birth mothers, see Hequembourg, "Unscripted Motherhood"; Layne, "Creepy, Freaky, and Strange"; Karina Luzia, "'Beautiful but Tough Terrain': The Uneasy Geographies of Same-Sex Parenting," *Children's Geographies* 11, no. 2 (2013): 243–55; Nelson and Hertz, "Donor-Insemination Motherhood"; Padavic and Butterfield, "Mothers, Fathers, and Mathers"; Peel, "Moving

beyond Heterosexism," 34. For some firsthand accounts by non-birth mothers, see Harlyn Aizley, ed., *Confessions of the Other Mother: Non-biological Lesbian Moms Tell All* (Boston: Beacon Press, 2006); N. A. Naples, "Queer Parenting in the New Millennium," *Gender & Society* 18, no. 6 (December 1, 2004): 679–84.

BIBLIOGRAPHY

Agigian, Amy. *Baby Steps: How Lesbian Alternative Insemination Is Changing the World*. Middletown, CT: Wesleyan University Press, 2004.

Aizley, Harlyn, ed. *Confessions of the Other Mother: Non-biological Lesbian Moms Tell All*. Boston: Beacon Press, 2006.

Akker, O. B. A. van den, M. A. Crawshaw, E. D. Blyth, and L. J. Frith. "Expectations and Experiences of Gamete Donors and Donor-Conceived Adults Searching for Genetic Relatives Using DNA Linking through a Voluntary Register." *Human Reproduction* 30, no. 1 (January 1, 2015): 111–21. https://doi.org/10.1093/humrep/deu289.

AncestryDNA.com. "AncestryDNA™ US | DNA Tests for Ethnicity & Genealogy DNA Test." 2017. https://www.ancestry.com/dna/.

"Average Size of Households in the U.S. 1960–2017 | Statistic." Statista. Accessed April 25, 2018. https://www.statista.com/statistics/183648/average-size-of-households-in-the-us/.

Bay-Cheng, Laina Y. "The Trouble of Teen Sex: The Construction of Adolescent Sexuality through School-Based Sexuality Education." *Sex Education: Sexuality, Society and Learning* 3, no. 1 (2003): 61–74.

Becker, Gay, Anneliese Butler, and Robert D. Nachtigall. "Resemblance Talk: A Challenge for Parents Whose Children Were Conceived with Donor Gametes in the US." *Social Science & Medicine* 61, no. 6 (September 2005): 1300–1309. https://doi.org/10.1016/j.socscimed.2005.01.018.

Beeson, Diane, Patricia Jennings, and Wendy Kramer. "A New Path to Grandparenthood: Parents of Sperm and Egg Donors." *Journal of Family Issues*

34, no. 10 (May 27, 2013): 1295–316. http://jfi.sagepub.com/content/early/2013/05/22/0192513X13489299.

Benkov, Laura. *Reinventing the Family: Lesbian and Gay Parents.* New York: Harmony, 1995.

Bergstrom-Lynch, Cara. *Lesbians, Gays, and Bisexuals Becoming Parents or Remaining Childfree: Confronting Social Inequalities.* Lanham, MD: Lexington Books, 2015.

Berkman Center. "Pew Research Center Release Findings on Teens, Social Media and Privacy." *Harvard Law Today,* July 15, 2013. https://today.law.harvard.edu/berkman-center-pew-research-center-release-findings-on-teens-social-media-and-privacy/.

Bernstein, Anne C. "Stepfamilies from Siblings' Perspectives." *Marriage & Family Review* 26, nos. 1–2 (1997): 153–75.

Blake, Lucy, Polly Casey, Jennifer Readings, Vasanti Jadva, and Susan Golombok. "'Daddy Ran Out of Tadpoles': How Parents Tell Their Children That They Are Donor Conceived, and What Their 7-Year-Olds Understand." *Human Reproduction* 25, no. 10 (October 1, 2010): 2527–34. https://doi.org/10.1093/humrep/deq208.

Blake, Lucy, Vasanti Jadva, and Susan Golombok. "Parent Psychological Adjustment, Donor Conception and Disclosure: A Follow-up over 10 Years." *Human Reproduction* 29, no. 11 (November 1, 2014): 2487–96. https://doi.org/10.1093/humrep/deu231.

Blumer, Herbert. *Symbolic Interactionism: Perspective and Method.* Berkeley: University of California Press, 1986.

Blyth, Eric. "Genes r Us? Making Sense of Genetic and Non-genetic Relationships following Anonymous Donor Insemination." *Reproductive BioMedicine Online* 24, no. 7 (2012): 719–26.

Boyd, Danah. *It's Complicated: The Social Lives of Networked Teens.* New Haven: Yale University Press, 2014.

Braithwaite, D. O., B. W. Bach, L. A. Baxter, R. DiVerniero, J. R. Hammonds, A. M. Hosek, E. K. Willer, and B. M. Wolf. "Constructing Family: A Typology of Voluntary Kin." *Journal of Social and Personal Relationships* 27, no. 3 (April 22, 2010): 388–407. https://doi.org/10.1177/0265407510361615.

Branje, Susan J. T., Cornelis F. M. van Lieshout, Marcel A. G. van Aken, and Gerbert J. T. Haselager. "Perceived Support in Sibling Relationships and Adolescent Adjustment: Sibling Support and Adjustment." *Journal of Child Psychology and Psychiatry* 45, no. 8 (November 2004): 1385–96. https://doi.org/10.1111/j.1469-7610.2004.00332.x.

Burton, Linda M., and Cecily R. Hardaway. "Low-Income Mothers as 'Othermothers' to Their Romantic Partners' Children: Women's Coparenting in Multiple Partner Fertility Relationships." *Family Process* 51, no. 3 (2012): 343–59.

Cahn, Naomi R. *The New Kinship: Constructing Donor-Conceived Families.* New York: New York University Press, 2012.

Cahn, Naomi R. "The Uncertain Legal Basis for the New Kinship." *Journal of Family Issues* 36, no. 4 (March 1, 2015): 501–18. https://doi.org/10.1177/0192513X14563797.

Carsten, Janet. *After Kinship*. Cambridge: Cambridge University Press, 2004.

Carsten, Janet. "The Substance of Kinship and the Heat of the Hearth: Feeding, Personhood, and Relatedness among Malays in Pulau Langkawi." *American Ethnologist* 22, no. 2 (1995): 223–41.

Cherlin, Andrew. "Remarriage as an Incomplete Institution." *American Journal of Sociology* 84, no. 3 (1978): 634–50.

Cohen, Glenn, Travis Coan, Michelle Ottey, and Christina Boyd. "Sperm Donor Anonymity and Compensation: An Experiment with American Sperm Donors." *Journal of Law and the Biosciences* 3, no. 3 (December 1, 2016): 468–88. https://doi.org/10.1093/jlb/lsw052.

Cookson, Peter, and Caroline Persell. *Preparing for Power*. New York: Basic Books, 1985.

Cookson, Peter, and Caroline Persell. "Preparing for Power: Twenty-Five Years Later." In *Educating Elites: Class Privilege and Educational Advantage*, edited by Adam Howard and Rubén A. Gaztambide-Fernández, 13–30. Lanham, MD: Rowman and Littlefield, 2010.

Cooley, Charles Horton. *Human Nature and the Social Order*. 1902. New Brunswick, NJ: Transaction Books, 1983.

Crawshaw, Marilyn. "Lessons from a Recent Adoption Study to Identify Some of the Service Needs of, and Issues for, Donor Offspring Wanting to Know about Their Donors." *Human Fertility* 5, no. 1 (2002): 6–12.

Crawshaw, Marilyn, Damian Adams, Sonia Allan, Eric Blyth, Kate Bourne, Claudia Brügge, Anne Chien, et al. "Disclosure and Donor-Conceived Children." *Human Reproduction* 32, no. 7 (May 2017): 1–2.

Crawshaw, Marilyn, Lucy Frith, Olga van den Akker, and Eric Blyth. "Voluntary DNA-Based Information Exchange and Contact Services following Donor Conception: An Analysis of Service Users' Needs." *New Genetics and Society* 35, no. 4 (October 2016): 372–92. https://doi.org/10.1080/14636778.2016.1253462.

Davies, Katherine "Siblings, Stories and the Self: The Sociological Significance of Young People's Sibling Relationships." *Sociology* 49, no. 4 (2015): 679–95.

Deater-Deckard, Kirby, and Judy Dunn. "Sibling Relationships and Social-Emotional Adjustment in Different Family Contexts." *Social Development* 11, no. 4 (2002): 571–90.

"Developmental Concerns in Adopted Children." Accessed December 15, 2017. http://www.internationaladoptionhelp.com/international_adoption/international_adoption_developmental.htm.

Di Leonardo, Micaela. "The Female World of Cards and Holidays: Women, Families and the Work of Kinship." *Signs* 12 (1987): 440–53.

Douthat, Ross. "The Post-familial Election." *New York Times*, November 5, 2016. http://www.nytimes.com/2016/11/06/opinion/sunday/the-post-familial-election.html.

Durkheim, Emile. *The Elementary Forms of the Religious Life*. 1912. Translated by Joseph Ward Swain. New York: Free Press, 1965.

Edin, Kathryn, and Maria Kefalas. *Promises I Can Keep: Why Poor Women Put Motherhood before Marriage*. Berkeley: University of California Press, 2005.

Edwards, Rosalind, Melanie Mauthner, and Lucy Hadfield. "Children's Sibling Relationships and Gendered Practices: Talk, Activity and Dealing with Change." *Gender and Education* 17, no. 5 (2005): 499–513.

Ehrensaft, Diane. *Mommies, Daddies, Donors, Surrogates: Answering Tough Questions and Building Strong Families*. New York: Guilford Press, 2005.

Eriksen, Shelley, and Naomi Gerstel. "A Labor of Love or Labor Itself: Care Work among Adult Brothers and Sisters." *Journal of Family Issues* 23 (October 2002): 836–56.

Ertman, Martha M. *Love's Promises: How Formal and Informal Contracts Shape All Kinds of Families*. Boston: Beacon Press, 2015.

ESHRE. "6.5 Million IVF Babies since Louise Brown." *Focus on Reproduction, the Blog of ESHRE's Magazine*, July 5, 2016. https://focusonreproduction.eu/2016/07/05/6-5-million-ivf-babies-since-louise-brown/.

"Fairfax Cryobank—Fees." Accessed May 5, 2017. https://fairfaxcryobank.com/fees.

Finkler, Kaja. "Family, Kinship, Memory and Temporality in the Age of the New Genetics." *Social Science & Medicine* 61, no. 5 (September 2005): 1059–71. https://doi.org/10.1016/j.socscimed.2005.01.002.

Finkler, Kaja. "The Kin in the Gene: The Medicalization of Family and Kinship in American Society." *Current Anthropology* 42 (2001): 235–63.

Fischer, Claude S. *Made in America: A Social History of American Culture and Character*. Chicago: University of Chicago Press, 2010.

Freeman, Tabitha, and Susan Golombok. "Donor Insemination: A Follow-Up Study of Disclosure Decisions, Family Relationships and Child Adjustment at Adolescence." *Reproductive BioMedicine Online* 25, no. 2 (2012): 193–203.

Freeman, Tabitha, Vsanti Jadva, Wendy Kramer, and Susan Golombok. "Gamete Donation: Parents' Experiences of Searching for Their Child's Donor Siblings and Donor." *Human Reproduction* 24 (2009): 505–16.

Freeman, Tabitha, Sophie Zadeh, Venessa Smith, and Susan Golombok. "Disclosure of Sperm Donation: A Comparison between Solo Mother and Two-Parent Families with Identifiable Donors." *Reproductive BioMedicine Online* 33, no. 5 (November 2016): 592–600. https://doi.org/10.1016/j.rbmo.2016.08.004.

Frith, Lucy, Eric Blyth, Marilyn Crawshaw, and Olga Van den Akker. "Searching for 'Relations' Using a DNA Linking Register by Adults Conceived Following Sperm Donation." *BioSocieties*, 2017, 1–20.

Furnham, Adrian, Natalie Salem, and David Lester. "Selecting Egg and Sperm Donors: The Role of Age, Social Class, Ethnicity, Height and Personality." *Psychology* 5, no. 3 (March 2014): 220–29.

Furstenberg, Frank F., Jr. "Fathering in the Inner City: Paternal Participation and Public Policy." In *Fatherhood: Contemporary Theory, Research and Social Policy*, edited by William Marsiglio, 119–47. Thousand Oaks, CA: Sage, 1995.

Gamson, Joshua. *Modern Families: Stories of Extraordinary Journeys to Kinship*. New York: New York University Press, 2015.

Gerstel, Naomi, and Natalia Sarkisian. "Explaining the Gender Gap in Help to Parents: The Importance of Employment." *Journal of Marriage and Family* 66 (May 2004): 431–51.

Giddens, Anthony. *The Consequences of Modernity*. Palo Alto, CA: Stanford University Press, 1990.

Goffman, Erving. "On Face-Work: An Analysis of Ritual Elements in Social Interaction." *Psychiatry* 18, no. 3 (1955): 213–31.

Goldberg, Abbie E., and Katherine R. Allen. "Donor, Dad, Or . . . ? Young Adults with Lesbian Parents' Experiences with Known Donors." *Family Process* 52, no. 2 (June 2013): 338–50. https://doi.org/10.1111/famp.12029.

Goldberg, Abbie E., and Joanna E. Scheib. "Female-Partnered and Single Women's Contact Motivations and Experiences with Donor-Linked Families." *Human Reproduction* 30, no. 6 (June 1, 2015): 1375–85. https://doi.org/10.1093/humrep/dev077.

Goldberg, Abbie E., and Joanna E. Scheib. "Female-Partnered Women Conceiving Kinship: Does Sharing a Sperm Donor Mean We Are Family?" *Journal of Lesbian Studies* 20, nos. 3–4 (October 1, 2016): 427–41. https://doi.org/10.1080/10894160.2016.1089382.

Golombok, Susan. "Disclosure and Donor-Conceived Children." *Human Reproduction* 32, no. 7 (July 1, 2017): 1532–36.

Golombok, Susan. "Families Created by Reproductive Donation: Issues and Research." *Child Development Perspectives* 7, no. 1 (2012): 61–65. http://onlinelibrary.wiley.com/doi/10.1111/cdep.12015/full.

Golombok, Susan, Jennifer Readings, Lucy Blake, Polly Casey, Laura Mellish, Alex Marks, and Vasanti Jadva. "Children Conceived by Gamete Donation: Psychological Adjustment and Mother-Child Relationships at Age 7." *Journal of Family Psychology* 25, no. 2 (2011): 230.

Golombok, Susan, and Stephen Wilkinson. *Regulating Reproductive Donation*. New York: Cambridge University Press, 2016.

Grace, Victoria M., and Ken R. Daniels. "The (Ir)Relevance of Genetics: Engendering Parallel Worlds of Procreation and Reproduction." *Sociology of Health & Illness* 29, no. 5 (June 6, 2007): 692–710. https://doi.org/10.1111/j.1467-9566.2007.01010.x.

Grace, Victoria M., Ken R. Daniels, and Wayne Gillett. "The Donor, the Father, and the Imaginary Constitution of the Family: Parents' Constructions in the Case of Donor Insemination." *Social Science & Medicine* 66, no. 2 (January 2008): 301–14. https://doi.org/10.1016/j.socscimed.2007.08.029.

Graham, Susanna. "Stories of an Absent 'Father': Single Women Negotiating Relatedness through Donor Profiles." In *Relatedness in Assisted Reproduction*, edited by Tabitha Freeman and Susanna Graham, 212–31. Cambridge: Cambridge University Press, 2014.

Granovetter, Mark S. "The Strength of Weak Ties." *American Journal of Sociology* 78, no. 6 (1973): 1360–80.

Greenfeld, Dorothy A. "The Impact of Disclosure on Donor Gamete
    Participants: Donors, Intended Parents and Offspring." *Current Opinion in
    Obstetrics and Gynecology* 20, no. 3 (2008): 265–68.
Hansen, Karen V. *Not-So-Nuclear Families: Class, Gender and Networks of Care.*
    New Brunswick, NJ: Rutgers University Press, 2004.
Harmon, Amy. "Hello, I'm Your Sister. Our Father Is Donor 150." *New York Times*,
    November 20, 2005, sec. National. http://www.nytimes.com/2005/11/20/
    national/20siblings.html.
Harper, Joyce C., Emily Jackson, Laura Spoelstra-Witjens, and Dan Reisel. "Using
    an Introduction Website to Start a Family: Implications for Users and Health
    Practitioners." *Reproductive Biomedicine & Society Online* 4 (2017): 13–17.
Harper, Joyce C., Debbie Kennett, and Dan Reisel. "The End of Donor
    Anonymity: How Genetic Testing Is Likely to Drive Anonymous Gamete
    Donation out of Business." *Human Reproduction* 31, no. 6 (June 1, 2016): 1135–
    40. https://doi.org/10.1093/humrep/dew065.
Hequembourg, A. "Unscripted Motherhood: Lesbian Mothers Negotiating
    Incompletely Institutionalized Family Relationships." *Journal of Social and
    Personal Relationships* 21, no. 6 (December 1, 2004): 739–62. https://doi.org/
    10.1177/0265407504047834.
Hertz, Rosanna. "The Father as an Idea: A Challenge to Kinship Boundaries by
    Single Mothers." *Symbolic Interaction* 25 (2002): 1–31.
Hertz, Rosanna. *Single by Chance, Mothers by Choice.* New York: Oxford
    University Press, 2006.
Hertz, Rosanna. "Turning Strangers into Kin: Half-Siblings and Anonymous
    Donors." In *Who's Watching? Daily Practices of Surveillance among
    Contemporary Families*, edited by Margaret K. Nelson and Anita Ilta Garey,
    156–74. Nashville: Vanderbilt University Press, 2009.
Hertz, Rosanna, and Jane Mattes. "Donor-Shared Siblings or Genetic Strangers: New
    Families, Clans, and the Internet." *Journal of Family Issues* 32 (2011): 1129–55.
Hertz, Rosanna, and Margaret K. Nelson. "Assisted Reproduction Technology." In
    The Social History of the American Family: An Encyclopedia, edited by Marilyn J.
    Coleman and Lawrence H. Ganong, 81–84. Sage, 2014.
Hertz, Rosanna, and Margaret K. Nelson. "Donors and Donor Siblings." In
    Encyclopedia of Family Studies, edited by Constance L. Shehan, 1–4. Hoboken,
    NJ: John Wiley and Sons, 2016.
Hertz, Rosanna, and Margaret K. Nelson. "In-Depth Interviewing of Parents and
    Children: Lessons from Donor-Conceived Families about How to Conduct
    Research on Sensitive Topics," in SAGE Research Methods Cases (Health, Part
    2), 2017. http://dx.doi.org/10.4135/9781473970564.
Hertz, Rosanna, Margaret K. Nelson, and Wendy Kramer. "Donor Conceived
    Offspring Conceive of the Donor: The Relevance of Age, Awareness, and
    Family Structure." *Social Science & Medicine* 86 (June 2013): 52–65.
Hertz, Rosanna, Margaret K. Nelson, and Wendy Kramer. "Donor Sibling
    Networks as a Vehicle for Expanding Kinship: A Replication and Extension."
    Journal of Family Issues 38, no. 2 (February 24, 2018): 248–84.

Hertz, Rosanna, Margaret K. Nelson, and Wendy Kramer. "Gendering
     Gametes: The Unequal Contributions of Sperm and Egg Donors." *Social
     Science & Medicine* 147 (December 2015): 10–19. https://doi.org/10.1016/
     j.socscimed.2015.10.049.
Hertz, Rosanna, Margaret K. Nelson, and Wendy Kramer. "Sperm Donors
     Describe the Experience of Contact with Their Donor-Conceived Offspring."
     Facts, View & Visions in Gynecology and Obstetrics 7, no. 2 (2015): 91–100.
Hine, Christine. *Virtual Ethnography*. Thousand Oaks, CA: Sage, 2000.
Inhorn, Marcia C., and Zeynep B. Gürtin. "Cross-Border Reproductive Care: A
     Future Research Agenda." *Reproductive BioMedicine Online* 23, no. 5 (November
     2011): 665–76. https://doi.org/10.1016/j.rbmo.2011.08.002.
Jacobson, Heather. *Labor of Love: Gestational Surrogacy and the Work of Making
     Babies*. New Brunswick, NJ: Rutgers University Press, 2016.
Jadva, Vasanti, Tabitha Freeman, Wendy Kramer, and Susan Golombok.
     "The Experiences of Adolescents and Adults Conceived by Sperm
     Donation: Comparisons by Age of Disclosure and Family Type." *Human
     Reproduction* 24 (2009): 1909–19.
Jadva, Vasanti, Tabitha Freeman, Wendy Kramer, and Susan Golombok.
     "Experiences of Offspring Searching for and Contacting Their Donor Siblings
     and Donor." *Reproductive BioMedicine Online* 20 (2010): 523–32.
Jadva, Vasanti, Tabitha Freeman, Erika Tranfield, and Susan Golombok. "Why
     Search for a Sperm Donor Online? The Experiences of Women Searching for
     and Contacting Sperm Donors on the Internet." *Human Fertility*, April 28,
     2017, 1–8.
Jociles, María Isabel, Ana María Rivas, and Consuelo Alvarez. "Strategies to
     Personalize and to Depersonalize." N.d.
Johnson, Katherine M. "The Price of an Egg: Oocyte Donor Compensation
     in the US Fertility Industry." *New Genetics and Society*, October 20, 2017.
     http://www.tandfonline.com.ezproxy.middlebury.edu/doi/abs/10.1080/
     14636778.2017.1389262.
Jones, C. "Looking Like a Family: Negotiating Bio-Genetic Continuity in British
     Lesbian Families Using Licensed Donor Insemination." *Sexualities* 8, no. 2 (May
     1, 2005): 221–37. https://doi.org/10.1177/1363460705050856.
Jones, Christine. "Openness in Adoption: Challenging the Narrative of Historical
     Progress." *Child & Family Social Work* 21, no. 1 (February 1, 2016): 85–93.
     https://doi.org/10.1111/cfs.12113.
Kahn, Susan Martha. *Reproducing Jews: A Cultural Account of Assisted Conception
     in Israel*. Durham, NC: Duke University Press, 2000.
Kimmel, Michael *Guyland: The Perilous World Where Boys Become Men*. 2008.
     New York: Harper Perennial, 2009.
Kimport, Katrina. *Queering Marriage: Challenging Family Formation in the United
     States*. New Brunswick, NJ: Rutgers University Press, 2013.
Kirkman, Maggie. "Parents' Contributions to the Narrative Identity of Offspring
     of Donor-Assisted Conception." *Social Science & Medicine* 57, no. 11 (December
     2003): 2229–42. https://doi.org/10.1016/S0277-9536(03)00099-6.

Kovacs, Gabor Thomas, Sarah Wise, and Sue Finch. "Keeping a Child's Donor Sperm Conception Secret Is Not Linked to Family and Child Functioning during Middle Childhood: An Australian Comparative Study." *Australian and New Zealand Journal of Obstetrics and Gynaecology* 55, no. 4 (2015): 390–96.

Krogstad, Jens Manuel. "5 Facts about the Modern American Family." *Pew Research Center* (blog), April 30, 2014. http://www.pewresearch.org/fact-tank/2014/04/30/5-facts-about-the-modern-american-family/.

KrKroløkke, Charlotte. "Eggs and Euros: A Feminist Perspective on Reproductive Travel from Denmark to Spain." *International Journal of Feminist Approaches to Bioethics* 7, no. 2 (2014): 144–63.

Lamb, Michael E., and Brian Sutton-Smith. *Sibling Relationships*. Hillsdale, NJ: L. Erlbaum Associates, 1982.

Lamb, Michael E., and Brian Sutton-Smith. *Sibling Relationships: Their Nature and Significance across the Lifespan*. New York: Psychology Press, 2014.

Landau, R., and R. Weissenberg. "Disclosure of Donor Conception in Single-Mother Families: Views and Concerns." *Human Reproduction* 25, no. 4 (2010): 942–48. https://doi.org/10.1093/humrep/deq018.

Lareau, Annette. *Unequal Childhoods: Class, Race, and Family Life*. Berkeley: University of California Press, 2003.

Layne, L. L. "'Creepy,' 'Freaky,' and 'Strange': How the 'Uncanny' Can Illuminate the Experience of Single Mothers by Choice and Lesbian Couples Who Buy 'Dad.'" *Journal of Consumer Culture* 13, no. 2 (July 1, 2013): 140–59. https://doi.org/10.1177/1469540513482600.

Levy, Karen E. C. "Intimate Surveillance." *Idaho Law Review* 51 (2014): 679–93.

Luzia, Karina. "'Beautiful but Tough Terrain': The Uneasy Geographies of Same-Sex Parenting." *Children's Geographies* 11, no. 2 (2013): 243–55.

Luzia, Karina. "Travelling in Your Backyard: The Unfamiliar Places of Parenting." *Social & Cultural Geography* 11, no. 4 (June 1, 2010): 359–75. https://doi.org/10.1080/14649361003774571.

Mac Dougall, Kirstin, Gay Becker, Joanna E. Scheib, and Robert D. Nachtigall. "Strategies for Disclosure: How Parents Approach Telling Their Children That They Were Conceived with Donor Gametes." *Fertility and Sterility* 87, no. 3 (March 2007): 524–33. https://doi.org/10.1016/j.fertnstert.2006.07.1514.

Mamo, Laura. "Queering the Fertility Clinic." *Journal of Medical Humanity* 34 (2013): 227–39.

Mamo, Laura. *Queering Reproduction: Achieving Pregnancy in the Age of Technoscience*. Durham, NC: Duke University Press, 2007.

Mamo, Laura, and Eli Alston-Stepnitz. "Queer Intimacies and Structural Inequalities: New Directions in Stratified Reproduction." *Journal of Family Issues* 36, no. 4 (March 1, 2015): 519–40. https://doi.org/10.1177/0192513X14563796.

Markens, Susan. *Surrogate Motherhood and the Politics of Reproduction*. Berkeley: University of California Press, 2007.

Massey, Douglas S. "The Age of Extremes: Concentrated Affluence and Poverty in the Twenty-First Century." *Demography* 33, no. 4 (1996): 395–412.

Mauthner, Melanie. "Distant Lives, Still Voices: Sistering in Family Sociology." *Sociology* 39, no. 4 (2005): 623–42.

McHale, Susan M., Kimberly A. Updegraff, and Shawn D. Whiteman. "Sibling Relationships and Influences in Childhood and Adolescence." *Journal of Marriage and Family* 74, no. 5 (2012): 913–30.

McIntosh, Ian, and Samantha Punch. "'Barter,' 'Deals,' 'Bribes' and 'Threats': Exploring Sibling Interactions." *Childhood* 16, no. 1 (February 2009): 49–65. https://doi.org/10.1177/0907568208101690.

McKinnon, Susan. "Productive Paradoxes of the Assisted Reproductive Technologies in the Context of the New Kinship Studies." *Journal of Family Issues* 36, no. 4 (2015): 461–79.

McNeill, Tanya. "Sex Education and the Promotion of Heteronormativity." *Sexualities* 16, no. 7 (2013): 826–46.

Mead, George Herbert. *Mind, Self and Society.* Chicago University of Chicago Press, 1934.

Millbank, Jenni. "Numerical Limits in Donor Conception Regimes: Genetic Links and 'Extended Family' in the Era of Identity Disclosure." *Medical Law Review*, January 28, 2014: 325–56. https://doi.org/10.1093/medlaw/fwt044.

Miller, Claire Cain. "Egg Freezing as a Work Benefit? Some Women See Darker Message." *New York Times*, October 14, 2014. http://www.nytimes.com/2014/10/15/upshot/egg-freezing-as-a-work-benefit-some-women-see-darker-message.html.

Miller, Daniel, and Don Slater. *The Internet: An Ethnographic Approach.* Oxford: Berg, 2000.

Moore, Mignon. *Invisible Families: Gay Identities, Relationships, and Motherhood among Black Women.* Berkeley: University of California Press, 2011.

Mroz, Jacqueline. "One Sperm Donor, 150 Sons and Daughters." *New York Times*, September 5, 2011, sec. Health. http://www.nytimes.com/2011/09/06/health/06donor.html.

Mukherjee, Siddhartha. *The Gene: An Intimate History.* New York: Simon and Schuster, 2017.

Nahata, Leena, Nathanael Stanley, and Gwendolyn Quinn. "Gamete Donation: Current Practices, Public Opinion, and Unanswered Questions." *Fertility and Sterility* 107, no. 6 (2017): 1298–99.

Naples, N. A. "Queer Parenting in the New Millennium." *Gender & Society* 18, no. 6 (December 1, 2004): 679–84. https://doi.org/10.1177/0891243204269396.

National Center for Chronic Disease Prevention and Health Promotion. "ART 2010 National Summary Report." National Center for Chronic Disease Prevention and Health Promotion of the Centers for Disease Control and Prevention, December 2012.

Nelson, Alondra. *The Social Life of DNA: Race, Reparations, and Reconciliation after the Genome.* Boston: Beacon Press, 2016.

Nelson, Margaret K. "Fictive Kin." In *Encyclopedia of Family Studies*, edited by
   Constance L. Shehan, 1–3. Hoboken, NJ: John Wiley & Sons, 2016.
Nelson, Margaret K. "Hollywood Sperm Donors." *Contexts*, Winter 2014.
Nelson, Margaret K. *Parenting Out of Control: Anxious Parents in Uncertain Times*.
   New York: New York University Press, 2012.
Nelson, Margaret K., and Rosanna Hertz. "As Anonymity Disappears the Focus
   Becomes Limits on Donor Offspring." *Journal of Law and the Biosciences*,
   October 20, 2016. https://doi.org/10.1093/jlb/lsw050.
Nelson, Margaret K., and Rosanna Hertz. "Donor-Insemination
   Motherhood: How Three Types of Mothers Make Sense of Genes and Donors."
   Journal of GLBT Family Studies, December 15, 2016, 1–24. https://doi.org/
   10.1080/1550428X.2016.1249585.
Nelson, Margaret K., Rosanna Hertz, and Wendy Kramer. "Gamete Donor
   Anonymity and Limits on Numbers of Offspring: The Views of Three
   Stakeholders" with Margaret K. Nelson and Wendy Kramer. *Journal of Law and
   the Biosciences*, October 29, 2015, 1–29.
Nelson, Margaret K., Rosanna Hertz, and Wendy Kramer. "Making Sense of
   Donors and Donor Siblings: A Comparison of Donor-Conceived Offspring in
   Lesbian-Parent and Heterosexual-Parent Families." *Contemporary Perspectives in
   Family Research* 13 (2013). http://www.wellesley.edu/sites/default/files/assets/
   making_sense_of_donors_and_donor_siblings.pdf.
Nordqvist, Petra. "Choreographies of Sperm Donations: Dilemmas of Intimacy
   in Lesbian Couple Donor Conception." *Social Science & Medicine* 73
   (2011): 1661–68.
Nordqvist, Petra. "The Drive for Openness in Donor Conception: Disclosure
   and the Trouble with Real Life." *International Journal of Law, Policy and the
   Family* 28, no. 3 (December 1, 2014): 321–38. https://doi.org/10.1093/lawfam/
   ebu010.
Nordqvist, Petra. "Origins and Originators: Lesbian Couples Negotiating
   Parental Identities and Sperm Donor Conception." *Culture, Health &
   Sexuality* 14, no. 3 (March 2012): 297–311. https://doi.org/10.1080/
   13691058.2011.639392.
Nordqvist, Petra. "Out of Sight, out of Mind: Family Resemblances in Lesbian
   Donor Conception." *Sociology* 44, no. 6 (December 1, 2010): 1128–44. https://
   doi.org/10.1177/0038038510381616.
Nordqvist, Petra, and Carol Smart. *Relative Strangers: Family Life, Genes and
   Donor Conception*. New York: Palgrave Macmillan, 2014.
Nuffield Council on Bioethics. "Donor Conception: Ethical Aspects of
   Information Sharing." 2013.
Ortiz, Ana Teresa, and Laura Briggs. "The Culture of Poverty, Crack Babies, and
   Welfare Cheats: The Making of the 'Healthy White Baby Crisis.'" *Social Text* 21,
   no. 3 (2003): 39–57.
Padavic, Irene, and Jonniann Butterfield. "Mothers, Fathers, and 'Mathers':
   Negotiating a Lesbian Co-parental Identity." *Gender & Society* 25, no. 2
   (April 1, 2011): 176–96. https://doi.org/10.1177/0891243211399278.

Pande, Amrita. *Wombs in Labor: Transnational Commercial Surrogacy in India.* New York: Columbia University Press, 2014.

Passuth, Patricia M. "Age Hierarchies within Children's Groups." *Sociological Studies of Child Development* 2 (1987): 185–203.

Payne, Jenny Gunnarsson. "Grammars of Kinship: Biological Motherhood and Assisted Reproduction in an Age of Epigenetics." *Signs* 41, no. 3 (2016): 483–506.

Pazanowski, Mary Anne. "Legal Checks on Fertility Clinics Lacking, as Cases against Industry Expected to Grow." Research Paper No. 17-284, Legal Studies Research Paper Series, University of San Diego School of Law, May 4, 2017. https://papers.ssrn.com/abstract=2967574.

Peel, Elizabeth. "Moving beyond Heterosexism? The Good, the Bad and the Indifferent in Accounts of Others' Reactions to Important Life Events." *Psychology of Sexualities Review* 3, no. 1 (2012): 34–36.

Perry, Samuel L. "Adoption in the United States: A Critical Synthesis of Literature and Directions for Sociological Research." Accessed August 5, 2017. https://www.researchgate.net/profile/Samuel_Perry2/publication/317902781_Adoption_in_the_United_States_A_Critical_Synthesis_of_Literature_and_Directions_for_Sociological_Research/links/59511ab50f7e9be7b2e84f28/Adoption-in-the-United-States-A-Critical-Synthesis-of-Literature-and-Directions-for-Sociological-Research.pdf.

Persaud, Sherina, Tabitha Freeman, Vasanti Jadva, Jenna Slutsky, Wendy Kramer, Miriam Steele, Howard Steele, and Susan Golombok. "Adolescents Conceived through Donor Insemination in Mother-Headed Families: A Qualitative Study of Motivations and Experiences of Contacting and Meeting Same-Donor Offspring." *Children & Society* 31, no. 1 (January 1, 2017): 13–22. https://doi.org/10.1111/chso.12158.

Powell, Brian, Catherine Blozendahl, Claudia Geist, and Lala Carr Steelman. *Counted Out: Same-Sex Relations and Americans' Definitions of Family.* New York: Russell Sage Foundation, 2010.

Prokosch, Mark D., Richard G. Coss, Joanna E. Scheib, and Shelley A. Blozis. "Intelligence and Mate Choice: Intelligent Men Are Always Appealing." *Evolution and Human Behavior* 30, no. 1 (January 2009): 11–20. https://doi.org/10.1016/j.evolhumbehav.2008.07.004.

Putnam, Robert D. *Bowling Alone: The Collapse and Revival of American Community.* New York: Simon and Schuster, 2001.

Rodino, Iolanda S., Peter J. Burton, and Katherine A. Sanders. "Mating by Proxy: A Novel Perspective to Donor Conception." *Fertility and Sterility* 96, no. 4 (2011): 998–1001.

Rubin, Lillian. *Worlds of Pain.* New York: Basic Books, 1976.

Ryan, Maura, and Amanda Moras. "Race Matters in Lesbian Donor Insemination: Whiteness and Heteronormativity as Co-constituted Narratives." *Ethnic and Racial Studies* 40, no. 4 (March 16, 2017): 579–96. https://doi.org/10.1080/01419870.2016.1201581.

Scheib, J. E., M. Riordan, and S. Rubin. "Adolescents with Open-Identity Sperm Donors: Reports from 12–17 Year Olds." *Human Reproduction* 20, no. 1 (2005): 239–52.

Scheib, Joanna E. "Sperm Donor Selection and the Psychology of Female Mate Choice." *Ethology and Sociobiology* 15, no. 3 (May 1994): 113–29. https://doi.org/10.1016/0162-3095(94)90035-3.

Scheib, Joanna E., and Alice Ruby. "Contact among Families Who Share the Same Sperm Donor." *Fertility and Sterility* 90, no. 1 (July 2008): 33–43. https://doi.org/10.1016/j.fertnstert.2007.05.058.

Scheib, Joanna E., Alice Ruby, and Jean Benward. "Who Requests Their Sperm Donor's Identity? The First Ten Years of Information Releases to Adults with Open-Identity Donors." *Fertility and Sterility* 107, no. 2 (February 2017): 483–93. https://doi.org/10.1016/j.fertnstert.2016.10.023.

Scheib, Joanna E., Alice Ruby, and Stephen Lee. "Relationships with Families Who Share the Same Donor." In *Encyclopedia of LGBTQ Studies*, edited by A. Goldberg, 1108–13. Thousand Oaks, CA: Sage, 2016.

Schwyzer, Hugo. "The Benefits of Men and Women Being Friends, Even If One Is Married." *The Atlantic*, May 1, 2013. https://www.theatlantic.com/sexes/archive/2013/05/the-benefits-of-men-and-women-being-friends-even-if-one-is-married/275467/.

Shange, Savanna. "Black on Purpose: Race, Inheritance and Queer Reproduction." *The Feminist Wire* (blog), October 10, 2014. http://www.thefeministwire.com/2014/10/black-purpose-race-inheritance-queer-reproduction/.

Silva, Jennifer M. *Coming Up Short: Working-Class Adulthood in an Age of Uncertainty*. New York: Oxford University Press, 2013.

Simmel, Georg. *The Sociology of Georg Simmel*. Edited by Kurt Wolff. Glencoe, IL: Free Press, 1950.

Small, Mario Luis. *Unanticipated Gains: Origins of Network Inequality in Everyday Life*. New York: Oxford University Press, 2009.

Spar, Deborah L. *The Baby Business: How Money, Science, and Politics Drive the Commerce of Conception*. Cambridge, MA: Harvard Business Review Press, 2006.

Stacey, Judith. "Cruising to Familyland: Gay Hypergamy and Rainbow Kinship." *Current Sociology* 52, no. 2 (March 1, 2004): 181–97. https://doi.org/10.1177/0011392104041807.

Stacey, Judith. "The Families of Man: Gay Male Intimacy and Kinship in a Global Metropolis." *Signs* 30 (2005): 1911–35.

Stacey, Judith. "Gay Parenthood and the Decline of Paternity as We Knew It." *Sexualities* 9 (2006): 27–55.

Stacey, Judith. *Unhitched Love: Marriage, and Family Values from West Hollywood to Western China*. New York: New York University Press, 2011.

Stack, Carol. *All Our Kin: Strategies for Survival in a Black Community*. New York: Harper and Row, 1974.

Strauss, Anselm L. *Mirrors and Masks: The Search for Identity*. New Brunswick, NJ: Transaction Books, 1997.

Sullivan, Maureen. *The Family of Woman: Lesbian Mothers, Their Children, and the Undoing of Gender*. Berkeley: University of California Press, 2004.

Sulloway, Frank J. *Born to Rebel: Birth Order, Family Dynamics, and Creative Lives*. New York: Pantheon Books, 1996.

Suter, Elizabeth A., Karen L. Daas, and Karla Mason Bergen. "Negotiating Lesbian Family Identity via Symbols and Rituals." *Journal of Family Issues* 29 (2008): 26–47.

Tallandini, Maria Anna, Liviana Zanchettin, Giorgio Gronchi, and Valentina Morsan. "Parental Disclosure of Assisted Reproductive Technology (ART) Conception to Their Children: A Systematic and Meta-analytic Review." *Human Reproduction* 31, no. 6 (2016): 1275–87.

Tanskanen, Antti O., Mirkka Danielsbacka, Markus Jokela, and Anna Rotkirch. "Sibling Conflicts in Full- and Half-Sibling Households in the UK." *Journal of Biosocial Science* 49, no. 1 (January 2017): 31–47. https://doi.org/10.1017/S0021932016000043.

Thompson, Charis. *Making Parents: The Ontological Choreography of Reproductive Technologies*. Cambridge, MA: MIT Press, 2007.

Torgler, Benno, and Stephen Whyte. "Selection Criteria in the Search for a Sperm Donor: Internal versus External Attributes." Center for Research in Economics, Management and the Arts, 2013. http://www.webmail.crema-research.ch/papers/2013-22.pdf.

Turner, Victor W. *Ritual Process: Structure and Anti-Structure*. Chicago: Aldine, 1969.

23andMe. "Our Health + Ancestry DNA Service—23andMe." 2017. https://www.23andme.com.

Vanfraussen, K., I. Ponjaert-Kristoffersen, and A. Brewaeys. "An Attempt to Reconstruct Children's Donor Concept: A Comparison between Children's and Lesbian Parents' Attitudes towards Donor Anonymity." *Human Reproduction* 16 (2001): 2019–25. https://doi.org/10.1093/humrep/16.9.2019.

Visser, M., M. H. Mochtar, A. A. de Melker, F. van der Veen, S. Repping, and T. Gerrits. "Psychosocial Counselling of Identifiable Sperm Donors." *Human Reproduction* 31, no. 5 (May 1, 2016): 1066–74. https://doi.org/10.1093/humrep/dew037.

Warr, Deborah J. "Gender, Class, and the Art and Craft of Social Capital." *Sociological Quarterly* 47, no. 3 (2006): 497–520.

Weeks, Jeffrey, Catherine Donovan, and Brian Heaphy. *Same Sex Intimacies: Families of Choice and Other Life-Experiments*. London: Routledge, 2001.

Wellman, Barry. "The Place of Kinfolk in Personal Community Networks." *Marriage & Family Review* 15, nos. 1–2 (1990): 195–228.

Weston, Kath. *Families We Choose: Lesbians, Gays, Kinship*. New York: Columbia University Press, 1991.

Wojciak, Armeda Stevenson. "'It's Complicated': Exploring the Meaning of Sibling Relationships of Youth in Foster Care." *Child and Family Social Work* 22 (2017): 1283–91.

Wong, Karen-Anne. "Donor Conception and 'Passing,' or; Why Australian Parents of Donor-Conceived Children Want Donors Who Look like Them." *Journal of Bioethical Inquiry* 14, no. 1 (2017): 77–86.

Wrobel, Gretchen Miller, Harold D. Grotevant, Diana R. Samek, and Lynn Von Korff. "Adoptees' Curiosity and Information Seeking about Birth Parents in Emerging Adulthood: Context, Motivation, and Behavior." *International*

Journal of Behavioral Development 37, no. 5 (September 1, 2013). https://doi.org/
10.1177/0165025413486420.

Wyverkens, Elia, Veerle Provoost, An Ravelingien, Petra De Sutter, Guido
Pennings, and Ann Buysse. "Beyond Sperm Cells: A Qualitative Study on
Constructed Meanings of the Sperm Donor in Lesbian Families." *Human
Reproduction* 29, no. 6 (June 1, 2014): 1248–54. https://doi.org/10.1093/
humrep/deu060.

Wyverkens, Elia, Veerle Provoost, An Ravelingien, Guido Pennings, Petra De
Sutter, and Ann Buysse. "The Meaning of the Sperm Donor for Heterosexual
Couples: Confirming the Position of the Father." *Family Process*, April 2015.
https://doi.org/10.1111/famp.12156.

Yardley, Elizabeth, Adam George Thomas Lynes, David Wilson, and Emma
Kelly. "What's the Deal with 'Websleuthing'? News Media Representations
of Amateur Detectives in Networked Spaces." *Crime, Media, Culture* 14, no. 1
(2018): 81–109.

Zadeh, Sophie. "Disclosure of Donor Conception in the Era of Non-
Anonymity: Safeguarding and Promoting the Interests of Donor-Conceived
Individuals?" *Human Reproduction* 31, no. 11 (November 1, 2016): 2416–20.
https://doi.org/10.1093/humrep/dew240.

Zadeh, Sophie, Tabitha Freeman, and Susan Golombok. "Absence or Presence?
Complexities in the Donor Narratives of Single Mothers Using Sperm
Donation." *Human Reproduction* 31, no. 1 (January 2016): 117–24. https://doi.
org/10.1093/humrep/dev275.

Zadeh, Sophie, Catharine M. Jones, Tanya Basi, and Susan Golombok. "Children's
Thoughts and Feelings about Their Donor and Security of Attachment to
Their Solo Mothers in Middle Childhood." *Human Reproduction* 32, no. 4
(2017): 868–75.

Zelizer, Viviana A. *Pricing the Priceless Child: The Changing Social Value of
Children*. New York: Basic Books, 1985.

Zhang, Liuyan, Suhua Chang, Zhao Li, Zhang Kunlin, Du Yang, Ott Jurg,
and Wang Jing. "ADHD Gene: A Genetic Database for Attention Deficit
Hyperactivity Disorder." *Nucleic Acids Research* 40 (2012): D1003–9.

INDEX

adolescents. *See also* children; Michael's
   Clan; 7008er network; Tourist
   network
   and donor identity, 45–48
   use donor for self-assessment, 43–45
   use donor to separate from
      parents, 41–43
adoption, 10, 66, 82, 247nn21, 23
age. *See also* birth order
   of children in respondent families,
      228, 231
   and contacting donor, 211
   and hierarchical and moral order
      among children, 269–70n8
   and historical moments in creation
      of donor sibling networks, 193–96
   and interpersonal dynamics of
      donor siblings, 76, 133–34, 155–56,
      199–200, 269n7
AIDS epidemic, 83, 263n2
anonymous donors. *See also* 7008er
   network
   and adolescent
      self-assessment, 44–45

children's opinions on, 122, 258n12
correspondence with, 198
and donor selection, 25–26
parents' attitudes toward, 253n10
revealed identity of, 139, 146–51,
   156–57, 211–12
autism spectrum disorder, 160, 161–63,
   170, 209

birth narrative, 33–35, 106, 271n18
birth order, 133–34, 135, 157, 192, 199–
   200, 269n7. *See also* age

catalytic moments, 197–98
children. *See also* adolescents;
      Connected Soul Mates network;
      Social Capitalists network
   co-production of donor by parents
      and, 37–41
   of donors, 147–48, 262nn2, 3
   and donor siblinghood, 71–74
   identity construction of, 63–69
   production of donor by, 33–37, 69–71
   sex education and, 35–37, 256–57n5

donor sibling networks (*cont.*)
  historical moments in creation
    of, 193–96
  internal dynamics of,
    196–204, 214–15
  involvement in, 2–5
  likelihood of joining, 261n11
  means of communication in, 259n3
  reasons for joining, 108–11, 124, 163,
    164, 173, 177–78, 220
  role of donor in, 209–14
  social resources and costs in, 204–6
  validation and trust in, 207–9
donor sibling registries. *See* online
  registries
Donor Sibling Registry, 49, 258–59n1
donor siblings. *See also* donor sibling
  networks; genetic strangers
  chance discovery of, 58–61, 270n12
  choice and "problem" of, 7–8
  choosing between, 123–29
  and chosen family, 8–12, 118–20
  disappointment regarding, 107–8
  and equalization of nongestational
    parent, 271n16
  establishing social order among, 133–
    34, 199–200
  failure to create bonds among,
    138–39, 155
  as family, 168–69, 221
  as genetic strangers, 4, 245n8
  and identity construction, 11,
    63, 65–69
  impact of, 64–69
  and insights regarding donor, 63–64,
    69–71, 111–12, 115
  intentional, 260n5
  interpersonal dynamics among,
    76, 133–34, 155–56, 198–202,
    221–22, 269n7
  media interest in, 259n2
  meeting, 52–55, 56, 57–60, 66–68,
    142–43, 144, 145, 154–55, 159–61,
    166, 190, 261n9

  in Michael's Clan, 96–101, 102
  and new perceptions of genetic
    origins, 65–69, 89–91, 103, 114–15
  parents' attitudes toward, 262n13
  relatedness among, 6
  search for, 49
  selectivity among, 128–32, 134,
    205, 222
  in 7008er network, 114–17
  similarities among, 61–62, 65–70,
    89–91, 103, 114–15, 126, 134, 143–
    44, 154–56, 170–71, 210, 217
  in Social Capitalists network, 188–90
  strained relations between,
    123–32, 134
  and understanding of donor
    conception, 271n16
  use of term, 240
  weak ties among, 269n4
donor tape, 120–23, 257n8

education, of respondents, 232
egg donors and egg donor families, 55,
  109, 187, 189, 212, 226, 250n33,
  251–52nn3, 5
embryos, cost of, 252n5
employment, of respondent parents,
  232, 264–65n3

Facebook. *See also* internet
  Connected Soul Mates members
    connect through, 166, 167
  interacting with donor on, 213–14
  as means of connection for donor
    sibling networks, 49–50, 57, 119–
    20, 195–96, 209, 210–11, 259n3
  and modern transient
    strangers, 268n3
  7008er network members connect
    through, 108, 126, 127–28
  Social Capitalists connect through,
    179, 180–81, 186
  Tourist network members connect
    through, 141–42